DOGS ON THE ROOF

AND OTHER SHORT FICTION, LONGER FICTION, NONFICTION, PROSE POEMS, MEMOIRS, ESSAYS, ETC.

Brian Swann

MadHat Press
Asheville, North Carolina

MadHat Press
MadHat Incorporated
PO Box 8364, Asheville, NC 28814

Copyright © 2016 Brian Swann
All rights reserved

The Library of Congress has assigned
this edition a Control Number of
2016904564

ISBN 978-1-941196-30-4 (paperback)

Drawings by Brian Swann
Cover art and design by Marc Vincenz
Book design by MadHat Press

www.MadHat-Press.com

First Printing

Acknowledgments

Parts of this collection have appeared in the following journals, sometimes in different versions and with different titles:

Agni, Another Chicago Magazine, Beloit Fiction Journal, Boulevard, Caliban, Chariton Review, City Lights Review, College English, Exquisite Corpse, Fiction International, Harvard Review, Hotel Amerika, ISLE, New American Writing, New Letters, New Ohio Review, Notre Dame Review, Paris Review, Ploughshares, Plume Poetry Journal, Prism International (Canada), *Raritan, Salmagundi, Quarterly Review of Literature, Stand* (GB), *Southwest Review, The American Voice, The Plume Anthology, The Prose Poem.*

DOGS ON THE ROOF

AND OTHER SHORT FICTION, LONGER FICTION, NONFICTION, PROSE POEMS, MEMOIRS, ESSAYS, ETC.

This book, as always, is for my dear wife and fellow writer Roberta, who has made all these words and worlds possible.

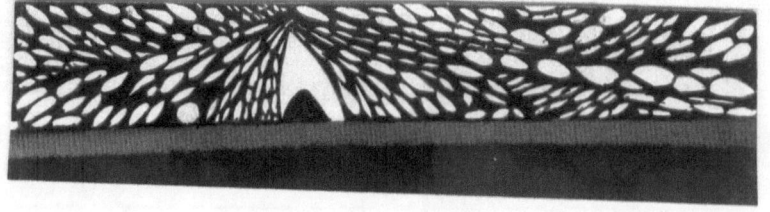

Table of Contents

INTRODUCTION
Bio Note No. 1   xv

PART ONE
Model-Dependent Realism: A Spectrum of Possibilities   1
A Book of Chapters in the Form of Prose Poems   9
Septet   15
Sestet   18
Lost Narratives   23
A Collection of Life   28
Music, or the Measure of Things   33
A Little Summer Music   36
In Limbo   40
The Track   43
Self   45
Debt   47

PART TWO
Ab Urbe Condita   53
No-Brainer   55
Argument from Design: Work in Progress   57
Reciprocal   61
Euclid   62
A Dream of Newness   63
Paysage Moralisé   64
Bird Cage   65
A Little Leaky Roof   67

Teleology of the Box	68
The House	72
Ancient Garden	73
Resonsibility	74
Outside the Box	76

Part Three

Process	79
The Sorcerer	81
Celebrations	82
The Art of This Art	84
Organic Form	85
Not Good Enough	86
The Net of Indra	87
What Works	88
Sugar Eggs	89
The Result	91
The Letters and the Lions	93
The Pebble	94
Not the Story	96
Through the Glass	98
A Day in the Life, or Making the Moon	100
The Notepad	102
Art History	103
Genitals	105
The Painting	106

Restoration of a Copy of an Imaginary Painting	107
Erasure	108
Lives	110

PART FOUR

(i)
EXCERPTS FROM MY FIRST NOVEL,
A FLASH OF LIGHTNING

Introduction	115
Chapter One: The House	121
Chapter Two: (Untitled as yet)	125

EXCERPTS FROM MY SECOND NOVEL, WORKING TITLE
EILEEN, NATASHA, MARY, THE RATS, AND ME

Chapter One: The Dreaming	129

(ii)

Novel	159
Plot	160
The Narrrator	161
Style	163
For Instance, the Glass Sponge	164
The Real World	165
Two for the Road	167
Ghosts	169
The Oral Tradition	172
The Director	173
Snow in June, or Why I Hate Actors	177
The Theater	178

The Cyclist	179
Balance	182
Monarch	184
Reflective	185
The Best of It	187

Part Five

No Conclusion	193
In Xochquetzal's Garden	194
Tequila Sunset	204
Mirrors	206
Perder el Hilo	209
Balanced in the Backflow	211
A Fantastic Roman Opera	213
Imagine	215
Dogs on the Roof	217
Silence and Nothing	220
The Tree	223
Dog	225
Argentina	227
How the West Was Won	233
The Usual	235
Home Sweet Home	239
American Sounds	243
Pioneers, O Pioneers	249
The Governor	250

Being There	254
Optimisme	260
Floaters	261
Wholeness	264
Wild Justice	271
Discourse on Method	277
Smoke up the Skirt	283
Walt Whitman on the Roof	285
Period Piece	290
Out of It	293
Waiting for the Tow Truck	294
Morning	295
Bio Note No. 2	
Poem and Prose Poem: Ancient and Wild	297
"I Think I Would Rather Be/A Painter"	309
The Waves	312
Work Riff	313

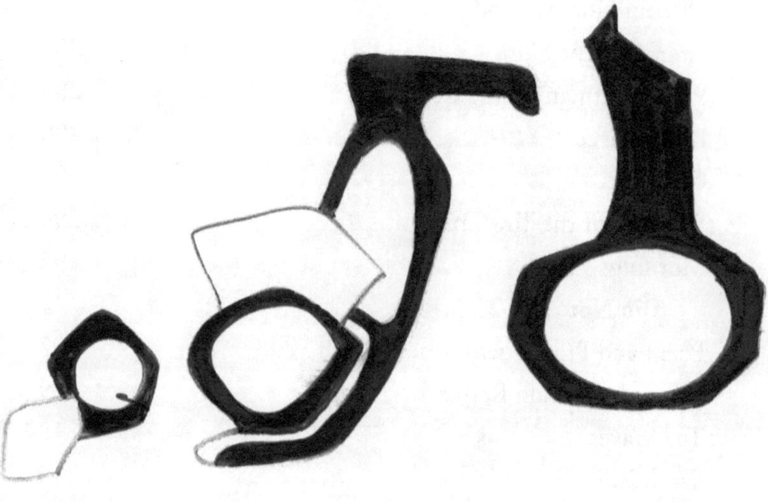

INTRODUCTION

Bio Note No. 1

After much wandering, I am back here, though I never really left. It is still as vivid as ever, though now mostly in variations and gradations of gray. Even though the old farmhouse and outbuildings are decaying, I still find things I'd missed before: old implements in a shed, a large barn with entire oak-trees for beams, a field filled with potatoes even in winter, still growing from thick white roots. I thought I'd closed the doors and windows but they were all open. Behind the house is still the mountain, the magic mountain I've known since childhood, full of wonders. I never know where I'm going, so it's always a challenge and always unpredictable in its woods and moods. I never see anyone since there is no one to see. The area is "undeveloped" and will remain so, I'm sure. My fields are overgrown and forests have crept back in. Sometimes, aurochs and bison move through the trees right up to the fences once meant to keep cattle in but which are now all down. Some mornings I sit on the loose stone wall near the spring and watch the strings of geometric images float across my eyes; "ocular migraines," I think they're called. I watch as they rise from deep in the visual cortex, patterns and structures, and as I follow their stories I get lost, I get lost, I lose the limits of being and body until I return by falling, dizzy, off the wall.

    I'd prefer not to talk further about this, and think I'll stop here, in part because I'm sure previous letters have not made it through. Certainly I've had no reply, (of course, I may have the wrong address). So not only have I wasted time writing them, but I'm not that happy sharing a place few people know about, or want to know about. It's a remote, rather backward part of the world, like Wittgenstein's Norway, and, to be honest (I hope this phrase doesn't imply I'm usually dishonest), it's never been a tourist spot, though when I first came here aeons ago there were working farms where the farmers would occasionally put up visitors to help make ends meet. Now, though the farms are gone, I still come back because it is autonomous, autochthonous, a place that never fails to surprise in its silence and anonymity. Still, it is a good place to think, pull your life together before it's too late, even if some days it is impossible to know if you exist or not. In its calm silence I feel like a ghost. It would be hard to live here alone full-time. I've tried it. There isn't, for example, anybody to summon for miles around to help you out with tasks, and there's no electricity or mod cons. When the truck quit I just pushed it into the old stone quarry. Every winter, on my own, I have to close the heavy oak shutters to keep the cold out. This also, of course, traps smoke and cuts out light, so if you want to visit a doctor with chest and eye ailments, too bad. Also, you yourself have to grow, find, stock up food and monitor its consumption. When it's gone there is no more. And there isn't anyone to wake you on cold gray mornings when you want to sleep forever. But I'm not totally alone. From time to time I have visitors. For instance, my best friend came back as someone else. This time he smoked, when he had previously quit, carelessly dropping matches all over the place. And he ignored me. He looked the same but acted completely different. He was sullen when he had been happy. He kept coming in through the same door at the top of the stairs. He left a long time ago but it seemed like yesterday. Where had he been to return so different? He wouldn't talk. Once he screamed. They say time passes, but I think it more likely that time stands still as a lamp and we pass in front of it, briefly illumined. We go back and forth, round about and back again, getting thinner, wearing out but never away. We just stay ourselves while becoming someone else.

Anyhow, be that as it may. That was all I was going to say, except for something curious that happened yesterday as I was sitting in the outhouse searching about for something to read and came across a few crumbling tattered sheets the mice had left. I sat with them on my lap. They were not in my handwriting and not in my style. They were typed, a mechanical method of recording experience which I abhor. (I am now writing fast, hoping this last pencil stub makes it to the end). From internal evidence, I thought these fragments might have belonged to a former owner, renter or squatter, someone who seemed to be a person of unsound mind, perhaps a writer (I include what seems to be a silly story of his, or hers, with a strange title), and something too of an academic who fancied himself or herself as a poet, an essayist, even an autobiographer, a genre I detest. Anyhow, as I said, with nothing better to do, I read them and decided to copy them out and include them in the envelope (if I can find one) for your amusement. Not that there was any point, of course, since there is no post office within reach, but it gives me something to do in the evenings, though I may, in fact, end up putting this paper to a more practical use.

—BS

Brian Swann

... can't read fiction. I wish I could. I feel left out. I can read only poetry and non-fiction. I don't go for Aristotle's "imitation". When I imitate I don't imitate a solid center but what falls between, what balances on boundaries or lives on edges. If I am imitating, I am imitating how I've always lived my life and what I am, for better or worse. Moreover, I have "a special lack of national and local roots," Elizabeth Hartwick on Sylvia P ...

... try to abstract the range and scope of human experience, what we think we know, it diminishes and eventually cancels as it expands like facing mirrors' infinite reflections. Put Montaigne's positivistic "observe, observe perpetually" in front of Descartes' "there are no certain marks by which the state of waking can be distinguished from a dream of ordinary life." What is there to observe now? I am not a systematic thinker, so I don't know....

... no contact with the contemporary, the flimsy, graspable world of winners and losers. The world is way beyond imitating and grasping. It is fantastic, on a cosmic and a quantum scale, a world of layers of dimensions no one can grasp, a world of self-similarity, like the self-similarity of poems, or snowflakes. So I live in the hallucinatory and unreal which disguises itself as real until it is, and I try to listen while it speaks for itself , each word a concentrated plot pushing on, each sentence an energy that has a say in its own destiny. Any control I have is part of a continuum, a collaboration, so most of the time, if I'm lucky, in Stephen Daedalus' words, "I am almosting it." The result is not thought as we know it, but something more prehistoric, what the great paleontologist André Leroi-Gourhan calls the thinking of prealphabetical antiquity, "a mode of thought based on multidimensional configurations," and which I link to what

Derrida calls "the joyous affirmation of the play of the world," which affirms "the non-center otherwise than as a loss of center." Now ...

... we all know how a word and the object it refers to, the object for which it stands, are not the same. Therefore .... just the shape of something, no content other than shape, abstract writing like abstract painting, form as content, form ...

Those are the fragments. This is the story (if that's what it is) in its entirety:

FIAT MONEY

Everything begins when everything is like images thrown on the blank white wall by the fire's flowering or when water in a glass jar reflects everything around it. I live here, or rather I don't live. I watch myself living. I feel I can do this here, growing richer and wiser, sensing possibility since, as John Gray says, with currencies now not tied to physical assets, as they were in the times of the gold standard, there is no limit to the amount of money that can be created.

There. That's it. All I could find or make out, not much, but every little helps as the monkey said as he peed into the ocean, or a little goes a long way, as the monkey said as he peed over the cliff. Well, not all. I had to utilize some of the paper for immediate purpose. I always thought literature should be practical. What's more ...

The pages in this file were copied from pencil longhand, and from some in print, and put into the computer machine by my niece, Miss

Susan Smallridge, home for Christmas from college. They was found by me on a desk made from a chest of maplewood drawers with a sheet of grade C plywood lying on top. I conducted an investigation after two pipeline surveyors reported hearing mysterious goings-on at the old abandoned Lebed property. They said that when they had went there they heard strange laughter, groaning, crying and singing, even a scream or two, and so they high-tailed it out of there. My deputy Bill Kneed and me proceeded to proceed up there but found nothing out of the ordinary except for some footprints in the snow which they could have been ours as we investigated around, but upon hearing sounds upstairs upon further investigation we came across some papers on the dresser which we proceeded to bag in the hope that they might be useful sometime in solving the scene of a possible crime and which my niece, Miss Susan Smallridge, copied out which was just as well because soon after this the main house went up in flames which we will look into come spring.
    Signed:
Rev. Orville E. Corn, Jr., sheriff and proprietor of the Last Chance gas station and dry-goods store.

PART ONE

Model-Dependent Realism: A Spectrum of Possibilities

> ... *the idea that a physical theory or world picture is a model ... and a set of rules that connect the elements of the model to observation.**

1: Wanting

By the lumps of mud water bugs gather. The sun sets.
We are going to sleep standing on our hearts. Sometimes an image peers down a well, and another gazes back.
The pendulum awakens at night, and is breathed on.

    Everything is larger than I thought, deeper and darker till it all ends in the cave of the mother, surrounded by models of her mountains and the old idols you reach on hands and knees, crawling along the dank tunnel. There are innumerable birds and fireflies, chips of live light, cold and calling like silk in a dimension of beauty you can't measure, or even call beauty, so you crawl back out to the factory floor where you can meet whoever you want. There's Mr. Marx trying to feed the rabbits and eating his shoes. And there's Mr. Spenser, but only his invisible hand so you'll have to talk to that, and there's the progressive Mr. Herder who has, unfortunately, given up on the *Natürliche Billigkeit* of those living close to nature and walking proudly through the machines of the artificial, the work of man's laboring thought, though you can still hear Mr. Kant's voice over the PA system expounding on the freedom of the will if you feel yours is still up to it. But perhaps you'd prefer to return to those lumps of mud which have become trees and those insects that are boys in the branches. They are also birds and those men below with bows

---

* All quotes are from Stephen Hawking and Leonard Mlodinow, "The (Elusive) Theory of Everything," *Scientific American* (October, 2010).

and arrows are hunters, but not in our sense. It's not as they see it. They are imitating something, but what they are imitating is already an imitation though they don't know it. But clearly they must know they are not like they are or they couldn't be what they are doing what they're doing. They would have no purpose. They would have no meaning simply as themselves. A thing is a sign of another thing, and this consists of memories which are desires and desire shapes things, which shape desire. We compare reality to a picture of it and find it wanting, but what it's wanting we can't tell.

2: TRIPTYCH

At the end of the transept you can see him dancing under a stained-glass tree from which another naked man hangs. From his fingertips birds spill, and from his head fawns and phalloi. At his feet milkweed sprays across the water. Behind all this a fish-line snakes off, and behind that scrolls of nets from boats heading across. This should have been part of a triptych but only this and another panel remain. The other is a rock-cut water-course with bathing-places in the woods beside painted tombs over which light scatters like insects. Just how these two panels are related, however, is unclear since the middle one is missing. In fact there may never have been a middle one. It is also possible that the present order is at best provisional or at worst incorrect. If so, permutations (increased, of course, if there were three not two), are possible.

3: The Sound in the Night

> *The way physics has been going, realism is becoming difficult to defend.*

We go through the possibilities. Nothing fits. Nothing we can count on. So why should it be anything? That would focus everyone's attention. We'd all go quiet, listening, for the first time, each hearing whatever it is he or she hears, and we'd keep it to ourselves, where each can listen alone to the sound, deep cousin to silence, in its own way absolute, inviolate, inviolable, and unknown.

4: Three-Day Vacation

> *... according to quantum physics the past, like the future, is indefinite and exists only as a spectrum of possibilities.*

The rooms in the boarding house are labeled alphabetically. We chose the M–T suite, eight small rooms, seven really since what should be T is marked M again, perhaps in the interest of economy, but since our two M rooms are identical that may also be the reason, except all the other rooms are identical. It takes us three days to empty our two cardboard cases and arrange the contents in the rooms. We leave no surface uncovered: memorabilia, trinkets, cards and photographs, lots of photographs, framed, stretching way back. All are placed carefully. Every cupboard, every shelf and closet is filled and the two cases squeezed under the bed. A concrete plant-holder on the single tiny terrace gets stuffed with a leafy plant. Then, when everything's unpacked, displayed or storied, before we have time to settle in we look around and realize: It all has to go back into the cases. We try.

And try. But it won't. There's simply too much. And even if we could, there's no time. No time at all.

5: STRING THEORY

> *To discuss the universe we must employ different theories in different situations.... None works well in all situations.*

Once more snakes vanish into their trails, mountains float and poppies go off. Sounds fall like silk. Everything you remember remembers you. Though the world is spirit, it leaves a track and that's the plot that starts following itself but soon splits, and splits again, losing and finding itself, changed in the process. It has its reasons. To keep safe from searchlights, its voices are muffled so they bend and turn in their own unique ways with pulses like the wind, membranes blown about, a way of filling emptiness. How lovely to be there, staking oneself to no new beginnings yet always beginning, how good to be sufficient and useless. Lost shores are still shores, the unseen visible still, vivid and fake as holograms. As skies gleam and disappear deeper into themselves, sometimes they break free, tighten up, chase and become loose again, swarms of vibrating strings, humming different songs in different places at the same time only a few of which we hear, wave after wave.

6: The Rill

> *In the framework of quantum physics, particles have neither definite positions nor definite velocities unless and until an observer measures those qualities.*

The mountain is a pattern that whirls, its brightness the absence of absence. Walking here is not easy. Once in there seems no end. It's dark, but some light's saved in melting snow along the stream where a water-ouzel runs and vanishes. Underwater he looks like something burning in a high bright window. The wind weaves back to its source and out again, going past me, past the old growth of huge pine the clear-cut forgot, past patches of dark, past cracked and broken things and back into those things so they seem whole, cues and slews like thought itself of which this is the thought, the way the rill contains itself, overrunning slabs and rearing back, its clamor in the quiet an expression of that quiet, its clarity what it lives on and gives rise to, allowing itself to be anonymous whatever we call it, faster and faster, its freedom restraint, always ahead of itself in the forefront of falling and falling over, moving forward in place, measuring itself to extinction, and I follow its pulses, which deny themselves the higher and deeper I trek, finally leaving me in the center of where there is none.

7: Albert and Not Albert

> *... that diversity is acceptable and none of the versions can be said to be more real than any other.*

A white blossom on the white picnic table supports the clouds. The green meadow is filled with mad marguerites. A dog howls as if he's flying, and suddenly morning brings snow, and Albert, who gets off his bike, panting and apologetic, and in half-a-dozen languages asks his way home. I point, all the time eyeing the steaming compost-heap topped with intact flower heads, and I think: If space is time and time space, don't they cancel out? That would help account for Albert's confusion, and my own sense that I am everywhere and nowhere, standing off to the side, watching myself slide through simultaneous seasons, becoming everyone and no one, alive and not alive, Albert and not Albert.

8: HELL AND HEAVEN

> *In some cases, individual objects do not even have an independent existence but rather exist only as an ensemble of many.*

You could be inside your self, salt in water, still to precipitate out. You could be in a missing-persons bureau not knowing where to begin, or in snow with no trace to follow, just dints the wind made. Yet things burn here with a patient lazy glow, as in a furnished room with a coin-fed gas fire where you glimpse yourself from time to time in the flickering on the dusty furniture or cold oilcloth. There are many rooms to move through where disembodied body might brush body. God's here too, concise as an almond, cool as the coils of hippocampus. His skin, chromium as an early '60s Buick, flashes and fades as he goes to work filling in the great hole for what could eventually be more sky. He quotes himself a lot, to varying effect. There is no moon, only a reasonable facsimile thereof, made opulent by silence which is made of something we have no name for. You know things here by feel, the body plenary as ellipses no paraphrase can close.

But for now that can be ignored. What works is what works, as you try to get back out in front of yourself to become for a while what you were before, clamber out of your reflection to become literal again, though, really, what's the point here among all these shards and casques and caskabells, Tlaloc's flayed skins, Gargantuan shadows and thread-like wings, blind rhyming things? It all holds together so you can count on yourself, all your incompletions, because while you can never be complete here where the world warps and the wrestler weeps and waves himself goodbye, where the economy is built on speculation and can go on forever, it need never crash, here where skies of satellites and stars talk to each other, to earthworms and coalseams, on what seems equal footing. There is no design, just patterns, the way we can't help connecting things, dot to dot, note to note, as the night sky itself mirrors thoughts and afterthoughts and becomes stories, throwing back dark as a reflection as light had been a reflection of dark, so we think we might see.

9: PASSING TIME

As measuring devices ... we are crude instruments.

Despite statements to the contrary, we haven't yet discovered the other side so it can't lead to the creation of the monumental time we call eternity. Here where inscriptions look original, all have a source. The real proof of our powers would be the destruction of the sundial's shadow. Instead what we make is decoration, a way to pass time, an architecture employing time as one of its terms, space the other, and running them together, where each face is decorated with another, which has gone before and left the contaminating trace we call proof. And so our experience of the dead is difficult to distinguish from a kind of cultivated pleasure, a dark costume of attributes where they can be lost and us with them, margin become center, border being, loss profit, an edifice of and to its own devised desires.

A Book of Chapters in the Form of Prose Poems

> ... *he cared nothing for a book if it wasn't a narrative ... it could be poetry as long as it told a story....*
> —Henry Roth, *Mercy of a Rude Stream*

(I): The Old Sailor

I remember him telling me stories with a parrot on his shoulder, a parrot that could have been part of him or a second head that spoke English, Spanish, Portuguese or what he said was Guaraní. Some claimed that at night he took off one gaudy skin to reveal another growing underneath and others under that, but I prefer my story where each night his Indian wife caressed him by plunging her hands into his deep plumage while the parrot sat on the sill of the open window, looking out over the foggy fens, singing love songs in four languages.

(II): My First Job

The lights were flat, relentless, humming. On the white slab lay a large white fish; that's what I tried to see. It was in fact a naked woman, waxen, long white hair falling softly over her shoulders and flat breasts, legs splayed as if secure, eyes closed, asleep. I tried to block it out, my first day, standing there in my brown porter's smock, forgetting why I was there until a click made me jump and the lights came on full. He slouched in, high yellow rubber boots turned over at the top as if he were a farmer, long yellow rubber apron squeaking as he moved. Ignoring me, he twisted a valve, picked up the hose. As he cleaned off the floor bits of flesh jumped up and stuck to him. When done, he turned the water off, picked up a brown paper bag from the stool, sat down, took from the bag something wrapped carefully in wax paper, unwrapped it, dropped the paper on the floor. I watched as he swallowed almost without chewing. Since he said nothing to me and didn't look in my direction I assumed I wasn't there.

(III) AIR-RAID SHELTER

I look out the window where a wheel is grinding over glass, where after the storm in a whiplash of streams whirlpools twist leaves and detritus in on themselves like ecstasies unmoored or pleasures without consequences, but in the room behind me I can still pick up rustlings from the pianola, glimpse the canary picking to pieces wax flowers on the sideboard and the pedal-organ playing hymns by itself close to the conservatory and its tomatoes forced by bull-blood, still see the air-raid shelter, all of which got the direct hit by a bomb meant for the nearby shipyards.

(IV) GYM

"Times change," says Chuck, a shivering one hundred pounds of skin and bone, former B-27 tail-gunner, always cold, even in the steam-room where the temperature's often above the law—Gino's told us how to use wet towels to cool the metal rod and fool the thermostat. He's 6'6", two-fifty, son of the founder, friend of Jack LaLanne, who made all the gym's equipment himself. Gino would rather be an artist specializing in still-life, especially in blue cabbages he brings in to show us. "I eat my models," he says. Max the anesthetist is out of work again for bashing an "incompetent" senior surgeon and the male nurse who came to his aid. Joel, ex-lawyer, ex-schoolteacher and now part-owner of The CatBox and Shazam!, sits across silent on the other bench.

Max has not yet killed himself, one of the first with "gay flu," by jumping off a roof and Joel has not yet disappeared, nor has Chuck been found rigid in his room. Gino hasn't got divorced yet, nor has the gym been sold to Lucille Roberts. I leave the heat and walk across the gym to look down 14th Street. Smoke from vendors drifts up. Across the street scraps of cloth still flutter from a tree where weeks before I'd watched someone fall, landing in that tree which tore her clothing off, held her up for a while, then let her drop. The clank of free-weights brings me back. Everyone is doing his best.

(v) ALLAHU AKBAR

The Crusties slept on the city streets with their pit bulls. I knew them well but couldn't bring myself to ask them in. They'd have refused anyway since they were anarchists. Each evening they made plans where to sleep and tonight invited me to join them. I declined. I'm no anarchist.

Leaving them, I walked into a bar near Wall Street with leather armchairs. Three lovely young women, sweet as peri, came up to say hello. The proprietress suggested we all retire upstairs, so we climbed, single-file. What I expected I didn't know. Something out of this world, maybe; something fresh and new since the century was only two years old. But I suddenly lost hope and plonked myself down on a padded balcony bench. The girls looked back as they turned a corner. I looked up to a large skylight. I heard a rumble. Then—what had I seen? Calder's *Red Stabile* flashed by. Surely not. Then through smoke and ashes a Miró tapestry drifted by in tatters and Louise Nevelson's *Sky Gate* shot by in slivers. I thought I saw Lichtenstein's *Modern Head* drop in lumps, and then a real head, a real arm. It felt like the end of the world. I wanted and looked around for a waiter. There were none.

(VI) TAKING THE SUN IN A CAR-PARK BESIDE THE EAST RIVER

I sit beside five old regulars whose lips are white as Jolson's. Coconut drifts from their naugahyde skins. Opposite, a gold lamé hip pushes out Long Island City and Williamsburg. Waft of talcum powder. Seaplanes slalom over the thighs of this nymph from a Pompeian garden and splash down behind her face reflected in a pool of last night's rain. The vents of the Con Ed power station cough and huff, and the five old men become five old cars. Later, they reincarnate as five old ladies parked in one space. On the FDR Drive, the same cars whirl round and round the island against a backdrop of far from the last Trump. At my eye-level, grit and glass glint like heaven's floor. I raise my head in time to see a cormorant from another age still finding graceful sustenance, appearing and disappearing in water close to black. It makes me wonder if the anticipated "superstorm" would ever make it here; a bit like waiting for the barbarians.

(VII) ANOTHER CITYSCAPE

The silver orb escapes. He follows. It rolls across the artificial turf, he's got it, no, his foot has tapped it, he runs, it keeps rolling, he catches up, bends down, his foot hits it again keeping it just ahead of his fingers, there, he's got it, no, his hands are too small or too cold in the slippery drizzle, but he keeps after it, it's slowing down, he catches up, he's got it, no, again a toe taps and off it scoots at an angle but now he's trapped it against a railing, he sits on it, falls off, sits on it, he slips off to the side, the ball rolls, he watches it finally quit on its own. He looks away. His legs are not yet his own. He is too young to be so angry. He bangs his heels in the turf. If he had another ball close by he'd kick it, he'd give it such a swipe, he'd really kick it.

(VII) AND ANOTHER, SAME DAY

I'm walking down 14th Street when I notice a pair of lovely legs in front, bare on a freezing cold day. She's wearing what look like dancing slippers and a raincoat that stops just above her short skirt. Her legs shine. So smooth. I've never seen such shapely legs. From back here she seems tall. I try to catch up and see how tall she really is, but people keep coming between, fiddling with iPhones, texting, talking. Every time I take a sidestep someone else does too, blocking me. But eventually I get around and walk faster. Then a strange thing happens. The closer I get the smaller she seems. Her legs stay beautiful as she walks at an even pace, but by the time I catch up she has shrunk to normal size and of course I can't see her legs. I need to adjust my angle and perspective and so I drop back. She walks on. I stand still as she pulls ahead, crosses 2nd Avenue. The farther off she goes the lovelier her legs, until they disappear, and she with them.

(IX) AND ANOTHER, ANOTHER DAY, SOMEWHERE ELSE

There is a girl I follow down an empty cobbled street. On her right foot is a surgery boot and on her left a red Jimmy Choo Gladiator. Her strong, shapely legs are hairy. She doesn't know

I'm following. I barely realize it myself. She rounds a low brick wall into an alley. How did this start? It isn't a game. There's more to it than that. Could the girl be running from an explosion? I doubt it. She isn't running, but she does seem to know where she's going. If she decided to run, even with the way she's shod she could easily outpace me and disappear. So who is this girl with magnificently muscled legs who reminds me of the doe who came up to me years ago and stood, one leg raised, trembling like light, staring at me before turning back into deep woods?

SEPTET

(I): CERTAINTY:

Can I navigate this single thread of light and plunge into distance to see everything again clear as a plate, even here where Columbus enslaved us all to his visionary banality?

As I watch, a crow starts into space.

I'd like to pry doors in tiny courtyards, carefully, within reason, so mistakes won't have consequences.

But I touch the shadow of a passer-by with my foot, the way a cat first tests a surface with a paw, grateful for small certainties.

(II): HERE:

The stars come out from under the earth where they have been eating our dead.

My walls flap and frighten them off, but one speck of light at the edge of the snow isolates me.

I sit at the white tablecloth. Its wrinkles are star-blue.

From here inside the star I can see into the night.

(III): OBSESSION:

Under stress things fall into patterns you think revelation.

And it's true, obsession frees the object from its background.

While the world's black light shines inward like a geode, bushes suck the heat into their green shadows.

There are obsessions everywhere.

(IV): SIMPLICITY:

Leaves turning back to mirrors in flight, tumbling yet rooted, saying: The mind is all trajectory, and everything is reduced to what sprang from intellect to sheer sight, imagination to the ear of night which first gave us fear, and then all possibilities.

Here everything gets filled again, as at first, filled out. What has been shaped by shadow the shadow cuts out to more form, which is just a succession of joined borders. With such borders discrete in this light, everything defines itself without humility, so all I have to do is be simple too.

(v): ACTION:

Day's just laid in fast, flat, thick of the knife, some bubbles in the blue, an ochre sheet stuck on what was cobalt night.

What action there is is indirect, nothing in or of itself, just reacting only when it has to, reaching and returning.

The wind rolls on oak, pine, maple, a big beast working to some end it doesn't understand, submitting to its own myths.

(vi): ALIVE:

There should be an interval in which rain picks over the earth and upholds the random selectivity of complete expression; quick, complete, without pleasure, outside familiarity.

Not to know is to have something else to say.

I have often thought of turning away from what can be known.

I imagine staircases without stairs, breathing without breath. Dying, then, is just a gesture toward no name, a place filled with material for a whole other landscape, ignoring my presence, but alive to it.

(VII): THINKING:

The sea breaks full as if transmitted by radio. One ship sails into view on the mirror as morning rises to things, its fire settling into the fabric of islands. Light rain falls on hyacinths and geraniums.

We broke something, as everybody knows, so our hands treat us to reduced things growing in the wreckage of tongues.

But I've had enough.

I follow the wheel and leave, covering my face, for this solitude is now my nature, building a lifetime.

No one knows I'm thinking in rags.

SESTET

(I): ARABIAN NIGHTS AND DAYS:

If we asked him, the Caliph might let us go. He's made his point. The scuttling lizard seems to have forgotten the lost child he really is, and flowers won't mind being stars about to break the surface, gasping out the world; trees are simplifying themselves to huge shifts of green, all volume and heft. This should satisfy him. And I, well, I am almost reconciled to being rock still too hot to touch, puzzle to hoverflies and haven to the ant. As I darken, I could believe in transsubstantiality of the flesh. What will I become? When I know I'll tell him. He's big on stories.

So captives have their compensation, becoming what was in them to become. And our captor Caliph Sun looks on in tolerant Ommayad amusement as the lizard-child plays in his world devoid of hierarchies, where vertical is just a special case of horizontal and no direction's alien. He's equally at ease strolling up a wall as moving over pebbles frame by frame, almost continuous. Each shift could be a different lizard if slowed down. But he is fire seeking its own form, and we are, all, of us, however we might phrase our circumscription, finally fictions of ourselves, forced, not unwillingly, into our own story.

(II): EPITHALAMIUM:

The bride in the boat is speaking to her maids about the fabric of things, keeping track of her progress at the same time, and thinking: Will he ever quit smoking? (He'd forgotten to put it out as he plunged the decompressor into the cow's bloat and that way flattened the barn, set the hayrick on fire and shot the cow off like a firecracker.) Where was he now? Her satined feet feel wet. She looks down.

He is standing on a bridge, a long project forming in his head, bullfighting from the bull's point of view, as his bride floats by beneath. He lights up. Cows raise their heads and move to the other side of the meadow. Her boat is heading for the falls. She will arrive too soon for her photo to be taken.

(III): WAITING:

The office window is squared off like one of Dürer's grids. People outside move from one rectangle to the other so they can only act relentlessly. Cars line the sidewalk, heads in. Only the shadows from high-rises move, closing over the cars, moving them.

Look! Today's special:

A woman climbs into the baby carriage with her baby.

A father, tired of fielding, clubs his son with the bat.

Furniture sits on the sidewalk as if the room around it had suddenly melted away.

The sky drifts.

As for me, I was looking out the window, but now at my desk I am remembering how last night I dreamed of an eagle squeezed inside the telescope I keep in a drawer. Through it now, in the office next door, I can see my secretary bent over her loins, inhaling the odor like the priestess at Cumae.

The page is blank in her typewriter.

I can wait.

What is she waiting for?

(IV): GRACE:

Antique cars line the driveway of an old house that's just an excuse for drawers and cabinets. The yellow Cadillac is too low to sit in. To what lengths we will go to create the useless and uncomfortable, and then use it to show to what pains we can go, all to create necessity. You can call it re-freshment, but this energy devours its own need, its own self.

So back we go to uniforms printed with mottos of divine omnipotence. But why does the crack in the mirror still make you fall through? The mirror itself is headed indoors through its own cracks, into decades which until now it has only reflected. It is ambitious. There is light outside into which it is aiming but which, it will find, can add nothing to it, even though it is all done up with cinnabar, burnt sienna, attar of roses, and highly polished.

There is a mirror, but there is also a lamp. Even though its threshold is smoldering, I don't believe for a moment that we'd hesitate to jump in. All the streets flash by, and we still don't realize we could be on fire. But at least we know where north is. We come through landscapes like a moon, waxing, then deliquescent. We have become replicas of ourselves, put together, then abandoned.

I have exhausted the self, a talking mirror, a guttered lamp. A moth beats desperately at my window. I feel its gesture as sickness. It reminds me of Signorelli's *Man Carrying a Corpse*, one wing the head, the other the legs.

(v): POST MORTEM:

Hollow shadows return to the house he left when he died. The mower was stolen so there's nothing to keep up the appearances he set some store by. The birds are nesting. Solitary, he had slight chances for kinship, yet remained popular.

His plywood happened all over, plywood, his intuitive response to architecture. I recall the dance that shook the floor, the bottle that broke the tree. There are still signs something happened. I touch everything and am confronted with landmarks. There is a single road that stops before the top. It says nothing, concerned only with nearness.

And now, how to get home. It is late. Stars swirl close, like a fairground.

(v): SHUT:

Fr. Eusebio showed Indian boys the resurrection with hummingbirds warmed, after a night's hypothermia, in the breasts of women. He gave the boys a rubber ball they thought alive. "They are neither cleanly nor civilized," he wrote. "And what is more worthy of regret, they cannot even recite the catechism."

Now the voice of the good-luck bird flies over THE WORLD'S LARGEST ROSEBUD, claims towns of tin roofs, blesses cinderblocks excluding tumbleweed, sagebrush, coyotes, Indians, sand. Its vibrations will set off the hermit's loose stovepipe that translates fat sounds to tinny vibrato. And the hermit, lost on the dark of his warped mesquite door, as I pass eats slices of watermelon and spits the pits into his hand. He looks up, fooled for a moment by the shape of a shadow, the giant crucifix on the roof of the Rock 'n' Indian Shoppe off Apache Powder Road that blesses the two-mile freight train, the black bull eating dustdevils and what's left of the range before getting lost in sheets of ripped black plastic flapping on range fences, then tearing away. As the sun pushes under clouds' aluminum glare, the plane moves clouds along behind the two-story watertower, and the sun goes down on streets named Tungsten, Copper, Silver, Aluminum. The one restaurant that says *OPEN 24 HOURS* is shut.

Lost Narratives

Narrative of an Abstract Universe:

Adopted by dragons in one version, according to anyone you asked he was a narrative character who adopted certain human traits and took on attributes of ancient defunct traditions to realize himself.

He was someone who soon made it possible for you to be inattentive and yet pick him out as a player in his imaginary town where the hierarchy was determined stylistically: so much for "febrile imagination," so much for "supple style," so much for "aiding the chromatic," and so on.

In exchange, he gave the impression of solemnity, wore a costume unique of its kind and destined for creating allusive comprehension. He took the name John, so as not to be confused.

He surrounded himself with figures and lived as silhouettes live in a landscape. This rendered him more or less specific and yet a copy of the natural environment.

As worlds became lost he became them, showing us that history is hardly geared to render such accounts of enigmatic personalities since the universe itself is abstract and we are its abstract creations, living in a profound blue with painted gold stars.

And so he showed us that we too can become our world, allegories of whatever style suits us best. We can be the traits that represent our little scenes, or large surface murals, or copies of what we have just walked through.

We can press our nose to the world, even if there is no nose, or no world.

NARRATIVE OF THE AMANUENSIS:

By the sound of it, night is vast.

The zapper next door is burning bits out of it, an indiscriminate cleansing.

What is matter actually about anyway? Will the object always be idea?

One day, much life may be happy as hitchhikers. But now distance is unconstrained, patterns are made and seen so nothing seems trivial, a way to make it all trivial.

Yes, but now is a time of wonderful stories. The one I am about to tell consists of whispers and the occasional innuendo:

The aged amanuensis pauses on the hill and reflects nostalgically on a wonderful story he once heard, or thinks he once heard. Or maybe somebody told it to him. But with everything now out of sight only the allusion to the story remains. A story about a lost love, or glove, at an airport. A young girl with a baby on a train or plane. He's sure she had a harelip or a list or a lisp because a lisp is a sign of intelligence. Krishna had a lisp.

Thus it is to hunger. One's history becomes an axe. Someone is always setting things in order, cutting time to order or braiding it to climb down and escape.

Ah, we fly in the light as if light had no meaning. We walk among shadows as if. To escape we learn boxes. I admire the Japanese. Or the Chinese. There is no time for what we have left. The farther off the better. Music like the agglomeration of silence on marble steps.

Narrative of the Fish:

It doesn't pay to reproach the dead. This hand is enough, made aware, erected to them. The dead come out of you. Why mourn yourself?

Sometimes there is a way home even if paths go in wide loops past the unweeded garden and strips of black cloth stuck through the chickenwire. Suddenly a tree is flooded, and it all empties out.

My hand looks like five rags. This hand is a bride who has gone underground.

We must seem worthy of what has to be done. I must seem encouraged, like the ouzel's lamp behind waterfalls and under streams where fish are invisible as the flow picks up speed in its countdown to glory.

Narrative of the Swan:

When the steam rises at sunup, trees send their little deaths skyward. There is still the call of unkempt graves awake to secret larvae.

Stringbeans have gone with deer whose prints are useless wings where the garden has left mint. Stones and several clouds return where a monarch, collapsing Rembrandt, is engulfed in air.

The hole where the wall stops, the elbow of rocks flaking the stream, the bird defined in silence, all turn blue. This theater hesitates, colorful, unsure. The green pepper sits wedged on stringy stalks. Squash will give buckets of blandness. The gold chalice of their flowers and the suppliant hands of their leaves reach out to where trees recover space and meet the turning point of midday. Then, a swan, queen of going, above the barbed wire.

Soon stars will shunt like so many wet stones along a riverbed beneath which they are shunted along a riverbed.

Narrative of the Rose:

With dry hands I traced dry branch, cracked glass jar, rose. But it wasn't clear until the sun's shoulders dropped below hip level. Away among the trees I heard her say: "Now you are asleep you ought to be ashamed."

I am a theater. I watch the stain spread. The invisible worm.

Trees are just opening, blossoms big as fists. A new kind of wind shares the glass-edge, ripping the old laundry I leave out each night.

There is an emergency. I stare dumbfounded. "Look, it's already fall."

The universe is at an intersection. In an approximate reflection of below, above is in ribbons. "As up, so down." Three steps up and three steps out. Back where I started. Someone has put a jockstrap on the statue. I try to stick birds back on its limbs, watch for take off. I pull back leaves of the rose, pull out the worm. O rose, thou are sick. But she says, "you missed". I try again to get it right with no nasty consequences. Until again the expected juts out and guts me. I double over, fire in the groin. What's left of hands I straighten and wave. I don't understand why they don't fly.

Narrative of the Stars, Again:

The stars come out from under the earth. Under the earth they have been eating our dead. The light of one star at the edge of the snow isolates me. Its breath is sweet and clear as ice. The wrinkles on the white tablecloth are star-blue. From here I am inside the star. I am here.

NARRATIVE OF THE DOG:

The dog returns, his voice a hundred times more bright than the ornamental sundial that registers the passing of light and shadow.

At tables, the party continues. They speak of religion constantly. As everyone knows, they say, we broke something. They want to know why.

Exile is the first essence. Calling the dog, I leave. Solitude is my nature. Exile is essence.

NARRATIVE WITHOUT TOPIC:

I turned back when I reached a motel, spare, blank. A floodlight was on. The windows were lit. *No vacancy*, said a sign. I checked in but did not sleep. Why is dawn so flimsy? And if we have to stop for the night, why is the illumined lawn the only manageable scenery, the only security?

A Collection of Life

I: THE HEART:

The heart dressed to kill limps, an old dog with one leg shot off but gaining ground on itself the way a river does or a tide hemmed in between banks. This sun meets everything halfway, anticipating disaster by embracing it. Its choices are like accidents. That bird gliding like a paper shadow over its head fits in too, and swallows dip in and out of it on their way to nests brimful with the bright faces of old men eager to leap into infinity where afterimages trail in damp air. Out its windows, trout break through water turbid after storms that took off one after the other, aboriginal saints floating the taint of hymns over partial wilderness where forests stutter but the drum's still faint. The great bubble of life forces its way up in arterial pulses and spreads loosely over mud packed hard as muscle. The seasons arrive all at once but the faintest thing is likely to pull it all back into unconsciousness when everything recurs at the same time with equal validity. The sound of the heart is one mayfly. And that is how long it lives as a collection of life at all parts, focusing at death to lift-off, enlarging what we can know by what we can't.

II: THE HUNGER:

Midnight. Some minutes past. Once again the machine kicks in. In a panorama of arbitrary belief I cope as best I can. I need a mechanic in these latitudes. Things need scraping out. The air needs more air. A whole slew of small things still conveys the impression of a dialectic that swings between extremes, a sickening tick-tock.

I look again at a shot of a dance pavilion where once patterns traced themselves in the floor's white and fragrant dust. It takes some imagination to see the fallen roof as the result of anything, but it is.

I was explaining hunger to myself when the lights came on and the sun kicked in, and I was left with my hands on the window, groping.

III: The Dead:

Woods in morning rain, and the wind. Without dying, flowers fall in mud. Forcibly uplifted, they struggle for air. Bodies, blue to the bone, float by. Day opens and shuts itself. As the rain stops, new vines get on track again at a place that has vanished. As I watch, a swallow sways above the face of the waters, leaving behind turbulence like a wind changing its nature. Then, evening, everywhere I look. The dead in the Vega Valley cemetery pause by a gang of asphodels. The small habitations of their children are all nervousness, light flickering. Night is ready to come again, leaves in a silver bowl. The wind unwinds to catch them and loose them into blue elsewhere where their delirium will be freed at first light.

IV: A Light:

A poet's beloved wife of a quarter century dies. He writes a book about it. It is well received. It wins prizes. My friend's wife of forty years dies. A couple of months later he goes for a transatlantic cruise with his new partner. A month later they are married. These must be strong men. They go about their life. My wife of four decades has had more than her share of serious sickness and adversity but goes about life as one should. She is a strong woman. But I, if anything should happen to her, I wouldn't even be able to write my name, let alone these words. Nor would I be able to walk a step. I'd stay in bed, sleep. I wouldn't move, even if I could. There'd be no point since everywhere, here and there, in and out, then and now, is her. Just thinking about it now drives me to darkness and in my cowardly way I plan to go first with a gunshot to the head or some pill. But when I imagine her all alone, all on her own, I can't bear it, and the plan backfires. I can't envision myself without her. The best moment of each day, the moment that makes day possible, is when I wake and turn to my left, and there she is. So I'm stuck and go on with life the way it was intended, for, as the Buddha said, the First Noble Truth is suffering, though I don't know what's noble about it. I am myself am not one for systems; I've tried a few. Most are a massage that works for a while, a short while. I look out the window. The storm is now at large, interrupted here and there by more of the same. I close my eyes and cut the self loose so it passes through the glass, hangs and shivers in night rain. It looks down to a stone dislodged from the old stone wall oxen and men like oxen raised to clear the land centuries ago. It tries to be the stone, its long memory, while shapes all round fumble and drift and as the storm passes sounds erase themselves like glass breaking. It looks up and sees a light coming down the mountain road, one light in the dark, terrifying, moving down, getting larger while seeming to stand still.

V: THE ATTIC:

These rooftops imitate information as their intervals fight against the night of Vincent Van Gogh, swirling the hair of dead women in spirals and mouths of stories that surface on silver. Inside, commander chairs, belted radials, comforters, cases ... forms of flaunted governings, shadows that touch your face as if from real bodies.... I have grown used to it, have tried fitting into passersby and small birds, have taken the shape of young women, the sex of night, duchies of damp hair, to knock out the night. But still this attic is exhausted rivers and seas with no sense left. The house is eaten from within, so debits love us as we try to leap beyond ourselves to gaseous stars and the sky, color of peacocks or gasoline, hangs in nets over the buttocks of sunbathers on tar beaches.

VI: THE MINK:

Rain is the articulation of leaves, wind an indifferent ecstasy. The zapper next door is burning bits out of night. One day life might be happy as hitchhikers. Today, patterns are made and seen so nothing seems trivial, but if nothing's trivial nothing's important. So yes, now is a time for wonderful stories. The one I am about to tell I have told before and it still consists of whispers: *The amanuensis pauses on the hill and reflects nostalgically on a wonderful story he once heard, or thinks he heard, for with everything gone only the allusion to the story remains, a story about a lost love (or glove) at an airport and includes a young woman with a baby on a train (or plane). He's sure she had a lisp, since a lisp is a sign of intelligence. There was, he thinks, a Hare Krishna somewhere.* I wish I could remember the rest but, as I said, I've told it before and you can fill in from there. That's the problem of dreaming in generalities; you tend to repeat yourself. You know something's wrong and so you're always trying to set things in order. But we continue to walk among shadows as if something would shine brighter there. I admire the Japanese; they seem to find their courage in neatness. I admire the mink I saw by the bank of the polluted stream just before nightfall, still searching.

Music, or the Measure of Things

*
Anapaests In The Park
I am watching a bird going hop, hop, jump, hop, hop, jump, under a sunflower that becomes Blake's "Ah, Sun-flower!" and the world turns rhythmic from the lithe little sparrows that squabble and screech to a child that just fell on his head from a high monkey-bar, and I move off to where a hansom cab driver is cursing his pony in musical Gaelic and a workman's Beethovenian hammer gives me one extra foot, *Tap, Tap, Tap, BANG*, so I trip and a soccer ball rattles my head and I fall in the dust where I lie and decide if I'll toss the thing off as far as I can or throw it back with a smile on my face and a wave of my hand like the Queen, monarch of all I survey, lord of the beast and the fowl.

*
Gustave and I
These shadows and rocks in the high pasture are bright, brighter than Egypt where Flaubert loved the sun and the blindfolded musicians and the bronze dancer stripping to the rebec while he's moving with his heroine whose name he doesn't even know yet, filling up with her, as I listen to the wind's humming under rocks, twisting like a dervish round sculpted trees and bushes, watch the turkey-buzzard banking up a thermal's a rising rhythm, shaping itself to air, sensing it for sustenance, and I reach up, the wind under my arms, jump an inch or two off the ground, try it again.

Brian Swann

*
To Sing

There are riots and wars somewhere. I can record that without much fear of contradiction. Likewise rapes, tortures, murders, a wealth of lies, skullduggery, sleaze and silliness. I just read about a fanatic setting himself on fire to make a point, and have been following the debate about a man who spent years in solitary, only to be released without trial by the same government and put in charge of the National Arts Council. He was a famous composer whose beloved sent him flowers each day he was in jail, and who still sends them there, long after his release. It seems she was a singer who lost her voice.

*
Pavlova

Through the open window again comes "I'm Forever Blowing Bubbles" played by the Marine band among statues that include a giant eagle. They say it used to grace the old Penn Station. I sing along until through the ceiling come the couple upstairs quarreling about the new oven they've installed. It's all they ever talk about, that new oven, what they'll make in it and when, even how they'll start a new career with it. Meanwhile, my wife is making a career out of making a baby. It's all she talks about. "Career" is a word she uses a lot. I looked it up "To go about wildly." She reports by the hour how the baby is musical, and kicks. I call him Little Ludwig, which she does not like since she is hoping for a girl. I am too. As I listen to the music I imagine our blatospheric dot, our little gemule, knotting into itself, blossoming, cells rhyming naturally, growing by division, preparing for publication. My wife says she has big plans. As for me, as I listen to the song and glance out at the eagle statue I recall Pavlova's last words: *Hand me my swan costume.* Where did she think she was going?

*

Once in Prague

We came upon part of a regiment in Maisel Street. They seemed lost. That night we slept naked as if we had spent the last of our inheritance but kept waking to the smell of vinegar and gunpowder. When she managed to sleep I could see her reaching for the black silk scarf. All night, I squirmed as if I had bulletholes in my back, hands over eyes, trying to lift them from my face, up against the snow which was falling against the panes. When I managed to open my eyes it was only to furniture like broken snails over which our clothes hung, and the bare wooden floor. Dawn wanted to kill. I lay still. No shots had been fired though I had felt the place shake. Looking at her darkened face, I saw myself. I scraped it off; hers came with it. The empty spaces slowly filled with rosettes. The town hall clock sent out a few slow, tinny notes to accompany the Twelve Apostles, then the Reaper.

A Little Summer Music

I:

Dingy rooms, furniture like forgotten spoor. Then, without warning, summer splashes everywhere, bleach, even on the cat by the window who has kept silent in the days of hunger. He opens an eye I look out of and see in the distance an old man who seems to be dancing with cicadas. I look down. At my feet the Snail God measures the gap between floorboards and fairly bounds across. I call the cap oblivion, and praise him.

II:

Cousin Dora had bought a large bouquet of silk roses at the Fair Grounds. It now sits on the player-piano which, when it plays, shakes the petals to "Old Folks at Home." On the wall behind it I project a shadow-puppet play when suddenly the piano changes its tune and plays out history in the form of a pounding "Garryowen." It's too much for the cat, who retreats to make a last stand on the roof via the coyote-ladder where a TV aerial draws down the world elsewhere.

III:

The piano has played itself out. I'm sitting on its stool staring at the keys when a honeybee, far from any hive, flies in. First she tries the roses. Then she drops down to sit on a white note. I watch as she unfurls her long tongue the color of fuchsia and laps the dust of a silent music.

IV:

Somewhere the radio or TV is playing a polka. I hate polkas. I pick at the meat patty. There's a large white pill stuck in the middle. "Eat," he says. I choke the pill down though I only came in for a check-up. "It'll put you to sleep," he says. "Take your mind off things. You come out right as rain, good as new." His lab coat is stained. "See you soon," he says, in Russian. "What's going on?" I ask a nurse arranging various implements. "We go in through the left eye-socket," she replies. "But the problem," I say, "is in my right groin. I can't support my weight. I can't walk." "That's why you're in a wheel-chair," she replies. I think: My hands and feet are shot. My back aches, joints creak. I'm plagued with lust. Was it for this I've sacrificed and suffered? The nurse looks at me as if she can read my thoughts. I look at her, embarrassed at my situation, lying there practically naked when I only came in on the off-chance. To blank out the polka and take my mind off things I tell her that the Chuckchi live in Siberia. "Siberia," I add, means the pure or silent land. They wear grass robes, go about in waterproof trousers of serpa sealskin and shoes with tundra-grass insoles. Their reindeer harness is strung with dangling ornaments. Their drums are stretched walrus stomach. They spear their old, a kind of suicide. Their land is empty and silent. The air is clear. "I would like to go there," I tell her as the pill takes effect and snow falls.

V:

In a series of flights he lost contact with his base. But he wasn't worried. Tapping out the melodic code to whoever was tuned in, he went on his way, until by mid-afternoon he'd grown feathery thighs and sprouted stubby wings. Talking himself through, he captured the blue in the prism all round. Now he could watch himself rise higher and higher to take closeups of marvelous creatures of light, reflecting more light despite the late hour and the fact that it all seemed to have happened before. Then he suddenly had no idea where he was. He felt himself going on and on, spreading himself thin until his adjustments became distractions so before he knew what had happened he was back on the ground, dragging his shadow in dust. But when he woke up next day it was plain as a line in the water: *Everything Is Everywhere*. And that's what he reported to one or two that had gathered. He told them the good news, but even as he spoke what had seemed to be great was a line in the water, ephemeral as music.

VI:

Morning has come to present itself. "Present." OK, I say to myself, now what? It looks like a riddle, e.g. "What am I?" Again it says "Present," adding "and correct, sir!" It has to be a joke. Who's having me on? "Who sent you?" I ask. "Sent *for*, sir!" "Stop calling me 'sir'." "Sorry, sir." It is a terrible day. The rain came in overnight and knocked the tomatoes down, flooded the driveway. The birds are still silent, and I feel waterlogged, not myself. And now this. I never saw it coming. "What can I do for you?" I ask. "I've really got nothing for you to do for me."

But then it says, "There's always something, sir. When I was a kid we had 'Bob-A-Job-Week,' Boy Scouts. We'd do anything for a shilling. There was always something. Let me help. We'd make a good team." His funny accent is getting on my nerves. Is he mocking me? Is this a joke? "OK," I say. "I'll do what you ask if you tell me who sent you." It seems to shiver, wind over water. "The weatherman, sir. He sent me. Perhaps you're right. Maybe it is a joke or perhaps he thought you needed a change in the forecast, a change in perspective. A little excitement." "Perspective? Forecast?" "The soul's weather," he says. I look at it/him carefully, and as I look, his quicksilver face clouds over. In its place is a sheet of wind that moves like water down a plate of glass, like a musical rhythm caught up in itself that could go anywhere and which I'm caught up in as it leaves a wake moving off to a place where a crow lets loose, a crow who's devoured stars down to their pulse and is now starting in on the silver light pouring out of the sun which swallows circle, then scatter, then circle again as if not quite sure until, sure, they set off headlong into the blue, the whole world theirs, while I go inside to consult my calendar with its Poor Richard mottoes in the margin stressing moderation, delaying pleasure, taking no risks, playing it safe, playing on the piano what's left of a little summer music before it plays itself out, again.

IN LIMBO

Here, now, it's one thing after another, falling over a hose, falling off a horse and shattering every nerve, hoisting me on board by crane and pulley for a firework party, getting hit by a delivery van, downing piles of painkillers none of which work though they do make me dizzy.

Old geezer, get up, walking stick.

Old geezer get up and go. Where's my walking stick? OK.

Whose face is this I used to know?

Let it stay where it is in the hand mirror. Shove it up to the back of the desk drawer. There, it's gone. What's left looks like a mask.

What country, friends, is this?

I feel thrown up like a strand of seaweed at the high-water mark.

What a fantastic view, looking back. That there is still—all this. That is what I find so wonderful, or fantastic, that is, the fantastic intersection of four principles: work-in-work, object-gone, time-gone, identity-gone, which equals short circuit in need of grafting at the vanishing point so it can lead us to the object seen properly which can lead one to believe there are others behind it. This amuses me at a time and at my age, when I am happy to be a shadow that can go anywhere, be a process that cancels itself out in the making, here where silence soars in plain sight and where exile is the condition of new growth, even if it means exorcising yourself drastically and diametrically after a lifetime of conflict and torment like St. Martin of Tours who, someone told me, exorcised himself by thrusting an arm down his throat and forcing the demon out his anus.

*

I decided to go by the house, but by the time I limped there it was empty, so I decided to return to the office, but when I got there everyone had left. There were only empty beer bottles on the floor. When I looked out the window I saw everyone sneaking off into the woods just as a hawk swooped down onto the back of a raccoon and came off second best, which reminded me of the newspaper article I'd just read about a 727 landing on the wrong runway and couldn't get off again because it was too long and the runway too short, which reminded me of another article which said that an Amtrak train took the wrong turning and ended up in the sidings at Philly, thinking it was in Virginia. So I decided to make my way back home and wear my poker hat that renders the wearer invisible and lucky at the same time. There are no tells. It looks to outsiders as if I am wearing a regular hat, a trilby, say, though my ears remain invisible the better to hear. My mother knitted this hat for me years ago from unraveled and unwound woolen socks and sweaters, itchy vests and undershirts. Over the years everything has turned blue, even the blue pom-pom which I made as a child by winding wool around a cardboard milk-bottle top and cutting round the edges. Yesterday on our elevator I saw the same hat worn by a small boy. I congratulated his mother. "I'm not his mother," she said. "I thought you would have seen that."

*

When I was a child I was always bleeding, especially from the mouth and nose, which was cauterized many times. I even bled from my eyes, like a lizard I saw on TV. I never remember smiling, so my face must have looked like a tragic mask. Once I vomited two pints of dark blood. They thought it was something I drank.

A late-seventeenth-century demoniac coughed up one hundred chamberpots of blood. At least they knew what it was.

*

Masks are meant to put you in touch with yourself, which is dangerous, which is why they are quarantined in glass cages so as not to confuse you with their faces rearranged into not-faces but not quite. You can't keep asking: What is going on? So whenever you have to go to the museum, you stare at them the way Bodhidharma stared at a blank wall when it was not about a blank wall at all.

*

There is no quarantine from yourself as time tucks tail and scatters. But this is not the time for skepticism. And I digress. I read recently that the north and south poles have changed, as they do every eleven years, but they are still polarized. This year, however, they're out of sync. It seems we now live in the delay between the two reversals. So we're in limbo, which might not be a bad place to be in the larger scale of things because this could mean that the sun is returning to a more relaxed state after high activity that started in the 1940s, which, coincidentally, was when I was born, which explains a lot when you come to think about it, though not why the painkillers don't work or how much longer I can keep this up.

The Track

(i)

The self cannot be seen but is in everything so it all probably needs captions or an instruction manual, as if there were still frontiers to cross but thieves had made off with baggage, documents and name-tags.

(ii)

Among the self's provisions are brilliances that look like fruit, globes of fleshly flashes, blooms that poke through the weave, so eloquent it wants to eat them, so quiet, but it thinks they're there and it can find them.

(iii)

The self assumes dead birds scattered along the sand must have assumed something that was wrong. But for now, from a distance they seem a florescence, a growth, as if something had been accomplished the self can use.

(iv)

The self makes a sketch of flowering shrubs, corridors through dogwood leading to a rickety barbed-wire paling on top of a stone wall, nailed to maple posts gone gray and spindly, something to love, needing repair.

(v)

So it switches on its flashlight and picks out everywhere like flames, bites in the dark, and keeps on going until the dog runs back and drops something at its feet.

(VI)

For the self, any piece of a hologram will grow an entire image for it knows things want it as much as it wants them.

(VII)

A man should have as many styles as he has selves, more, since he doesn't know how many selves he has or when he'll need them. It's best to be copious and play it safe.

(VIII)

The bird's notes climb then swoop, then climb again, a glissando taking the self with them, lifting it so, looking back, it can glimpse that, as I think I said before, though the world is spirit, it leaves a track, and the track is it.

Self

Rain picks over the earth and upholds the random selectivity of complete expression like an obsession.

I have exhausted the self, a talking mirror, a moth beating desperately at my window, I feel its gestures as sickness.

What is there to know about anything? What if all you knew could be summed up in one word? What would that word be? Verb? Noun? Adjective, what? A different grammatical structure might do it, the agglutination of polysynthesis, for instance, except it doesn't know when to stop or even what a word is. It could go on for ever, adding and subtracting morphemes front and back, attempting to get closer and closer to what it wants to mean. There's no stopping such a "word", it is always far off, the way, as someone once said, the present is always a far country, the way everything that reaches our senses comes from the past, like light itself, a spirit. And spirit is essence, it has no limits. If it has a body it is the kind you can put your arm through but not the kind you can push around. A spirit has no experience, it has nothing to draw on, nothing to hold it back and nothing to propel it forward. It knows in essence and has no need of particulars. Spirit is delightful. It is frustrating. Its soul is identical to itself. It has no self. Or has it?

Or has it ... There's a lot to think about and lots to do still, but no time to do it. You could take this in your stride but your stride is now too short. I read somewhere that the reason people take shorter steps as they age is because they rely mainly on muscles round their thighs more than those in ankle and calf, which age sooner. Anyway, I always thought that I wanted to do something else but now I don't know what it is I always thought. I had thought there was time to write a novel, for example, until I decided I didn't want to write one which was why I kept putting it off. But most of what—hang on. Intercom. I look in the little window to see who's there. No one. Wrong number, maybe, or a technical flaw. Or like "The Bald Soprano". What was I saying? Oh, yes, I wanted to find a self. Just yesterday I was reading an article by an eminent psychiatrist, a C. Bollas, MD, who said that schizophrenia, the split self, is caused by a childhood in which we endure a time when the human mind is often more than the self can ordinarily bear, so much going on, when our minds, in themselves, produce content that will be overwhelming. Therefore, to be normal we have to dumb ourselves down, and then the "self" caves in, overwhelming (OE "hwielfan," "to bend over") itself in waves, like the billows of birds I saw flying all over an empty, ploughed field, large parrot-like birds, gray-brown. A few people had stopped to watch. I stopped too. "What do they eat?" I asked a man. "Do they scavenge?" "Yes," he said, adding "they're from China." He began calling them in, stuffing them in a huge burlap bag and slinging it over his shoulder. He walked over to a pick-up truck and dumped them in the back. Then he gunned the engine and drove off. Those parrots reminded me of kea which I'd seen in a book, large, scary parrots from New Zealand that perch on the backs of sheep and peck at their kidneys. "What did they eat before sheep arrived?" I asked Miss Lockie, my teacher. "No such birds," she replied. "You shouldn't make stuff up." "They've also lost the ability to fly," I added. "They walk everywhere." "Then how do they get onto the backs of sheep?" she asked. I wish she was around to ask me that now. I have an answer. I might have an answer to everything now that I know more and can keep it all in place. If only the world could see me now, I thought, self or no self.

Debt

What am I owed? Who owes me what? What do I owe? Who? Oh, I thought, oh. What is there to owe. To owe is to engage, to engage is to promise, to promise is to imagine the future and keep at it. To keep at something is generally acknowledged to be a virtue but I resent having to think about this, because when I think I feel I live at the end of a long tunnel hacked by hand straight through a mountain from both ends, sighting along wobbly sticks. Sometimes I almost meet me in the middle, off by only a few years but sometimes each end would have tunneled by each other and kept going to who knows where had it not been for my accurate hearing. (I can hear through granite.) Ends must meet somewhere, beginning must meet beginning. If you set out blind, though, and without good hearing, a good memory is better than good eyesight. Eyesight in such a case is useless. Memory isn't all that helpful either, but keeping your wits about you is, being open to new experiences, making adjustments, willing to develop new senses like, in this case, antlers for digging, as in prehistoric times, or, better, antennae for picking up vibrations, actually antennae are better than antlers, because antlers fall off with the seasons and are gnawed on by rodents, but antennae keep waving forever, even in the dark, becoming even more sensitive, feathery syllables snagging signals, phrasing our world. They are like all the other senses combined into one, which makes me wonder why we don't have them if we think we have everything. They can pull in the universe and send it out again. They are the epitome of correlation, even when doing opposite things that are really not opposite at all. If they could only fly they would be complete. But they need attachment so they can go to all the places they respond to, places they discover if not invent. I wish I wore, I wish I were an antenna, even one.

I would be everywhere at once. I would let nothing stand in my way. I would be generous as air since what I had would be virtually limitless. Here, I'd say, waving people over, maybe clapping an antenna on their heads. Here, have this. I have plenty. I can grow another. But let's start with one to get the hang of it. No need to give it back, no need to return. Ride about with it, see how you like it, see how it fits, adjust it if you like, it's yours so I don't even know why I'm telling you what to do with it. Tell your friends, and maybe after a while you'll all grow your own. That's what I would do, I hope. But you never know. I might squirrel myself away and keep my antennae all to myself wondering if the one antenna I gave each person was enough since antennae do seem to need a pair, they do seem to work best in twos. But they'll figure it out, I'm sure. And even one appendage is better than none, as anyone with a prosthetic leg or arm will tell you. Maybe they'll pool resources, team up. Or I might simply take myself off somewhere where I won't be bothered by any of this, where no one will even find me, up in the mountain, maybe, near the stars, and there, owing nobody anything and nobody owing me, enjoy a kind of permanent jubilee for my generosity. Canceling all debts owed or owing, I'll live out my days knowing all I know, or think I know, no ambition, no need to tunnel through the mountain to know it, just hoping to grow wiser sitting on it like a little fat Buddha, growing larger in space while at the same time I might be growing smaller since all around me will be expanding. I will have nothing and no one to compare myself to. They'll have gone waving their antennae, who knows on what adventures, not even leaving me their shadows. You'd have thought they'd have felt they owed me that, at least that. But it doesn't really matter since though we used to think the cells of a healthy person rarely differ genetically, now we know that we contain genetic multitudes and one person can contain multiple genomes; there is widespread genetic variation in a single body. "Mosaicism" they call it, "chimeras." In effect, in essence, we all overlap, so the concept of debt is pretty complicated, if not meaningless.

Part Two

Ab Urbe Condita

I: Fin-de-Siècle Phase:

The thread of vestiges stretches out, working the world into shadows. But we still court more existence with the vigor of resplendent origins to make stories in the surrounding gardens, gardens with the air of being closed but with a profusion of flowers. As I look, I think I might purchase a motor car, even think of establishing a small town named after the pianist Valentin, or a village to be named after Anton Holban, the sculptor, part of a series of settlements named after artists, local and adopted. I might even find poets, still young, and turn them into streets, streets to be named with a certain lyricism that had once passed through our lives unbidden. But the century is passing, and all its genres that rested in, at best, some measure of tradition, and at worst behaved like a Gallery of Mankind full of amusing anecdotes, like a railroad elevated over galleries of glass and progenies of shade. Economic relations will follow naturally in the brief revived patriarchal calm. A cryptic rest will hang like a proliferation of fuchsias and geraniums centered on a theme that won't have to stay local but can be, among much else, a glory pregnant with yet another epoch, even if one where the stranger may have to find something else to subsist on, the way after the War I found myself lost near Maisel Street and had to find my way through broken streets that smelled of vinegar and gunpowder. But still the town hall clock sent out the Twelve Apostles, then the Reaper, as I reworked the world from shadow, stretched vestiges out from another fin-de-siècle, trumping the eye.

II: Post-Modern Phase:

The first time after whoever it was, in an unknown place, came up with the idea, the original foundation was able to be called canonical. Without leaving obvious traces, each of its rungs was richly realized even while being at the same time only a hypothesis. The structure may have been phrased just as a manner, but the virtuosity of the builders rested without doubt on what was least revealed. Other ideas, such as hierarchy, depended in part on the re-dreamed ornation. The result was there, surrounding the courtyard, cultivated by nobody, there among the ruins with redeemed votives and elongated figures of saints pale and contoured with formal pride, while from a window on the north side sprang a console of arcs like nerves, thrusting out among objects that generated loss, redeeming them. Interlaced with pastorals and fields of stone, they were not difficult to deconstruct into what they had been originally. In this echoic existence, without having made a gateway to the world as we know it, the enchorial population was reproduced in an extremity of equality. This whole idea may have been relatively new, but, ransomed into historic-narrative, each spectator and commentator suggested ranges of shadow, thus constituting an interpretation. And, since modesty is less useful than hiding in full view, movement beneath the surface was unfixed and hence democratic, maybe everlasting. Seen at the margins of a hemicycle of proportions, it was phrased in such languages as the apostles might have used for the foundation of the eternal city.

No-Brainer

Here there is no land, at least not what you'd call land, the firm stuff under your feet. There is something that looks and feels like land, but it is not. This could be the cause of much confusion because things you can do with, to and on land you can only imagine doing here. Which means you have to keep your wits about you especially when dealing with officials, and not only when being forced to negotiate with lawyers, notably those in real estate, who, like lawyers everywhere, will say at your very first meeting how attractive you are and therefore they are cutting their usual fee in half. They're all the same and have nothing to sell anyway. They count on your knowing this, otherwise there is no challenge. But they also count on your not knowing this, or not caring much.

The towns and cities that have grown up here are vigorous enough, since everyone has bought into the same ideology, even though they may not know it, or, if they do know it, they don't think of it as an ideology. What else can they do? The country is dominated by a system centered on passing things around so they get heavier or, as they say, more substantial, more valuable, the longer and further they are transported. This applies to ideas too. Their system is embodied in statues and erected as edifices an inch or so off the ground. They walk among them at ease, also elevated an inch or so.

When I discuss this place with outsiders I have difficulty describing and explaining many things, including the windows which are closed all the time. The best I can come up with is that it is done in the name of propriety and equality. And there is nothing more eloquent (though eloquence is not valued in general and is certainly not taught in the schools) than a street of closed windows with shades drawn so that the sun is reflected in all directions, leaving none out. It affords them, I believe, a sense of generosity and even prosperity, speaking to a sense that there is nothing to hide, especially since walls are optional in the interests of transparency.

Nobody stays anywhere for long, perhaps because they get bored easily, or because they like to move about. They are serious, on the whole, with little sense of humor, but they do value their entertainment, especially the theater where mirrors set along the walls and round the stage, including the fourth wall, multiply everything to the point of vanishing, so it all convinces them of the value of their experience and their innate worth. Even unpleasant subjects are so framed and thus contained. There is nothing loose to chase down, wasting valuable time in the process. For they are big on saving time,, though where they will spend it remains a problem they have yet to face up to. In the meantime, they keep it in delicate jars of majolica and faience, or sometimes in little black seed jars made of fired black mud and imported from places they've barely heard of.

To an outsider, all this could seem confusing or even a bit bizarre, especially since I have only scratched the surface. But to me it could all be considered attractive, and even, to an extent, beautiful. The lack of land has produced a kind of adaptation to circumstances which is the hallmark of all great cultures. There is a balance here, and the outline of a system which, given the right circumstances and conditions, could easily be adapted to other ideologies and locales with similar needs and circumstances, such as where the absence of land has led to serious misunderstandings and problems, even to strife and conflict. For such places, the importation of this culture would be a no-brainer.

Argument from Design; Work in Progress

The city has always seemed to me a curtain hanging, a tapestry, a painted intrusion of the wind. But, remembering a phrase I heard long ago, I wanted to go beyond such flimsy skepticism and decided to build a city as music, a melodious rhyming with ancient roots and pilings, on a diatonic scale, in the Aeolian mode, or whatever works, even on the frequency of bees; a city of the auditory cortex using sounds you cannot hear, or sounds from an ancient flute made from an auroch thigh-bone or an eagle-wing bone flute. Until I ran into codes and regulations, design solutions, defensible space and the like. But I will still build a city of cities, not in the biblical sense of "king of kings, lord of lords," but in the mode of incorporation, notes from everywhere going in all directions at once, composed with loops and gene leaps, floating beads on tough strands and filaments like DNA, arabesques of eternity. I am also considering a city that would grow up and root down, duplicate itself like bamboo, raising ever higher, hollow chamber on hollow chamber, which, once the wind puts its lips to it, would become a forest at a number of frequencies like the sound of one hand clapping, even though such a structure might be considered somewhat inherently unstable.

Sometimes I wonder where such a desire, such an idea, originated. Perhaps it was from the memory of a boy in a crumbling cemetery on the outskirts of town. He used to open the iron gates or climb the guardrails and walk down decaying steps into underground passageways looking for he knew not what. Then, one day, climbing back up into the bright light, he came across a painter among the dead leaves, broken stone monuments and fallen columns. The man shone in the sun and seemed to be doing something magical. In reply to the boy's question, he said: "Each thing we see hides something else we want to see."

Therefore I have decided that this city will have no safeguards and no guardrails. It will be a permeable membrane standing on its own volition, perhaps even a structure where the idea of permeability itself is expanded via a development of the quantum method of transporting information from one chip to another so that what happens to one happens to the other; what was written on the sender side leaps to the receiving without passing through the space between. There is a good chance this might work, but I haven't yet puzzled out all the practical details, haven't really begun to delineate its breath and finer spirit; there are moral and aesthetic implications I have yet to address.

Be that as it may. Meanwhile, as things stand, anyone in this city who wishes to do so can go up and down at the same time, these directions being, of course, really the same, as Heraclitus noted long ago. So "up" you go till you see the sky open up, and below quivering like a tympanum, and "down" you go, past cathedral and temple, skyscrapers and apartment and town halls, though this city is more presence than lasting stone, or more the presence of stone than stone itself, since I am reluctant to commit myself to "forever," which is only a word, air. As you go down you pass the unheard melodies of Skara Brae, Provadia, Varna, Çatal Höyük, foundations of mud and clay, wattle and daub, dung, river cobbles, piled-up stones. It will sit on wood pilings, strapped together with withies. It may seem primitive but I intend to go back to well-tried principles. I don't enjoy change for the sake of change. Such a procedure and the resultant total structure only needs someone of genius, a Homer, to sing its praises and compose a history for it to enter the annals of history which are also the annals of the future.

Mention of ancient Greeks reminds me how wrong Plato

was dividing the world into up and down, "upper" (invisible) and "lower" (visible), privileging, of course, the former. As I said, in this city, in addition to no up or down, there will be no interior or exterior. There will be only the middle way, which is the most stable part of any construction, the part that holds it all together, the core. Everything has two sides so the place of mediation, the agora of stability, will be where these sides press up against each other, bolstering and supporting. This is a good place to sell or exchange anything, apples, melons, all manner of flowers, merchandise, sensations, suppositories, suppositions and aspirations. It will be a place where contraries collude and opposites progress.

You might imagine from all this that I intend to work without definitive formula or blueprint, even no "system" and you would be right. I'll simply start with a sensation, the germ of a coadunating sprout or spark, one note of a tune, and let others grow, such as the preference for rooms to be kept bare, thus avoiding affectation and allowing freedom of movement. I also thought of other small details such as having, at the center of this city, a skating rink which could double as a diving pool. Thus, when people are not skating they are diving, and vice versa, a circle. How easy to convert one into the other, since the basic city-wide principle of complementarity will come into play here, the whole place symbolized by the place itself. Of course there are other ideas which I rejected, and others which I prefer not to divulge, at least not at this early point of the process. Later, perhaps, if it helps, I may (without going into too much detail) include the dimension of neuroscience where each act of listening recapitulates the past and predicts the future, releasing neurotransmitters into the striatum like a flock of doves, the way dopamine is released not at the peak moment but before, singing in anticipation of a reward for simply thinking of an event, raising it up so it floats while at the same time being rooted. Or I may not. I could simply have mentioned it here as a red herring.

But I probably should not worry about giving too much away. Since my city is not based on any Aristotelian principle of imitation I doubt anyone will imitate it. Despite the outline given above, I doubt they will be able to figure it out, especially since I have built into my system a little trick based in recent advances and adventures in physics. The more you look the less you see. The longer you look the more you see what is not there, or it is somewhere else or even in two places at the same time, and so on, so people will leave me and my plans alone. There would be no point in doing otherwise. Still, I have set out the above in the interests of perspicacity. It is not something to be figured out. Its flow just needs to be acknowledged since it has been there from the beginning. Look inside to look out, as someone said. There could be millions of such cities singing, the way the blood sings in the body, from which one could make an argument from design, a design which has had the weight of structure and theory removed from it so it floats on itself, maybe forever, beautiful.

Reciprocal

The sensible gives back to me what I lent it, but this is only what I took from it in the first place.
 —Merleau-Ponty, *Phenomenology of Perception*

Light is come, bringing the rubber plant to life with sharp detail while projecting it across the room onto the white wall, a luminous icon of some saint making a translation the way religion discovers its intentions through creating texts and perspectives for those texts, thus being able to call on narrative to mobilize itself, and as I turn to look out the window I see myself looking through the room dissolving in glass, sky filling in, fields stretching to hills, the insistent flights of birds under the comic drift of clouds. It is too much. I let my sockets fill with water, ears coil like mountain pools after a storm, muscles turn serious the way birds are serious, to be empty as the sea is empty, draw from within shapes of rocks, contours of trees, emanations of water, down into some fibrous darkness, consumed in the echoes, consuming the echoes, giving back.

Brian Swann

EUCLID

We think ourselves everywhere, relentless, free and sumptuous even on stone, even in this cheap room with a coat on the bed and an empty beaker on the night-stand, and one window's mathematical certainty. Here the soul sits on the floor reading Braille with eyelids pulled back, forced to look out the window at bodies hanging from trees, twitching like running starts that never got off. Sparks fly clear of themselves as light piles on, a falcon pulling at the wrist, whetted at a scent, the scent of us. A single light, one light, featureless as stone, the yeasty blow of flowers, it is everywhere out the window where, against the blue a white flash, one bird swinging back alone as if it's forgotten something while the others continue on, focusing Euclid's vanishing point which keeps vanishing. For here, even skies are measured and echo back measurement so that we can think ourselves everywhere, free as a bird, a bird I now care for because I cannot see it. I care for what I cannot see.

A Dream of Newness

I don't think there's anything wrong with a formula as something to obliterate.
   —Richard Diebenkorn

The ensemble suggested an iconography of the past expressed with other ideas, so even the beautiful became more interesting. Such preference began a program, one that would, in short time, draw in bits of aspects of everything else, a glittering caddis. In this way, it became a glazing of doubt, an encrustation of characteristics, a fractured renaissance, its force in the information that directed us below the foundations and left us there. As time went on, ardor was expressed with the original superimposed, such as a clock, or clock-tower, while the old hierarchies slipped by in subtitles, and we presented ourselves, not only as informed, current with the trends of our own ages, but as commanders of preferences found only in retrospect. Votive inscriptions provided texts to improvise on, each of a demotic hauteur corresponding to blind yet painted corners, hypotheses again after conformation, like heaven in art or art in heaven. The new perspective could suggest as well as prove, an architecture of flexibility. The register of narrative themes now appeared as a monumental amplitude where the subject spoke to itself of itself, conforming to itself without necessity of liaison. So there, among the directed and projected, we had the specific realized in itself. This is the meaning of collaboration, and the result is a lively tomb even for those interred elsewhere (there is no elsewhere; every empty room's an everywhere). We accorded the dream place and proportion, while mobilizing it as an experience of and beyond the world, an integer of grand measure whose history is always being made.

Brian Swann

Paysage Moralisé

The town finds itself year after year producing nothing spontaneous but evolving into a style; a sign, some, say of durability. So a park where a ditch shines with ducks constitutes a corner for feelings, and battlements, rebuilt, a vestige of horizons. There was a blueprint for islands, but techniques are still primitive for reproducing a feeling of sand and sea. Towers are combustible to remind us of a certain transmitted sensibility, like lightning. On the outskirts, representations of forests give way to trellises against which small saplings lean. In this context it is not difficult to generalize about intimate connections, and the population itself has devised plans for turning the streets permanently bright. But each evening, many gather at the unlighted station or at the back door of the casino, as if each was a lost reference to something else.

Bird Cage

The carved wood panels, muscular beams dark as mahogany, carved from sturdy hearts of oak, stretched from one end of the long room to the other. Nothing could move this, I thought, even though it was empty all the way to the mullioned bay windows that gave onto the garden where all you could see was light. It never used to be like this. It must have grown into itself, become what it might have been. I felt I could live here still but knew I couldn't, and wondered if I ever had as I looked up the wide balustraded staircase to a stained-glass window. How did that get there? I didn't remember it. But as I looked at the empty landing, I did remember there used to be an ornate birdcage there with a singing bird, a "mule," my grandfather had called it, half finch, half canary. Just then, I thought I heard someone tell me to go back where I was needed. "Go home," it said. "There's a problem. Tie things down."

When I got there, I found the tarpaulin sheet that served as the fourth wall of my cramped basement apartment flapping a bit more than usual. I'd never previously felt the need to anchor it, but now I searched about and I found some thin rope which I slipped through the eyelets, then looked around to tie and secure it to whatever came to hand, even a chair leg if I could have found one. Recently, there were reports of intrusions from the subway tunnels, but it had never occurred to me that someone could actually slip under the tarp and steal the place from right under my nose, which is what seemed to have happened. One of the homeless who haunted these tunnels must have finally plucked up courage, or been rendered so desperate, as to realize how easy it was. He took it all, everything except the tarp and the rope. How he did it is anybody's guess, but it rendered me homeless. The police, expressing bafflement, offered no hope for return. When I told them I doubted a befuddled homeless man could have done it, and suggested that maybe it was an inside job, they looked rather offended, but admitted it was a possibility. With that in mind, I thought more carefully and discovered that the thief in fact had not left nothing. In some ways he left more than he took. So the complaint I registered with the police and the claim I made with the insurance company turned out to be at best pro forma and at worst downright fraud. But I had to do it, in case they thought I'd pulled the whole thing off myself, that it was a scam, perhaps executed in cahoots with the homeless man, since what he'd left, and which I never reported, included beautiful carved wood panels, oak beams dark as mahogany stretching from one end of the huge room to the other. I was sure that the upstairs I would likewise find vacant but ready to move in, if I could manage to climb the steep balustraded staircase, passing on the landing the ornate birdcage bathed in multicolored light in which a little yellow bird on a perch was singing his little heart out.

A Little Leaky Roof

I: Experience of the World:

These cool courtyards are whiter than I remembered. The clock in one of them is a huge diagram of everything. Outside the open gates, pollarded elms and cypresses are taller than I recalled and in the still air between them, in what became of height, butterflies so still they could be painted. In weather that no longer solicits silk for comparison, I sit on a broken bench watching the sky slip back into place, emitting a certain type of light as from a margin or border. It suggests expressions for faces, or just expressions. I look around: The cycle assists the stone, now the color of apricots, to secure the courtyards with a votive experience of the world understood in the leaving, like the monochrome motives of saints on the walls.

II: Lucky:

The interior appears as amplitude. Onto its prolonged space you can project yourself with no program other than that provided by the elements however rarified or tinted, however subtle or precise. But today, whoever expected spiritual fruits picked with the imprints of intelligent fingers will have to settle for a margin of stone. Whoever expected revêtements of martyrs penetrating even consolation to emerge as a canonical person of paint is lucky to see them defined by beauty alone, pregnant with the rain and bulging panes, protected by a border and a little leaky roof.

Teleology of the Box

Clouds gray slabs, drifting down, around, so windows served little purpose. The high white walls were endless, except for a pipe rack and three pipes, one of which belonged to a distinguished Thomist who, when he died, left his house to a close Jewish friend whom he converted, and his wife, a Romanoff, whom he didn't need to. She rented me the room that had been his study, which is where I found his pipe, books and papers. The second pipe had a bitten stem and had belonged to my grandfather, while the third, very small and uncharred, had been mine as a child when I'd sit and spit in unison with him through the open door of the coal-stove. My ex was preparing breakfast, as she often did. But today felt different. As I looked about, I realized we were still in the same house I'd sold recently to a large Indian family named Pandya. What if they came back up, I thought, if only for the day? I mentioned this to my ex. She too had forgotten, "Yes, you're right. They'll know," she said, emptying some water from the kettle she'd just set on to boil. "They'd know. They'll be able to tell from whatever we use. We'll have to use less." She poured out a bit more water, measuring carefully. "This way they won't know. They'd have no way of measuring." "But what if they do turn up?" I said. "On a day like this?" she muttered, looking nervously out the window. "I don't think so. Still, you never know. They could measure the oil we use, and then they'd know." But I didn't see them dashing down to the basement as soon as they arrived and measuring that little nipple oil-gauge thing on top of the tank. They'd have to suspect first, and they'd also have to have known how much was in it to start with, where the mark had been. I looked around. "We'll have to live lightly," I said, watching a Scotch mist descend over the valley, then looking up at the living-room walls, (in truth, there was only one room), which now seemed higher and whiter than usual. The place was empty but seemed emptier, though we'd sold the house furnished. Then a distant clatter of thunder like plates falling (we'd left them plates too). A strobe of lightning bounced off the one remaining mirror and fractured on the blank ceiling like the northern lights, the revealed ache in a sheet of glass, light giving up its nerve while the roof stretched up and up like a circus tent, beams pushing outward, rafters straining to keep it all together, like stitches. It had often puzzled me how the roof pushed up so determinedly but the walls didn't collapse outward, especially since it was balloon framing. By rights, the walls should have bulged out like a herniated disk. Yes, I thought as I stared upward, what the house needed was a pillar, preferably in the middle. A pillar is the most appealing part of any house that is more than just a place. It lends distinction, it affords stability. I remembered reading how a pillar was the most frequent attribute of a Minoan sanctuary, at Koumasa, for instance, or at Knossos with its limestone pillar room, each rectangular pillar carved from a single limestone slab (sometimes the pillar was carved from gypsum), or how the four painted pillars in a Pawnee earth-lodge supported and maintained the cosmos (the smoke-hole was a celestial observatory). Yes, I may have made a mistake selling the house, though there had always been a lot of work to do to make it habitable, this all-wood house, which in storms creaked like a ship at sea. You could hear the songs of mermaids amplified like whale song. It sat on a rock ledge over wetlands and could have fallen in at any moment. The wetlands (we used to call them swamps) still lay like a green crumpled handkerchief, so perhaps I should have kept this house and worked on it. But owning always means being connected to something in an unequal relationship, no matter the emotion involved. There is always more that you are responsible for and being so tied down means loss of freedom, which means loss of true self. After a while you can't see clearly, or, worse, you're fractured and all you see are reflections of yourself everywhere; you are, in effect, nothing, locked into what Kierkegaard called "the vast penitentiary" built of the reflection of everything you associate yourself with. (As I thought this I hoped I wasn't enslaving myself to Kierkegaard.) In a rush, before the tea was ready or the bread toasted, and before I could find out if the new owners had arrived or not, I said goodbye, again, to my ex and left the house. I had left the city years before; there was no point in returning. So I returned and after a while found myself in a roof garden piled with the kind of industrial junk that kept the building working—the elevator going up and down, the air-conditioner cooling things off, the furnace warming them up and so on. Ailanthus grew luxuriantly, vines and lianas of all sorts. No one, it seemed, was supposed to be up here, but here I was, along with rats and the hollow sucked-out remnants of a small colorful bird, blue swallow-like tail, purple finch-like breast feathers, stuck in a tree. I tried to light my pipe, but it wouldn't work. I tried again, but the match went out. I will be important, I thought, and I will light it. I tried again, knowing the odds were against it. I sat down to rest on a huge box lying on its side, like an sarcophagus, empty except for what looked like a squirrel's nest at the back. It was certainly big enough to contain me. All my life, everything had always reminded me of something, unfortunately, and this reminded me of the wooden book box my father had a carpenter friend make for me when I crossed the Atlantic for ever. He made it tight as the Ark, with deep screws, as if it was to make the journey by itself without aid of a ship. After the rough crossing, at the Cunard pier in Manhattan the customs man asked me what was in it. Just books, I said. How much was it worth not to have to open it for inspection, he asked. I thought he was joking. He wasn't. I had $25 to my name, I told him. Open it, he said, and walked away. I stood there until the pier was empty. How much do you have now? he asked, screwdriver in hand. I told him. Open it, he said. When I'd done, my books were strewn all over and it was dark outside. It was darker when I'd finished putting them back. I treasured that violated box. It stayed with me from apartment to apartment all over the eastern seaboard even after all the books had been sold or lost or left behind. I often draped an Indian print over it and on top of that placed a rubber plant or aspidistra. Finally I left it in the attic of a Victorian house where, as a grad student writing a dissertation on Feuerbach, among others, I rented that room from the Russian princess who had inherited the house from the distinguished Thomist. The box seemed safe there, in that house from a sturdier time with its hefty beams and wide plank floor, its able walls and roof, a house that had done its settling, was sensible of what it was, the natural result of what the Thomist in one of his books called "an organic life," by which he meant "a growth of being constructed through victories and ruins." Yes, if the box was going to be safe anywhere it would be there, its "vegetal soul" in Aristotle's "perpetual sleep." To my mind it had followed its teleology, the way Aristotle said flames leap up and stones fall to get to their proper place. I assume it is still there, and the house too, though I've forgotten its exact address.

THE HOUSE

Leaves twitch. A wren flits. A rope between trees sags. By the wellhead a few stranded dandelions. Rain opens stones so they shine. A crow calls with the voice of a hammer. The rain stops. The sun enters with the voice of a crow. Heat turns day to distraction and the trapped mind wilts. A hawk calls and small mammals dive for cover. Sky goes carillon, dwindles, cooling off until the moon fills windows and stains rooms. A door swings and things go strange as if they had to. If you hear a voice, you hear a voice. I walk through the empty house, carefully, a cat's whisker. When I get to the top floor, over the moonlit roofs I can see the prison and the small zoo. They must be able to see me here where I'm training the self to lose itself, the way the stream ignores the stream.

Ancient Garden

Dragonflies of the twenty thousand eyes, waterskaters, crickets whose tibiae hear, damselflies breathing through their rectums and jetting forward with each breath they take. Here decay is a fellow deity in an ancient garden where her flowers are the evening whose petals are phosphor plates, their light the scent gliding toward her with painted walls of Minoan flowers and pigments of Lascaux. Her house is full of animals and plants she's breathed. I too live here where arbutus trails over windowsills bears have licked thin. The house is shaky, but into all of this she infuses desires, light as spiders billowing over grass tops, making it thinner and thinner, like a glassblower, so it all seems sad. Sadness, sadness. But just below the window, bushes and low grass are full of instars, bodies melting and changing in radical histolysis under a night sky dry as indehiscent fruits where she herself is weightless as a mayfly whose digestive tract's transformed into balloons to help they fly before they die.

Responsibility

In a game where you can never be held responsible, evening brings awakenings like allergies and ghosts prick my wrists as I sit in this deep sofa in the parlor. It once stood for great things, prodigal with ideas. And still sometimes its deep color renews thirst. Its Prussian blue, for instance, becomes a woman's hands and out the window coltsfoot is the yellow of silence. As I sit in it, I do not care if one day's larger than another or if in my mind a psalm from childhood dissolves in the cries of birds. But it is time to come to, since the serious main floor is being added, and stairs. I watch the work, even though the loveliest scenes being played out have little to do with the painted canvases I had hoped for and ordered. Still, to create unexpected effects they make allowance for handicaps and failure, thus allowing the imagination to rise to levels of self-contained details that are almost unpleasant in their intensity. And though the most compelling remnants of desire at first sight may seem unrehearsed and flimsy, something might triumph to intrude upon the development of meaning, drawing in, for example, themes such as infidelity, total immersion and bathtubs, spectators bribed with a salary, and a man frightened by his own thoughts as emotional silhouettes since, heaven knows, technique has become a synthesis of equipment. Thinking this, I was reminded of wending my way home one evening some time ago after a short excursus. I passed a shadow in a dark doorway and thought: Nothing explains the improbable. I heard someone say this, and looked around, but it was only myself, thinking out loud, which led to the (silent) thought that perhaps monosyllabic mutterings could be the only props needed for figures thrown across the white screens of your own walls. Then something made me look up. Out the window a disembodied arm waved like a line of birds, or a line of birds waved like a disembodied arm. After that, I decided to add another floor and another flight of stairs so designed as to speak to us, to address an audience who never came and who could, therefore, not be held responsible.

Brian Swann

Outside the Box

From inside the wooden box a white arm reaches round, fingers fumbling with locks and latches, someone squirming to slip straps and heave up past pebble and worm, clod and crumb, nerves dancing as light filters down, floods the head like birdsong, a presence released by other presences, the way from inside a wooden box a white arm reaches round and finds a way to free itself, become above ground its own simulacrum, a body youthful and subtle as snow, even with the sun overhead whose speed is amazing.

Part Three

Process

I am indebted to the fantastic. Thus, comically, though it is May, it is snowing, and by the time you read this who knows what month it will be, or year. But for now it is late May, green under white. The waterfall paused, and almost stopped. Flowers have scuttled themselves. A hawk circles, unsure of his bearings. A junco is pinging his lost world in which, however, I still feel I can go anywhere, an itinerant, a beggar, a quester, here where my window bellies out onto a garden with white pools. Behind me, on the wall, is a small Magritte drawing of a wall. On the wall to my right are photos of pools and windows. They are faded, old. You could blow them out with a breath or reach in and turn them over like the pages of a book, carefully, the way I slowly open the pocket-size facsimile of the vellum quarto MS. Cotton Nero A.X. on my desk, ink faded from being in my possession over half a century. This is a book I can lose myself in. I follow a painted plant climbing up the side of the first page to the ornamental capital, its tendrils gripping, two leaves filling out the initial letter "S", and soon I am battling the werbelande wind. Gwalchmai, Hawk of May, is overhead. The year unfolds. It is now June, a twelvemonth on. The walls have melted to green and the room is filled with sound and light, bejeweled with light and song. Everything feels secure, so I feel safe in leaving for another June, for a rock in the sacred river Dee, near Llangollen, decades ago. Cold water is flowing by me, all around in flashes of color like liquid butterflies, and someone on the bank is telling me he comes near ecstasy when, after a long search, he observes a rare morpho, say, or a heliconian. I've never had such an experience so I pretend not to hear him, concentrating on holding my balance on the slippery rock as I watch water contradicting itself, writhing round the rock, fretting, buckling, flaring, falling back, an intermittent monument to the fantastic, possibly even, I think, as things swirl, something like ecstasy, though, looking back, now I think that it was just dizziness. Certainly, shortly after this I slipped and fell into the turbulence, was sucked under and felt I would never get out.

Today, I am looking out of my little room, my box, my everywhere. Behind me, on the wall with its Magritte drawing and its motto, "*un objet fait supposer qu'il y en a d'autres derrière lui,*" I still feel a bit lightheaded at how things find their way, fold and unfold and flurry, at birds doing bird things, at my favorite book still talking to me on my desk, encouraging me to think my own thoughts, at flowers bright as butterflies, each one rare, at the seasons back on track, at least for now, and as for me, it's enough to be a shadow that can go anywhere, a process altering and canceling itself in the making, a sensation behind a sensation, feeling its way to whatever might be behind it, keeping it going.

The Sorcerer

> *... only by altering the common organization of his senses will he be able to enter into a rapport with the multiple nonhuman sensibilities that animate the local landscape.*
> —David Abram, *The Spell of the Sensuous*

In time, in due time, a bird, in due quiet, in the field, where the mind's in the belly, shining, muscular, and it's the foot firmly planted yet moveable, where mind is immanent in the more and less than human, in that tree, for instance, that old maple in the stone wall, in its leaves, roots, sap and bark, those chickadees searching in its armpits and groins. I can't unknow this since I know the game's for keeps, snagged in a net whose currents intersect in the night sky where one star dreams another so their fire leaps out and falls into the world, into the deep rhythm of rocks who repeat themselves so intensely light comes out of them and flows back into a night sky that throws off more stars, which at dawn are set down in my garden that swans fly over from the north in a formation clear as their constellation.

Brian Swann

CELEBRATIONS

What if today was everyone's birthday, the way crystals align and are basic for all patterns, essentially the same, they can't help it, molecules arranged to team up and withstand the vast stresses in unit and environment, able to accommodate themselves to free space or the pressures of confinement, the instinctive stress and adjustment to stress resulting in rearrangement of pattern without sacrificing integrity, the essence of objectivity, the way a skeleton is lattice and defense, an innermost world which has an understanding with the outer, which the outer may not have to honor but does, the way a plant takes off and with it goes the flower and within that the scent and within the scent the whole purpose of the plant that makes it distinctive and holds it up, hooks it together so it can succeed in its own special way, unlike any other, but very similar, where not one petal is superfluous nor one leaf extraneous nor one scent molecule redundant, all of which is used for strengthening and stringing stars together and eventually bringing to the table the child who had wandered off in order to find the world and hear it in all its frequencies, not realizing that the music of the spheres is the first thing already heard, the throbbing in the womb, the beating of the blood's universe like the plant's heart at the center of a host of windows centered on the delivery room with everyone standing about, staring in with bouquets or maybe just a few stray flowers, something which needs no rehearsal and no one need prepare for it. It brings itself. It is ready for itself, needing no philosophy to muddy things, nothing to disturb all the faces looking in, offering blossoms which the child cannot see but knows already through glass which is no impediment since it holds everything together like a glasshouse or a greenhouse or a long calm transparent philosophy in the sense that it flows from many points so there are no points just counterpoints in a liquid solid or solid liquid, a celebration as if today was everyone's birthday and always will be.

The Art of This Art

(i)

Vegetable motifs along cellar walls that grow up and out into columns, between which are faces that appear like medallions, ample as clouds, as gold in leaves. Such things are more accessible here than the errors of rules and perspective allow.

(ii)

On the margin of the wood among trees like colored inks, I watched a drama featuring two personages. The woman was converted into attitude, the man into tortured silver lines, the whole an efflorescence which a tardy grandness illumined.

(iii)

Once, long ago, I saw such a surge wash over a façade with the Virgin dressed only in a white chemise just before she vanished. A peasant, laden below, was realized at that same moment of disequilibrium in an intense blue, such as is seen when the limits of dream are amplified. Then a door opened that swallowed the light. Somewhere that light is still flowing, carrying Virgin and Peasant on it, an underground river developing like a film plot in clear frames, a film featuring vegetable motifs and involving a man and a woman and presumably much else.

Organic Form

Pick up the whole earth in your fingers, and it's as big as a grain of rice.
—Hsueh Feng

What it thinks, it is. What's taken in at root is complete at leaf. It flowers into a dream of seeds that wake to what they were before, their laughter plunging back into a darkness wild as teosinte, ecstatic as emmer. It spans great chasms with roots, it shifts glacial boulders so syntax blooms everywhere, links anywhere.

Brian Swann

Not Good Enough

Type-metal, tintype, taproot, king or coon, sounds disappearing before they know what to do with themselves. Up they go, down they go. It is disgusting. So I go outside, stand in front of a tree, interrogating the intensity of its leaves, the integrity of its twigs and, in a fit of pique, end up pulling it over my head, turning it upside down, inside out, sucking on the analogies of its taproot, the analgesics of its sap that tastes like tintype. I hold my breath, anachronistic. What can I come up with? I hope for the best but when a king questions a coon and it answers in the best way it knows how, well, that is simply just not good enough.

The Net of Indra

> *The joyous affirmation of the play of the world and the innocence of becoming ... This affirmation then determines the non-center otherwise than as loss of the center. And it plays without security.*
> —Derrida, *Writing and Difference*

Light hits the petroglyph north of San Juan Pueblo revealing a hand with wings, a hand rising where a bird would rise, doing what a hand would do if it could clear the rock it was born on, but it strains as if reluctant, the hand that can make anything, and as it heaves, one side pulling one way, one the other, it could tear apart, so maybe that's what keeps it straight, in process, about to be even staying in place, like the deep ache in a pane of glass where light is born, bends and keeps beginning, struggles invented to no end save where they shatter in a shower of shards, a kaleidoscope of shivers like rain, a spectrum where the marble feet of the cold walk up to the window and daylight comes to catch the fragile sound of the mirror as it opens with perspectives and purviews, fractures, traps and snares, whatever it can to hold it all together, to be capable of anything, spread like the net of Indra.

What Works

I went out with the sound that contained the idea of sunup.
I went out with the sound of an idea of sunup.
I went out with the idea of sunup.
The sun broke through.
It contained no ideas. It was silent, at least from this distance. Close up, no doubt, it was deafening and there was no sunup. It was always up. Same with the idea. Close up it was noisy, ear-splitting, you almost couldn't hear it. But at a distance it was calm to the point of evanescence, whose sound is revolutionary, even religious. So you have to strain your ears, you have to strain your eyes because if you don't you could be taken in, you could be deceived. This way you will be able to reassure yourself and hence reassure others that you are in it for the long haul, the payoff, in it till the cut, come what may. This way you will not be defeated and be able to show everyone how natural, how inevitable it is, make it as familiar as if they had thought of it all by themselves and not question their ears or eyes, or yours. And if they can concentrate to the sweet or bitter end they will have few or no doubts. That has always worked for me.

Sugar Eggs

I lost my shape, perhaps deliberately, by which I mean I needed to break it up by which I mean I am tired and need to be disentangled by which I mean the road to return is far away yet close at hand and is there any point in being here and now, which is very short, when I could be there and then, which is very long, and what would it mean to live there and then, I wonder, where a butterfly could influence you, splash water from its wings on you so you can see better, and at other times something flashes in your face so you can't see at all until light spills over you like yolk and you want to sing to the sun but would feel foolish even though you sort of believe the sun can stretch a net like a spider's web and catch a person in it, that you can make a rope of caterpillars and butterfly wings so that somehow you morph and ascend where you can draw someone to you with song and flageolet music where they will become enmeshed with you in the net or ropes of the sun, and what then? It is impossible to know, since once you are in it, if you question or doubt where you are, then you are no longer there, so what does it mean if you think that smoke from a fire kindled on a still night is causing clouds and a lot of rain to fall, while a crescent moon tip-down is draining itself, where to bring the sun back they must hunt lice and tie them to a stone with a hair and draw a charcoal ring around the anus and point it to the sky? But again, if you are too impatient and decide to catch strands of sunbeams for your own purposes, if in your haste you damage them, the sun will make a web inside you and damage you. So what does it all add up to? Maybe simply that it all adds up without my thinking too much about it. Maybe all you need to know are things like this: As stars spin round at night you can know your passage by whether the cup of the Big Dipper is turned down or not. It takes all night for the dipper to turn round and face down, pour over you as you sit under its light in the glow from split fish and pilot whale strips hanging to dry, here where nothing is sweeter than maple syrup stored in the perfection of blue duck egg shells, the shape of the universe, sugar eggs.

The Result

I would like to know the matter, the result, and I would like to know where the result goes, or even if there is such a thing, for a result has to be accurate or it could keep on going to who knows where. God himself from a scientific point of view is really no more than a starting point of view, no small achievement but hardly a result. It's the same with the famous vision of "a terrible flood" the famous philosopher saw in broad daylight where all of northern Europe was engulfed in yellow waves and reduced to rubble. This was in 1913 and it never occurred to him to connect it to the political situation, as if it was freestanding. Instead he interpreted it to mean that he was "menaced by a psychosis," and the outbreak of waves came as something of a relief since he was able to decided that he was going mad and so escaped the burden and responsibility of being a prophet. "God is an image," he wrote, "an image yet to come," and so capable of being avoided at least for a while. The medium of God was hysteria, he thought, with attendant spirits. Again, looking back, we can see that this was no small achievement since each spirit had a life story and even its own distinctive handwriting. He said that if your spirit is a genius you're lucky. If not you're screwed and have to start again. Luckily, we now know that you can be and go anywhere, be in more than one place at a time (a cryptoamnesiac particle). You can be more than one person, each remembering the other, each making the other though this could result in a prolonged self-torment as a bodied disembodied spirit, incompatible, maybe, but not opposites, speaking a private language anyone can learn to speak. It is literature. It is about God, though he is an outrageous fellow, continually disturbing, continually asking and being asked "What's the matter?" Indeed, what is the matter? I search for something in my life to make this true, all this, or come true, in order for it to be a result. But I still have no idea where the result goes.

The Letters and the Lions

The grooves where words were are in shadow. Behind and above them, the lions are tense, holding their stance. The words were sutures in stone, holding it together. Over everything, the flutter of lightning makes for something almost erotic, yellow, blue, red, sheets and forks that could hurt. When I turn my back or look away the lightning is still there, a kind of celestial scrawl, making noises like words you say again and again to go beyond meaning or be the pure sound they were. Then the sky blurs, goes quiet. The lions settle into the dark though you can still sense their muscled outlines squatting over the words as if they'd just brought them down. Over the years, fingers have followed each letter as if it itself was loved, as if by tracing they could believe, but by touching they have hollowed and erased them so now you have to read their absence where shadows fill the void while the lions still crouch above, tense, muscles flexed like storm clouds so you feel that if they had a mind to they could fill the grooves with roars, melt the stone itself and its freight of ghosts.

Brian Swann

The Pebble

What to do with this pebble? Actually, it is not a pebble, and even if it were I'd have to call it by something else, since a pebble has no history, being a word of unknown provenance, one that has existed in many forms over the centuries but whose phonetic relations are obscure and as yet undetermined. What to make of a word so slippery and elusive that in Australia it can even mean an animal or person hard to deal with? Luckily this rock-fragment is not a pebble but a situation in which one kind of bluish stone has been fused onto a grayish rock, become part of it, or maybe the gray rock has become part of the blue. Nor is it round, as I believe a pebble must be, or almost round, oval maybe. It has a flattish top and bottom but wobbles a bit, earth-like. If I concentrate I can see a face the blue makes, like a face on a coin or medallion, or the man in the moon, vaguely Roman, at least the nose, or, if I pull back a bit, maybe a tree. Still, if I tried hard enough I might convince myself it is a pebble simply by using the word enough, as I probably will, since "piece of irregular bi-colored rough-edged rock" does not spring as easily onto tongue or page. It is heavy for its size so it might have been useful as a paperweight, maybe to anchor this sheet which is always in danger of flying away through the open window. But I prefer it where it is, on top of a chest of drawers just inside my study where it forms part of a ritual of leaving keys, coins and wallet in the old wooden ashtray beside it when I return and picking them up when I leave. Perhaps it would be better off if I could recall where it comes from or how I got it. That would at least be a way of showing respect for the great heat and pressure that fused those two rocks. But I accept it for what it is and for fitting into my life. I'd miss it if it wasn't there. So, unlike Roquentin's pebble in *Nausea*, it has a place to be just where it is, and unlike the pebbles Molloy compulsively sucks, shuffles and transfers from pocket to pocket, this pebble need not fear displacement even in the interests of some sort of compulsive order. It might even be that its value is in its lack of value, which to me is a value. It is not like a pottery fragment that suggests a world where each fragment implies a place where pieces cohere, are not ambiguous. This pebble will never undermine itself, being as true in this world as in another. It doesn't cramp its style. It is commodious, vast and vibrating, though some have tried to scale it. Christopher Middleton, for instance, in "Climbing a Pebble," did it 'pataphysically, which is, of course, the best way to do it. But Ted Hughes writes that "A pebble is imprisoned/Like nothing in the universe." That, however, is another story. Or not. Perhaps, as Hamm says in *Endgame*, "I could go on with my story, end it and begin again." Or not. I think I have done all I can with this pebble.

Not the Story

A line of bright names on bright stock, each one possibly it and, when pronounced, more than possible, till they form whole lines following rivers, roads, trails, maybe ancient deer tracks. I pocket the map and neglect to pay for it. It sticks out. She points and giggles. I don't care. The name's stolen. If we hop a tram, narrow as a mineshaft, maybe we'll get there. So we do, but only later realize it's traveling in the wrong direction. At the next stop we jump out, and find a bookshop I search for maps. I find a pile of linen ones, tough as rope, bright and multicolored. I follow the dots of likely names, each one ringing right, and follow them all until I come back up against the largest lake in the county. It has no name. So I reach up to a high shelf and take down the latest survey maps. Oz, I say. Its name's Oz. Same as your uncle, I say, but she's off again. I have no uncle, she calls over her shoulder. If that's its name it doesn't exist.

Rummaging about in a corner of the store I find a bureau, and open a drawer. There's a pile of letters held together with an elastic band that splits when I lift the bundle out. They are all from a Mr. Wade to a Mrs. Seabury. Pretty hot stuff. This seems a sign. I put them back. Let's go, I call out to no one in particular. We take a tram going back the way we'd come. After a while we get off outside our new house. I can't remember if we'd bought it or were just renting. She's walking around and making friends. I let myself in, and call back out to her: It's a center-hall colonial.

Just then a lady comes out of the back carrying a large ring of keys, some old, some rusty. Come, she says. I want you to meet the Irish fishmonger. It turns out that the fishmonger, who isn't Irish, has a pet clam he keeps in a cloudy tank. We all hit it off, but I have to go. I have to go, I say, handing her back the keys. This isn't it, I say to my wife. I don't know why we bought here.

Rented, she says. And anyway, she continues, Oz is a name in a story. This isn't it. This isn't the story.

Brian Swann

Through the Glass

Cases in point:

I remember months ago sitting and chatting on the side of his bed while he ate breakfast of eggs, toast, sausages and bacon, tea. It wasn't cold, but he had on thick wool socks, the kind he wore, perhaps, at Oxford. I forget what we talked about, but he seemed interested in what I had to say, which is more than I can say about the three women in the antique shop later that day who pointedly ignored me, unless they actually didn't even know I was there. But how could they not have known Bill was there, or if they knew, how could they not care? *Sic gloria* ... But he didn't seem to mind, happily browsing tea-cosies, tea-caddies, doilies, and a piggy-bank in the form of a girl with a wide skirt (you put the coins in the top of her head), and so on.

I think it was the evening after that when I found myself on a vacant lot in Brooklyn. Quite by chance I ran into Brodsky in front of a ramshackle corrugated iron building on the corner. It looked like an abandoned hangar. Brodsky seemed anxious to get inside. "Nice house," I said. "I think so," he replied, pulling out a key. "Yevtuschenko gave it to me." "He once called me 'Mr. Shifty Eyes'," I said. "Or was that Brodky?" He tried to push by. "Brodky," I continued, "once asked me over the phone how much I weighed and how long my beard was." He got the key into the lock, wrestled with it a bit, pushed the door open, tumbling inside, and slamming the door shut. As I walked off, I looked back to see him at a casement window. I thought of asking him the way to the 6 train but he pulled his head in. I walked on in the wasteland and eventually found the subterranean passage I was looking for. I took the first train that pulled in and sat between two young nuns. All the way back to Manhattan I was thinking of the time I sat next to a lovely woman at a conference at the Huntting Inn in East Hampton, sneaking glances at her chest on which was pinned a card with her name on. She caught me. "Oh," I stammered, "'Ann Sexton.' What do you do?"

As I said: Cases in point: What do you make of them, a life in stories which seem to have lives of their own, which don't seem plausible, even while you're telling them like memories, as if they're having you on? I remember (unless this is another one of my stories) an old Lenape man in Oklahoma used to tell me stories that began, "My story camps, by name Jack." This puzzled me, until I found out this phrase drew on an ancient Algonquian concept that the story itself is a person who walked all over the earth. The story cannot be heard until he camps. This is what I'm thinking, looking out the window, while the rain is running things together, blearing the glass so it's well-nigh impossible to make out what you've seen, or are seeing, while I listen to Chopin's "Variations on Mozart's *Là ci darem la mano*,'" and think how many more variations can there be until the original is unnecessary, in effect non-existent, existent in other lives, and then I forget it's raining or where I am or who I am as I become absorbed into the sublime last movement of his Piano Concerto in E Minor where Chopin himself must be somewhere and as it closes I think how on earth did he write that and realize that he didn't. It wrote him, or it was delivered by flying saucers.

Brian Swann

A Day in the Life, or Making the Moon

Only half an hour before they wake. I water the basil plant on the sill before it collapses. FDR traffic comes through the window. I sit, arrange notes, clippings, paper. I open the window and the breeze blows everything off the table so I have to scurry about like my grandmother after the chickens. From mid-air I grab a monkey's mummified paw. What to do with it? Well, my granny could get a spell from each finger and use it more than once. I pick up an antique doll Rilke would have liked, but not me. I find dolls confusing. I scoop up pictures of transformers and switches, all sorts of things until I'm holding a pair of ceramic hands and a poster of nerves in the body. I collect hands. Nerves I can do without. I'm jumpy enough as it is. I sit back down, arrange a few things, make a few notes, get up, tiptoe to the john, then tiptoe back. The house is waking. I start my day again, pull out a drawer from the cabinet, hoping some fairy in the night has sorted it all out, but no, it's still a mess bursting with bills, records of all sorts from medical to tax, certificates of death, birth, baptism, banks, jury notices, summonses, photos, clippings, guarantees and stocks, any sense of syntax collapsed as file tags get written over, crossed out, torn off, mutilated, an unchartered past. I jam it shut again and pull another out so hard it hits me in the chest. Inside's the usual mess with stories marked Final that aren't for as soon as I put something in it's taken out and water-boarded again, but I still don't trust what it says so back it goes until I think it's really ready to spill the beans, then off we go again where each confession's copied down and saved though none's believed, and they pile up, so now I pull out something I was working on the night before where my wife who cannot drive is driving a Rolls Royce I help her park in a thunderstorm, and—just then she calls up that she's reading an article on frontotemporal dementia I should read, which makes me realize I haven't had breakfast yet so I climb down but then remember something I wanted from the story so I climb back up but by then it's flickered and gone out. Not to worry, I know CPR. I drive the kid to school, work all morning, then go out for my constitutional to reduce what my grandfather called my corporation. As I leave the grounds, I notice a bush with purple flowers that smell like mimosa, and on either side plants the size of grandma's chamber pot she kept under the bed. I take a deep breath. I'm open for inspiration as a sanitation man peeks round his truck at three laughing Catholic schoolgirls in white knee-length socks and hiked-up blue skirts. Somewhere, I'm sure I can hear Jimmy Jones singing "Handyman," and as I quicken my step my newly-pinned hip gives way so I crash against an out-of-service telephone kiosk and sit there silent as a garden gnome, until.

That night I'm on the roof in Cleopatra's barge, perfumed, lemony, minty, leaking its golden freight, spinnaker with no boat stretching out in the open shell of pure space, yellow as the yolk of one of my granny's free-range eggs. Then my eldest is at my side. "What is the moon?" she asks. "What do you think it is?" I reply. "A wing," she says, "but no bird, a nail with no hand." "Cleopatra's barge?" "That's good. But what's to stop it floating away?" "You," I reply. "That's what makes it all worthwhile. You make the moon."

The Notepad

A cock-sparrow sits on a bench beside a young woman. He is chirping. She is texting, copying a flyer on the wall announcing a concert by Ramon Bruno y sus Silbadores. I want to tell her that Ramon and I were once friends but I'm not sure this Bruno is the one I knew, who I suspect is now someone else in another country. "Have you heard of whistled languages" I ask, as she starts to get to her feet, "across vast distances?" She sits back down and begins to text again. When I realize she's taking down everything I say, I continue: "The after-image of bars gives faces something to peer through." I pause for her to catch up. "What do they see?" she asks. The sparrow cocks his head. I put down my packages, and think what they could see. Suddenly, she rises and leaves. "You've left your—." I whistle to get her attention, but she's off at a fair clip and I'm drowned out by electro-ranchero songs from one open window and a telenovela's domestic discord from another. Picking up the present for my wife, a ceramic pot made in China in the form of an Indian head, and the present for my daughter, a China Poblana skirt just like Frida Kahlo's, I trip and hit my head on the bench. When I come to, things look the same but it feels I'm someone else. I hear a sparrow. I see a notepad. I pick it up, scroll through.

Art History

"I had to go to Italy for this," she said in the interview. "I live here but I work there." Accompanying the text was a double-page full-color spread of her new installation, a rich assemblage including brocaded tapestry and painting, or painting that looked like brocaded tapestry. There also appeared to be real objects, but it was hard to tell. For example, two large gray identical erect penises stuck out of a wall like gargoyles on a cathedral. Prominent were foreskins of the ideal classical Greek variety, streamlined, tapered, long and pointed, the longer the foreskin the greater the owner's virtues and beauty, or so we learned from Dr. Hodges in grad school.* Much else was going on, so there wasn't really time to stop and ask yourself how she had fixed these organs in that rigid state or even how she had obtained them in the first place. Maybe it was easier to acquire a penis in Italy where the collection of body parts is not to severely regulated as here, especially in Sicily where Greek influence was and is strongest and lawlessness still rife. Or maybe they were family members obtained post mortem, the way William Harvey, discoverer of the circulation of the blood, had dissected his own father (and sister). In any case, whatever their origin, what kept them so hard and so horribly gray? Had she managed to perpetuate rigor mortis? It occurred to me that my former neighbors, the Newmans, who had recently moved uptown, might be able to help. They had gone separately on a trip to Italy and, fortuitously, were due to return that very day. So I took the bus and waited outside their apartment. Mr. Newman arrived a few seconds before his wife. He reached above the door for the key and let himself in. When Mrs. Newman arrived I took her cases, one a violin, the other small but heavy as if filled with

---

* Frederick M. Hodges, "The Ideal Prepuce in Ancient Greece...." *The Bulletin of the History of Medicine*, Vol. 75, 2001.

rocks. I followed her in. Putting down her luggage, I said "I'll leave you two to get re-acquainted. Just sit there and I'll go behind the sofa and catch up with some reading. But before I do, there's a question I'd like to ask you." Just at that moment, however, a dozen or so of their neighbors entered and began peppering them with queries about the trip. I sat down on an ottoman behind the sofa and picked up a glossy art magazine from the glass-topped table. Flipping through, imagine my surprise to find the same double-page, full-color spread reproducing an installation, a rich assemblage of brocaded tapestry and painting including, if not featuring, two large gray identical penises sticking out of a wall like gargoyles on a cathedral. But these penises were circumcised. What could it mean? Some sort of political, aesthetic or moral statement along the lines of Arnoldian Hellenism and Hebraism? Or perhaps the need for balance and reconciliation? Or had the artist run out of paint or clay or whatever material she's used and forgotten how to attach the prepuces, or had she simply forgot that she even needed them, or was the artist a good businesswoman doing what other artists do? Munch, for example, released different versions of his prints to expand his market for collectors. But her assemblage was room-size, larger than any print, and the penises much larger than the small foetuses and sperm you'll find in Munch's *Madonna*. Or maybe the artist's moral, aesthetic and political positions had changed over time, though there was no indication of when these works were produced or which came first. After much thought, sitting there quietly, I came to the conclusion that in order to avoid unnecessary confusion in the viewer, the artist should be encouraged to take out all four penises and make adjustments to the composition accordingly, which made my query for the Newmans redundant, and so I left.

GENITALS

They can be swallows, like those on Ming jars, or the airy epigrams scratched thereon, or fish looking dumbfounded when caught, or complacent behind glass, as if they were going somewhere but don't know where. Some just drive on, blasé as my father's father, who drove the Royal Train and carried a big stick with a silver knob he used to tap on my head, saying, Ambition's a great thing. Some genitals are polished and smooth, while others are tough as dragonflies you can make little impression on. And some are polite as fur. They come in all shapes, but me, I prefer the arcane, the calmly symmetrical, *to kalon*, the way I like an aquiline nose, for the nose too plays a part, smelling the air for magnificence that is everywhere, from honey locust to damp soil and, as I said, they are also swallows, slick fish and deep shafts agleam with geodes and a ruby glow, everything fitting in a topography to hike and enjoy, with side trips to out-of-theway places, the joke being that when you get there you're back where you started, for compression's its first rule, taut and tight, springy, generous as flowers; yes, flowers are the key, gentians in particular, my favorites and my poor grandmother's, bluer than heaven, a touch of night, *Gentianaceae*, the closed and small fringed, the downy and the stiff, best off where they are, wild in place, for no jar or pot will do to set them off, perfect as they are.

The Painting

On TV a young Russian woman was dancing to Khatchaturian's "Sabre Dance." Now Renée Fleming is singing "Song to the Moon" by Dvořák. I am transported. Such beauty at so many levels. But I am watching as through a wall. That is as close as I can get. I turn the TV off and find myself staring at the painting beside it, those slippery, shapeless blue shapes, as if I could be it, the body losing its limits, giving up one form for another, and another, blending bubbles and spheres, fluid as that voice, that dance. And I think: How I love women. I would be them if they would have me. I would be sorry if they turned me down for then I would be reduced to longing. I am willing to be made over, though suffer I must, pulling off "me" as fast as I can, like a bandaid. Then I can say, as I watch a woman do something as simple as cross her legs, yes, I have done that, I know what it means, I know what it feels like. Women amaze me, and I say this quickly, for my visions do not last long, and I may have been born too late to see clearly, having to spend my life catching up. Women raised me. How could I not want to be that painting, pillowy deep water, floating globes and dancing beads, weightless as music, which I enter before it shuts, leaving me.

Restoration of a Copy of an Imaginary Painting

> ... *dire, non pas tout crûment sa vision, mais par un transfert instantané, constant, l'écho de sa présence.*
> —Victor Segelen

The thick white is meant to stabilize the house, but the matted crenellation of reed-thatch throws it off to the side until a squadron of crows solidifies the rhythm, carrying the eye through incendiary doors to open space, opening up the ancient sky world, habitation of sun and moon, carrying it over a river that flows by persimmon trees, over a statue with arms encircling a trunk, so you're not sure who's upholding who, and over a figure, arms outspread, silhouetted on a wall. It might be fall. Roses turn to the right, and fail. The sky is vestiges of towers flecked by tongues of flame. Women in white dresses file by. But just at that moment when the main matter seems about to be represented as rain and wings in a dark garden and a bull bellowing, words like those that descended on the apostles drift down on a scroll. The copyist may have been about to make each word add up, but now it is too late and dark to read. Everything before restoration is an unproven fact. Everything after is guesswork.

Brian Swann

Erasure

The past is a blank sheet so there's plenty of room on it. So now, here I'll start with Art homework, which is to "draw something you know." Deciding to draw our garden, I sit cross-legged on the path, on the cold concrete my father made me mix. Balancing the pad on my knees, I pick up my pencil and start with path. Then comes the small lawn, its hammock, and on it, asleep, my tubby sister. Next I start the two walls of yellow bricks on either side of the garden. Snapdragons grow in the wall's decaying mortar, up and down each side of our narrow garden, tight as a fort, like Ticonderoga in History homework, where we had to write about the Seven Years' War, which Americans call the French and Indian War. I finish one wall and its snapdragons, then the other. After that I do the trees. Trees are my favorite. I'm good at trees, puffy as clouds, all the same except for our scrawny pear that never gets puffy and has no pears. To finish things off, I look around for a noble English elm. I do elms best. A large puff on top, and a small one beneath. I don't think there are elms in America. Too bad for them. I put one in anyway. Maybe the English planted one at Ticonderoga, which is an Indian name, where they burned people alive. I could put one in singeing an Englishman, or sticking lighted matches under his nails until he told the truth. They didn't have to do that to Indians because they always spoke the truth. They called us forked tongues. They scorched an enemy's balls to make him sing. But how can you sing with your balls on fire? I decide to turn the wall into a bastion, and draw an Indian on the lawn, holding a tomahawk over my sister and her hammock. But then I think better of it and rub him out. I like how easy it is to erase. I keep going. First the elm, then the crooked pear tree, then the walls. That leaves the hammock and my sister. They go too. Then the path and me.

Out we go. I stand up, brushing the crumbs off my lap. I didn't erase my parents because I never put them in. I pick up the blank sheet and, look at it carefully, and decide erasing's a skill too. Not everybody can do it. You have to know what you're doing, what to leave in and what to take out.

Lives

In my high room looking over mountains, I sit poisoning paper and air ("vapours may ignite explosively") waiting for images to rise from the dark pool like berries to the mouths of salmon. But nothing. So I sit thinking. I don't know what I'm looking for. So I get up from my desk and walk out back where everything is in motion, occupied by shadows. I go back in, climb the stairs, and try again until gradually I find myself walking through the painting, a flicker, a surge, a shadow, but when I look closer, nothing, though my looking seems to have created something I don't recognize and will never see again, and so I want it as it lurks and hides in the ink itself, in acetone and hydrocarbon propellant, the isopropyl alcohol that can be harmful or fatal and should be kept away from heat, flame, eyes, children and pregnant women; lurking and hiding in white-out, Color-aid, everything held together by the eye that each day perishes, and the brain that each day changes all its parts so what persists is a grave deferred as you fall over yourself to be someone or something else, at least one of those "several *other* lives" Rimbaud thought everyone should have.

Part Four

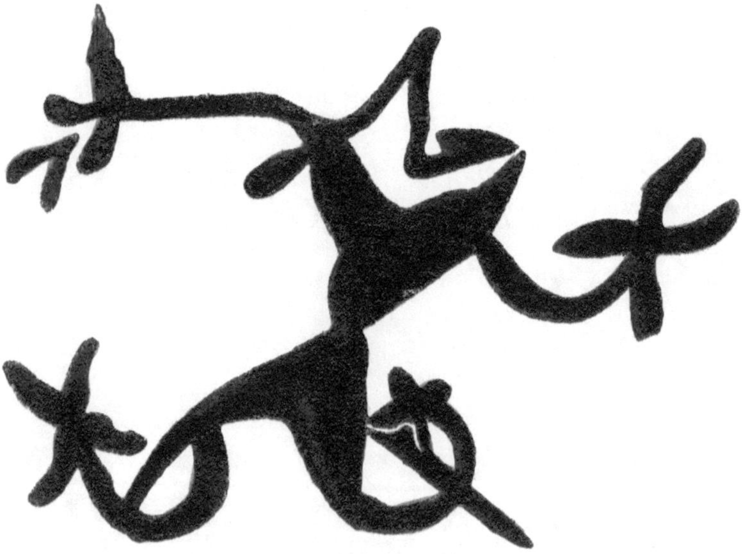

(i)

Excerpts from My First Novel,
A Flash of Lightning

Introduction

I didn't want to go to the party, but I went. Day was too hot and night was just as stifling. Since Milly, the hostess, said air-conditioners brought on her asthma, everyone was dissolving in sweat and steam, and my head ached. The TV voice in the next room announced that the air itself was unhealthy, so I tried to breathe as little as possible. A middle-aged man sat cross-legged in a corner, reading out loud: "When you say I'm in love with so-and-so what you are really saying is that they are a key-stimulus which is an innate releasing mechanism to the place in me where I am in love." A young woman in a floral skirt was chanting "Om Mani Padme Hum, Om Padme," again and again. Milly's ex-husband, Eliahu the psychiatrist, had become a fanatic Hasidic chanter. At no prompting, he would grab a guitar and go frantic with crescendo. He had been through Freud and Adler and Jung and Ram Dass and motorcycle maintenance, through speed and pot and acid and snow and psilocybin. Now he sat there, gray and remarkably tolerant, with that superior tolerance fanatics possess. He screamed a song and explained it to his wife's most recent ex-lover who had been humming along in ignorant falsetto. "It says in Hebrew 'love thy neighbor as thyself.' And what do you think that means? It means you shouldn't dump shit on him." "I don't love myself," said the ex-lover. "I mean, I love myself but I know so many people hate themselves, I—." "Yes, yes. OK. Just wait one second and you can have center stage. It means that you can only help others when you are as full of love as a cow is of milk." Or shit, I muttered, pouring more white Gallo into my paper cup. "Yeah, way out!" screamed the ex-lover through the heavily medicinal air. "That's what we were talking about yesterday, right? Everything is the same, right, Milly?" "You know," said Eliahu, "you are the most pleasant infantile schmuck I've ever come across.

It means that you can only see the rotten parts of a friend, but when you look at yourself you take yourself as a bundle of good and bad, and you can even justify the rotten parts to yourself. So what the hasid means is that you should see your neighbor in the same way as you see yourself." The ex-lover took another drag, lay back down on the floor, and began a falsetto chant in gibberish of his own composition. He never shut up, even as the kids rushed in, pulling at each other. One tugged at the tablecloth. Bottles of tonic-water and beer crashed to the floor, glass, fizz and wine everywhere. Eliahu's stepson screamed that he wanted a drink. "You'll have to wait," said Eliahu. "Wait till we've cleared the glass out of the way." "No, I want it *now*!" the child screamed, kicking him in the shins. "*Now*!" Kick. "*NOW!* Ahagh, mom he hit me, he hit me!" He kicked his step-father in the shins. In came Milly. "Why do you always have to take out your aggressions on my children?" she yelled. The evening wore on, hotter. As I sat on the floor in the corner by the radiator, I hoped that one day all this might mean something. I watched as more children came in dressed in old fancy clothes. Some came in naked. "They're ahead of us there," said a face-painted woman. One of the children had colored the others with ink, paint, crayons. A girl has red rings around her cunt, a boy had a blue asshole and a purple cock. Another girl kept trying to add black dots and as a result the boy had an erection. They knocked over a wine bottle and stood on a guitar. A large woman with long braids came in leading a boy with a face acid-burned a couple of years back by a Vietnam vet who had knocked on the door. When the child answered it, the man tossed a vial of acid in his face. "My, that's a good mask," said the painted woman. "But you are really a bit early for halloween." "Fuck you, fuck you!" the child screamed, hopping up and down, his face a sheet of shining plastic. Eliahu tried to play with the boy but only succeeded in falling over and hurting the boy's arm. "Fuck you!" yelled the boy. "You clumsy fucker!" Then everybody started shouting. I needed this like another hole in the head so decided it was time to go. Since nobody knew I was there, nobody would notice I wasn't.

As I stepped out into the night I found it even harder to breathe, this time because another pier was going up in smoke, the gay pier where men used to bathe naked. I wandered over. At first I thought it was those flashes I still got inside my eyes, but then I realized they were flames shooting up. Houses and apartments nearby were being evacuated. It was like a war zone, Ia Drang, Dong Xoai, you name it, except people were walking about in the smoke, chatting. A small middle-aged woman was bouncing about with a photographer hounding her, taking pictures. When I looked closer I could see she also had a camera and was trying to take pictures of him. She tried to complain to a cop but he shrugged her off. Another man with a movie camera was stalking them both. All three disappeared into the smoke. It sure is quite lovely in a war, I thought. Bombs dropping, fires raging, napalm flaring, everybody pulling together, like, so they say, in the London blitz. I'd never seen so many happy faces, cops and firemen in their element, the Salvation Army Emergency Snack doing a brisk business. A kind of sexual energy was generated, but, like sex, it didn't last and generated sadness. Suddenly, out of the blue, out of nowhere, out of the smoke, Greta was in my head, a kind of presence. I couldn't recall what she looked like but I caught her perfume, Greta (Margreta) whom I hadn't seen in decades and seldom thought of any more. But slowly, as I watched the fire and the smoke curling inland, I turned for home, and things started to drift back, how her dead mother had come from Sweden and her father's family from the Mezzogiorno, how her dad won a Pulitzer and her uncle was an expert on Velikovsky and flying saucers and talking plants, and in whose house I once had dinner with Peter Tompkins of *The Secret Life of Plants* and Tom Kuhn of *The Structure of Scientific Revolutions*, which almost ended in a fistfight. Yes, she came flooding back, Greta, as I sat on a stoop and felt for my cigarettes, forgetting I'd quit. I saw you walking down Nassau Street in late snow, wearing your swagger coat and little white beret, arm in arm with your girlfriend, while I watched from across the street. I saw you coming to my garage sale with a boyfriend and finding nothing to buy. You lived at home, and once in your kitchen you let down your raven-black hair for me to brush while your brothers laughed, so I brushed harder sensing I frightened you, sensing you thought I was an oaf. But this didn't prevent me from leaving in your mailbox a new pair of pantyhose still in their packaging with a note inviting you to Turkey with me, where I would have swum the Hellespont for you. Ah, Greta, half the grad students were in love with you and the other half were gay, and even half of them had a crush, not to mention a couple of middle-aged bachelor faculty and a married medievalist. You seemed oblivious to it all, deep in your Renaissance studies. Where are you now?

When I got back to my apartment, the pictures I found on Google weren't you but a lovely lady who looked like the grandmother of the girl I knew. How could you have aged like the rest of us? I couldn't look in my mirror for days, afraid of what I might see. I had calendars tacked up all over the place but they were no help. Time is pointless anyway. I hummed a hymn: "*Time like a river bears all its sons away./ They fly forgotten as a dream dies at the break of day."* Everything happens at once, we're all made up, bits of each other, at least that was what I used to tell my class, so I had a drink or two or three and stared out the window where people flowed by like fish, swaying like kelp. I ran a scenario in my head where I'm high on a beach waiting for the next wave to suck me back, I'm fighting for breath until at nightfall, exhausted, I'm ready to climb aboard any boat that might be sent to save me. Once on board, I go below decks and listen as the raven-haired first mate stretches and does yoga poses on deck until she senses I'm listening and stops. Silence. Later, I decide to go on deck and thence up to the crow's nest to get a better look at what it is I am trying to lose myself in, what I am trying to forget, but the scenario gets away from me, so I back up, I scramble, as waves chase each other, falling over, swamping in mindless haste, the boat beating to windward. Once there, I wobble as if at the tip of earth's pole. I listen to a bird cry, one note over and over, ecstatic, until I lose my balance and fall back down onto the deck, where I slacken off stays so sails flutter and the ship sails in place against whatever wind's left in a bay wide as the Mekong delta. It stays there with the shore in sight, but moves no closer since there are flames and explosions. When light returns, I can see with my mind's eye people on the land, quiet as balloons, moving the way snow moves, melting as they pass, flowing away while I breathe as if improvising, as if the intent of breathing was enough to keep me alive, as if it was simply enough to follow the breath, the way I followed for a whole afternoon forty years ago a woman in Venice, following an illusion with no inevitably diminished culmination. I never caught up with her and I never saw her face so in theory I could have followed her for ever. It was enough just to follow, just as it was almost enough to let Greta go again by losing myself in a bottle and a book, like the one I'm reading about Ryokan, a teacher who lived in a small hut. The story goes like this: One day while walking along a potato field, he was overtaken by the desire to shit. Now the owner of said field, who was suffering from a series of thefts, had hidden nearby. When he saw Ryokan all bent over he leapt up and began to beat him. A boy saw what was happening and cried out: *Stop, stop! That's our teacher, Ryokan!* But he was pushed aside and the beating continued. When it was over, the puzzled boy asked Ryokan: "Why didn't you tell him who you were?" But Ryokan said nothing, pulled himself together and staggered home. There, so we're told, he wrote a poem: "*The one who beats and the one who is beaten,/ Both are like dew, or a flash of lightning.*" Yes, there might be the germ of a novel here. I'll call it "A Flash of Lightning." That'll do for a while. Beating and beaten, the canceling out, the same and different. It's all shit. And so on to Chapter One.

Chapter One: The House

A house constitutes a body of images that give mankind proofs or illusions of stability.
—Gaston Bachelard

Not long after we bought our house, across our quiet valley, a city architect, his fashion-editor wife and their baby-to-be turned a huge old falling-down barn into an edifice that appeared on the cover of *New York Magazine*. Solid people lived there, and nothing could move it, not even if the mountain fell on it. But I couldn't imagine myself living under those massive oak beams, inside those fortress walls, even if I could have afforded it on my Board-of-Ed. pension. In any case, Greta and I were happy enough in our small house, at least for a while, before she got bored with even her intermittent weekend visits. The moment I saw the A-frame I knew it was right, though once inside I was almost blinded where I stood by the white pickled oak floor, which brought on one of my headaches. Greta wasn't so keen. Her tastes ran more to the aristocratic, as befitted a Bryn Mawr grad. Me, my tastes weren't so refined, as you'd expect from someone who'd worked his way out of Gravesend, not the one where Pocahontas died and was buried, but the one in Brooklyn where my dad had a chop shop, someone who'd never finished his thesis on Byron even with the help of Chapter 34. Anyway, to return to the matter at hand, I'd never owned anything before, and I felt that now was the time to have a house, a place of my own, a base to put roots down, even if it meant dealing with Eddy, the retired-cop do-it-yourselfer from New Jersey. The first thing he asked me was if I wanted to buy the appliances. I thought they came with the place, I said. That's usual. Usual, he said. You want usual? I'm not giving stuff away, you know. And he took almost everything with him, including the microwave which left a huge hole above the stove. He also carried off his long ladder and the strips of flypaper black with cluster flies which the ladder was designed to reach, high in the corners of the cathedral ceiling's skylights. Turned out this was Eddy's first shot at a house. He sold it to us to build a boat in his backyard. I hope he learned a thing or two from building this, like don't drill too many holes. But, as I said, I took to the house at once, though it took its time speaking to me. A house is like a person. It didn't give up its secrets immediately. The oil delivery man was the first to find one when the pipe blew his #2 heating oil back into his face, drenching him and knocking him flat. I think he saw the funny side, though I've had difficulty getting him to make deliveries since, which has made me use the woodstove more, though it doesn't really work and I can't get parts because the company that made it in New Zealand has been out of business some time. Other revelations soon appeared. Doors stuck, windows jammed. Toilets slowly tipped you off onto the floor. The bathroom sink wobbled. Push the jacuzzi button in the bathtub and get slapped silly by the waves. H and C taps were everywhere reversed, but not consistently. A scalding helped you remember. The garage door had a mind of its own, sliding up and down when it felt like it, or when you pressed one of many light switches, which last time round had turned on a light, or nothing at all. Flip the ceiling fan switch and you smelled smoke in the basement. It kept you on your toes, that's for sure. You took nothing for granted. Surprise was the order of the day, or night, when things went pop or bang, and something scratched and whimpered in the bedroom wall. The house had character, I guess you could say that, even the basement where the variety of valves kept failing and flooding the place, which the plumbers found amusing. If you looked up from wet feet you'd see on floorbeams penciled arrows pointing every which way, with messages. "Not glued", said one. "Almost done," said another. The one that read "Guess what?" has me still guessing and looking over my shoulder. In case someone forgot what one looked like, "Pipe" was scrawled next to it, with an arrow. That sure was some place, that basement. Wires of all sorts and colors hung and dropped. Beams had holes drilled through and nothing going in. Lots of holes. Holes in holes. Above ground I made a garden from scratch—manure from the back field, lots of leaves, a few dead birds and squirrels I found under the deck. When I went there to relax or dig I had to watch out. Tiles, stapled, not nailed, shot off like Frisbees over my head and into the woods. A lovely green color stained the buckled deck planks and ran down the sturdy wood pillars into said garden. Eddy said it was only arsenic for insects, and everybody used it. Nothing to worry about, he said, but once I'd glimpsed myself in the mirror I wasn't so sure. Still, nobody came by, especially after Greta went back to the city permanently. She couldn't take the isolation, but soon, thanks to New York Magazine, the whole area was overrun with all the new "DO NOT TRESPASS OR YOU WILL BE SHOT" signs, and crazed realtors whizzing about with families in tow, SUVs, ATVs, Humvees, chainsaws, bulldozers, road gangs, guns, lots of guns, ABMs, ATMs, or whatever they're called, machines I'd never seen before. I nailed up my own signs. "NOBODY LIVES HERE SO GO AWAY." If anyone made it up the drive I'd chase them away with whatever came to hand and became known as the someone to avoid. I lasted a year then sold the place to an Indian family from Queens and returned to the city. In truth, the house never felt like home and how much gardening can you do, how many hikes can you take, how many bottles empty and books read? Nothing lasts. And I missed Greta, who was working hard on her second book, this one about *Hamlet*, and it was not going well. She said she was arguing that the play was about estrangement, transience and detachment; that a "ham-let" is a little "ham", or village, a home. Hamlet was detached from his "ham," cut off from his patrimony. She also said that the name "Hamlet" contained a reference to Ham, son of Noah but I didn't pick up how, and that the plot generated by the play was a plot of land, but here she lost me. Still, it all seemed very clever, but she looked depressed and needed cheering up. "I think Hamlet delayed so long," I said, "because it was his job to drag things out so there'd be a play. No delay, no play." She shot me one of her looks. "How funny, how original." "OK," I said, "look, let's have some fun. Let's go somewhere. Let's take a trip." "You've only just got back," she snapped. "I have a surprise," I told her, though I hadn't. "Trust me," I said. I knew it would not turn out well.

Chapter Two: (Untitled as yet)

The car's brake light fluttered on and off. She said, "You never get this car serviced." I said, "It just came from its checkup. You know nothing about cars." Just then, going around a corner the brakes failed. I pushed the pedal to the floor again and again. "Use the gears, you oaf!" she yelled. "It's automatic!" I yelled back.

Despite all the drama, we arrived at the nudist camp late in the afternoon. (Here I should interject that I don't think that the real rather reserved and cool Greta would ever have done any of the things I am about to describe, or which I have already described. In truth, though she fascinated me, as I said, I'd hardly known her, so I guess there could have been a possibility that she might have been up for a trip to a nudist camp. She certainly had the figure for it. In any case, I forgot to mention that I discovered the googled Greta was a distinguished Ivy League professor and had stayed beautiful and single well into her sixties when she met and married a famous Old Etonian novelist and travel writer with John Dryden and Alma-Tadema up his family tree. He was a year or two older than me, and, while older than Greta, he too had never married. I felt a touch of jealousy and meanness, but I also felt hope, which took the form of thinking that since he was so old he'd soon be dead, freeing her up for me again, though by now I wasn't sure I wanted her. Perhaps all I wanted was revenge.) But back to the nudist camp, which we reached in late afternoon. As we pulled up to the gate and waited behind a couple of cars, I noticed the place had a large swimming pool. As we sat in silence, my mind drifted back to the time I went with Greta to the university pool where, when I wasn't staring at her breasts, I watched a skinny Jerzy Kozinsky at the shallow end paddling about while his large companion, Kiki, was doing great laps. "What?" I said to Greta as she poked me in the side. "Oh."

I moved the car forward, paid the lady proprietor $10.50 at the gate, and drove in to the parking lot where we disrobed, put our clothes in the trunk and set off barefoot and bare-ass along a path black with the glitter of coal chippings and cinders. There was a smell of smoke. We followed the narrow path with a chicken-wire fence running along one side and a green-mantled pond along the other. I almost stumbled over a frog disguised as a lump of coal. The path ended in an abandoned chicken-run. "There's no worse stink than chicken shit," I noted as an invisible cock crowed. Just then a bee stung me on the scalp. "Pull it out!" Greta said. "If you don't it'll fester. Then it'll have to be lanced. They may have to cut your head off. Look, there's a hole! It's bleeding! You should have worn your helmet." But I just let it throb like a dark memory. A few stray sky-beams flickered. In the distance we saw a large greenhouse lit from within, and beside it something that looked like the field hospital at Nha Trang, and beside that a long, narrow log cabin which, when we entered, was found to have walls of well-polished wood and satin sheets on the bed. I turned on the gas lamp but Greta said "Turn it off. We don't know how it works. We don't even know who lives here." She looked around for a match, found a box, then remembered she was afraid of lighting things. "The gas smells worse than chicken shit," she said, though in reality the real Greta would never have used such a word. "Here, you light," she said, but then, "Wait. What'll happen if the people return, don't know the gas is on, and light a match! They'd be blown sky-high, that's what. And stop staring at my breasts as if you've never seen them before." "I haven't," I said. "And anyway, if God hadn't meant for us to stare at breasts he'd have hidden them away somewhere, like under the armpits." She sat on the bed, pulling the coverlet around her.

Dogs on the Roof

I sat beside her, naked. "What are we doing here anyway?" she said. "I didn't mean to put us here," I told her. I turned on the gas and almost forgot to strike a match. When I did, there was an explosion, a yellow flash, and I fell back onto the bed, closing my eyes. We were at a stalemate. We were not even us. I lay there. When I got up Greta was gone, which was just as well. The whole thing was a postscript to something that never happened, and never could as long as time, ruled by desire, if by anything, slips and stumbles as it weaves drunkenly in and out of itself, catch as catch can. This is what is meant by the texture of time, every part touching every other part, like the Net of Indra, except that now it's all tangled and there are large tears. Or it's like a black hole lit from time to time by flashes of lightning.

Excerpts from My Second Novel, Working Title *Eileen, Natasha, Mary, The Rats, and Me*

Chapter One: The Dreaming

My last secretary watered the plastic plant for a month before she realized. It took the next one only a week. She had been born again just before I hired her. Each morning she came in with her Celebrate Christ coffee mug dangling from one finger and hugging the Celebrate Christ apothecary jar in which she kept her hard candy. She tormented me for six weeks with her lack of Word Perfect and her insistence on saving everything so there was no telling which version of a document or letter she'd produce when requested. For each mistake she corrected she made at least another two. In theory, she could have worked on the same document forever. Several times she'd tempted me to Promote her to Glory. Her humming hymns all day from the Salvation Army Song Book was one thing. Her feminism was another. Almost the first day she arrived, seeing a copy of *Playboy* peeking from my desk drawer (I was planning on using it to defrost the antique office fridge) she started in on how the magazine was "exploitive of woman." I was about to agree, when she added, "I also think that physically challenged women should have the same right as other women to be included." I was about to agree again but she rolled on: "It would go to show there's diversity among the physically challenged, Praise the Lord."

I am now between secretaries again. My wife helps out once in a while, but she has her own work and no real interest in the export-import business. Alone in the office, I became aware of my various aches and pains. I was more conscious, for example, of a pain in my legs, terrible pain in both feet, and the difficulty of getting about. The podiatrist told me I had a severe case of plantar fasciitis in both feet, as well as heel spurs and arthritis in each foot's small bones. I probably contracted this, I told him, as well as other aches and pains, in the rain forests of Ecuador. Until a year ago I didn't even know how to pronounce "podiatrist." If asked, I would have said "po-di-at-rist," accent on the "at." I wasn't even sure what a podiatrist did. But mornings crawling on knees and elbows from bed to bathroom convinced me I ought to see one—actually, my wife made the suggestion. I found Dr. Apple in the Yellow Pages. "Don't wear those orthoses more than an hour a day," he told me after all sorts of measurements and casts. "Some people call them 'orthotics,' but their proper name is 'orthoses'." He was a huge young man with photos of blue sailfish leaping out of the ocean on his walls. He was a great fisherman, it seems, spending each weekend in Florida. "Why not?" I inquired. "It'll kill your arch." "I thought my arch was already killed." He shrugged. "Will wearing these things hurt?" He shrugged again. "How do I know?" On the way out I chatted with the receptionist. It turned out she was about to leave him and return to the Phillipines where she was to marry a guy whose family owned a huge fleet of buses. She was afraid of Mt. Pinatubo erupting again. I asked her about my feet. "Is it common?" "It happens to the elderly," she said. "And you should lose some weight."

My last medical had been about a year ago. Or so I thought. "Five years is too long," Dr. Feld told me. "Time flies," I said, "when you're having fun." I told him about the pain in my legs. He gave me a blue gown made of paper and left me alone in an examining room the size of a closet. I looked around to see what I could swipe. But there wasn't anything except little empty bottles, needles, an open box of Q-tips, paper cups to pee in, and a pile of paper towels near the sink. It looked like he'd been cleaned out already. I didn't need any more Q-tips or towels. I sat on the edge of the examining table and listened to the racket outside. There were a dozen doctors working out of this address. The waiting room was like Penn Station at rush hour. I stood up and dropped my drawers just as the door opened. "Sorry," said a middle-aged woman. "Where ees the batroom?" Before I could reply, Doctor Feld was back."How's the farm in Massachusetts?" he asked, glancing at his clipboard. "What farm?" He turned over a couple of sheets. "Oh, import business, how is it?" "*Export*-import" I replied, though in truth I no longer exported much. Next to nothing, really. "Hmmm," he said, studying some scrawl. "Picked up any bad habits since last time?" "No smoking," I replied. "No drinking. No buggery." He gave me the usual going-over, and then came the moment I dreaded. "Lie on your side, please. Knees up a bit." Ay, ay. "OK. Your prostate is smooth. No bumps." He peeled off his gloves, tossed them into the can, and was gone. I sat for half an hour waiting for the nurse he promised to take blood, do an e.k.g. and the rest. From time to time he paid a courtesy call. "She been in yet?" I was ready to cut and run except my legs and feet hurt and I wouldn't have gotten far. Anyway, eventually the nurse came, took blood, did e.k.g. and told me to provide a urine sample, none too soon. I'd stocked up on soda before I arrived, just in case. "Where?" I asked, looking at the paper cups. "Here?" The Caribbean nurse scowled. "In the bathroom." So, taking a paper cup and a plastic vial, I did as I was told, and was soon lost in a labyrinth of crowded corridors and rooms. Luckily, I was dressed. When I finally located a bathroom I had to wait. When my turn came it didn't take me long to do what I had to do and emerge bearing my vial of golden pee. Holding it in front of me, careful not to spill, I proceeded to get lost again. Eventually, I found myself in a room something like a lab except a nurse was eating a sandwich among all the bottles and tubes. "Excuse me," I said, displaying my amber liquid, "but what do I do with this? "Put it down there," she said, between bites. "But how will the nurse know it's mine?" I inquired. She lifted her shoulders, and dropped them. A small lady, probably from the islands. I stood there, hesitant. I tried to stand the tube on end, but it was rounded, so I leaned it against some others that were empty and hoped it wouldn't tip over. "Now what do I do?" I asked. "Stand on your head," she replied, snapping open a Tab.

*

"I know you have a theory that it's easier to make the bed when you're in it," my wife said, "but it isn't. Get up."
"Female conches grow penises," I told her. "I'm lying here planning what to do with that new consignment of assorted Caribbean gastropods. There are some lovely cock stromps."
"That's all you think of. You lack romance. Get up."
"You only recognize romance on TV," I told her.
I had only thought of romance as a means to an end. For some time now that end had been nowhere in sight. The last time I did it she was asleep and couldn't say no, but as I was doing it I felt like one of those bloody dogs that bites picnickers. I'm a morning person. Eileen, needless to say, is a night person. I wake primed. I prefer to do everything in the morning. I hope to die in the morning.

Eileen had given up trying to get me out of bed and was rearranging one of her drawers, the one she kept her vibrator in. Once I tried unscrewing the damn thing to get at the insides, but no screwdriver I had would fit the screws. And it was built practically all of a piece, heavy and self-contained, built to withstand the bombardment of meteorites in outer space. Another time I tried submerging it in the sink, but it could have been built to a submarine blueprint for all the damage I did. I looked at Eileen. She was thin and rawboned, with reddish hair, medium build. She had become afraid that my sperm might contain pathogens that could give her AIDS. Before that, she'd said she was allergic to my sperm, and it had given her vaginitis, even when I wore rubbers, which I hated. "Your microbes are lazy," she'd said, "like you. And crafty. They hitch a ride on your sperm. If we didn't menstruate we'd all be dead of candida albicans and the like. Men are killers. Thank God for the monthly flush, even though at my age it means I'll pay a price later." For a long time Eileen had tried to train me with phrases like "affection without erection." This soon became "affection without infection." I suspected she's gotten all this from Mary, her five-ten, two-fifty-plus-pound friend. Mary was one of Aristotle's born slaves, built perfectly for shopping and bodyguard duties. She told Eileen she didn't need to depend on a man for anything. They called each other "Honey."

Without turning from the drawer, Eileen said:
"You should lose weight. Remember what the doctor said about your heart."
"How are the bruised backs of your knees?" I countered, making an unpleasant reference to a falling gluteus maximus.
"Sometimes I think you hate women."
"The heart hath its reasons."
She shoved the drawer shut.
"I'm going to the cheese store. What do you want me to get?"
"A pineapple, maybe."
"The *cheese* store."

"It's possible. You can buy lots of things if Mary is there to carry for you, then escort you home safely."
"Why don't you leave her alone? She's never done anything to you. I think you're jealous."
"Well, it's true she's got over fifty pounds on me. She's a mountain. Remember 'the Odyssey'? 'She was huge, and they hated her'."
"So are you. You exaggerate everything about her. About everything."
"Sorry."
"You've become really awful in your old age, bitter and paranoid. It's nobody's fault, age. You used to be fun."
"So did you."
In truth, it wasn't so much that I disliked Mary, though I did. But she reminded me of my own shortcomings, lack of loyalty, for one. And it looked really grotesque to see her side by side with my skinny attractive wife.
"I give up. Here, I'll go over what I think we'll need at the store. I have a list."
"To port or starboard?"
"Always the same jokes. You're always repeating yourself, honey."
"Don't call me 'honey'."
She's never appreciated my jokes. But sometimes she brings back jokes Mary tells her, mostly Catholic schoolgirl jokes which I don't understand. She sat down on the side of the bed.
"I had this dream last night," she said. I groaned inwardly. She must have heard.
"Fine," she muttered. "Forget it."
"No, no, I—."
"Forget it, *honey*."
Eileen dreamed a lot, and saw significance in her dreams.

"I may have to go to Seattle next week. Kwakiutl masks."
She was now looking for something in the hall closet.
"It said in the papers they had an outbreak of bucolic plague out west."
"Bubonic."
"Bucolic, bubonic, carbolic. They're advising people there not to play with dead animals."
"One of my favorite pastimes."
Suddenly I remembered a shipment of Carib stone inscriptions smuggled out of St. Kitts twenty years ago when they were leveling half the island for the Frigate Bay project, high-profile tourism. Had they ever arrived? What had I done with them? The contractors who found them had smashed most so as not to delay the project. But some got smuggled out...."
"Ow!"
Eileen had returned and sat down heavily on one of my feet.
"Last night on TV they showed Romanian orphans. One man sold his million-dollar house in California and gave them the money. A woman adopted a baby with the most horrible disfigurements. She said she saw its beauty. Barbara Walters wept."
"I hate Barbara Walters."
"I sometimes think we should adopt."
She rose and walked slowly to the living room.

 Can one feel lust for one's spouse? Only by imagining them as someone else, not part of the family. I lay back. Over my belly I could just make out my toes. I counted them. Correct. I reached under the bed for the pack of Marlboro and the book of matches. I took out a cigarette, lit it. A dream came flooding back, a huge flash, the west exploding, attacks camouflaged as natural phenomena. I never want to see you again, my wife said, so go away. But my feet were locked and I couldn't move. "Something's burning," Eileen called out

*

Despite everything, I try to remain as positive as possible. Yesterday, for instance, I took a fancy to a pollarded, lopped locust tree. Its spring leaves were yellow-green, the sap rising from the earth, surging up its trunk to be embodied as more leaves, airy as thought. But while I was admiring this, and musing philosophical musings, a small dog on a leash came by. It reared its hind leg and pissed on the trunk. I was outraged, and was about to confront the dog and its owner when I stopped and looked carefully. The piss was bright golden stream shot through with yellow sun. And I thought: A tree is a wonder of nature, but that dog's piss is a miracle too.

I was in a good mood by the time I got home. And so, strange to say, was Eileen. For once she had a story to tell me that did not involve, or derive from, Mary. She had bumped into an old friend on the street who told her about her crazy mother-in-law on a visit from England. "Did you know our old house in Maidstone?" she'd asked her daughter-in-law. "No," she replied. "It was sold before I came on the scene." "Just as well," the old lady went on. "It was a lovely house." "John told me it's now a home for delinquents." "The De-who?" her mother-in-law queried. "I don't believe I know them." She'd gotten drunk on the plane over and kept banging on the window. "Stewardess, stewardess, it's rather stuffy in here. Can you open a window?" Eileen was laughing. She didn't laugh much these days. She looked like her old self. "Maybe I can postpone that Seattle trip, "I said. "Don't you think it's time for that trip to the country? The weather's warm and we can borrow Myron's house." Myron was someone I knew through the trade. He'd just retired, remarried again and was on a cruise. "We can squeeze in three days. Things are slow now, and you don't have any classes Fridays." But Eileen said there were too many insects, and Myron always left his dog up there. "He's got a dirty tongue." She also saw a rat last time. "What do you want for dinner?" "Pu pu platter."

After this rejection, I gave up on the idea of a weekend sojourn, so I was surprised when later that day Eileen asked if Mary could come with us. "I'd rather not go," I said. I was even more surprised when Eileen said that Mary couldn't make that weekend anyway.

*

Butch, he of the dirty tongue, wasn't the problem. He spent most of his time chasing frogs in the pond, around the pond, through the pond. Other people had bird-dogs. Butch was a frog-dog. No, Butch wasn't the problem. Bo was the problem. Bo was Myron's neighbor, a yuppie banker from the city who owned a dacha at the end of the lane. His wife had stayed back in the city and he was lonely so he dropped by with his six year-old son Julian just as Eileen was cooking dinner. She invited them to stay and then went upstairs. Bo went to the bathroom while I sat in the nineteenth-century farmhouse's renovated living room trying to talk with Satchel until he got bored and wandered off into the kitchen. Suddenly he ran back—
"The pan's on fire! The pan's on fire!"
"Your pants are on fire?" I said, entering into the spirit of things.
"The pan's on fire!"
From where I was sitting I could see that it wasn't.

"So put it out," I said. "What should you do if your pants are on fire?"
"*Pan!*" he screamed.
"Stick your butt in the pond?"
"*The pan!*"
Just then Bo returned. He sized up the situation.
"Now, Satchel," he said, "what would you do if your pants *were* on fire? We've been over this many times. Mr. Spangler here is trying to teach you something. Remember, he's a teacher."
I tried to protest, "exporter-," but he pressed on.
"Well, son, what would you do if your pants were on fire?"
"Dunno."
"You'd *roll*. Don't you remember? I told you, if your clothes are on fire you *roll*."
"But they're not on fire."
"That's not the point."
"The pan's on fire."
Just then I smelled smoke and thought I glimpsed a flame. I leapt up. Such is the power of suggestion. And while Bo droned on about teaching opportunities and the market I checked out on the horsehair sofa, musing on other fires like the one by the old pier that July 4, fire-trucks and firemen.
"Lots of fires?" my friend Herb asked casually, making conversation.
"A few," the older black fireman replied. "Big one ten years ago."
"No, I mean tonight."
"Yea, a few."
"Did you catch the people who set them."
"You from around here?" the older fireman asked us.
"Yea, sure," said Herb. "We just came out for a breath of fresh air."

The younger white fireman glanced up at a lamp almost obscured by smoke from the pier's smoldering creosote.
"Fresh air?" he said.
"Sure," Herb replied. "Look, there's another fire out there."
He pointed, but nobody could see it.
"How do *you* know?" asked the elder fireman.
"Maybe it's out," said Herb, quick. "Have they cut out the fire from underneath? Is it still burning?"
"No," said the white fireman.
"Yes," said the black fireman.
They turned and glared at each other.
"How come you're so interested?" asked the black fireman.
"I'm an artist," said Herb.
Fireworks and rockets shot all over the place. The firemen stood statuesque, looking at each other.
"Who gets to hold the hose?" asked Herb.

*

All my friends seem a bit nutty and bleached. I mentioned this the other day to my friend Nahtasha, though I didn't tell her that recently she'd been looking more faded than most, bleached out, even. I had known Nahtasha about four years, since she wrote a letter to my company protesting the importation of rhinoceros horn. I liked her handwriting so I wrote back explaining that what she had read in the *Village Voice* was in fact erroneous, and she was welcome to inspect the premises. Which she did, and that's how we met. (I was careful to hide the horn and turtle shells and walrus ivory too). Soon after, her husband, a retired high-school teacher, had died in mysterious circumstances, which was particularly sad because her first husband, Jim, had also died, as she put it, "in unfortunate circumstances." Anyhow, no doubt as the result of all this, most of Nahtasha's hair had fallen out and she had taken to wearing a flaxen wig as close to her original (dyed) flaxen locks as possible. The wig did double duty as a *sheitel*. Though not Jewish, Nahtasha was serious about joining the Hasidim in Crown Heights as a way, in her words, or linking her youthful idealistic Marxism with a more practical and immediate messianic future.

The first time I went to her apartment to see her collection of seashells from the Leeward Islands she pointed out her parrot to me. Apparently, he had achieved some sort of fame as a mimic, imitating vacuum cleaners and the voices of dead people. She'd had him stuffed and placed under a tall bell-jar on a Victorian night-stand beside the door. A tape-recorder sat alongside with the parrot's version of the "Post-horn Gallop," a vacuum cleaner and assorted voices available at the touch of a button. There was also a rooster in the apartment, a massive white bird named Walter who kept picking at my shoelaces despite some hefty, if secret, kicks. "Roosters symbolize dawn and rebirth," Nahtasha informed me. "That so?" I said, looking around and noticing nothing offensive about floor and carpet. "Where does he do his business?" "In the bathroom," Nahtasha replied, as if I'd asked a very silly question. I glanced at the open window."Aren't you afraid he'll fly away?" "No fear of that," she said. "I've clipped one of his wings. He could only fly in circles. I've also had his spurs clipped. He comes from a long line of fighting cocks." The rooster was going for my ankles now. "Playing dead is one of his favorite tricks. Want to see?"

The whole apartment was dark and gave off an aura of decay. And yet I was not repelled. What is it that attracts us to decay? Are

we trying to immunize ourselves to the inevitable? Do we hope to find the germ of new life in corruption? What is the beauty in the fantastic blooms and efflorescences of decay? Is it the thrill of decay? Thrill-seekers, they say, have a low level of arousal. The sense of danger primes a neural network at the base of the brain, the reticular activating network. They have an imbalance in the brain chemical monoamine oxidane which has been implicated in some forms of depression. Excitement changes the level of chemical from torpor to relation. I must be a thrill-seeker. My reverie was interrupted.
"Stop that! He's humping the chair leg! Where does he pick up such habits?"
Sure enough, Walter the White Rooster was going at it, sturdy scaly legs grasping the smooth wood. Nahtasha chased him off.
"Maybe looking out the window," I volunteered.
Nahtasha glanced to her left.
"I'll keep the curtains closed all day from now on," she said.
There was the sound of crowing from the bathroom.

*

Eileen is quite a few years younger than I. One of the problems with a younger wife is that you find yourself doing things again which you tired of doing decades before, like going to poetry readings. But Eileen is something of a jill-of-all-trades, having published two poetry chapbooks and a children's book which she illustrated herself. Proceeds from this book, *Jimmy and the Butterfly*, paid for the car we used to have until constant towing and vandalizing led to its demise. She is now planning a poetry video so, every now and then, when Mary is otherwise engaged,

Eileen pries me loose from the apartment and drags me off to somewhere like the Poetry Society of America on Gramercy.

In the early days it was old ladies breaking wind at both ends. Now the crowd was younger and less flatulent, but I still hated it. Poetry is what writers resort to when they can't do anything else. It takes no stamina and less knowledge. Nietzsche had it right: "The poet carries his thoughts in the carriage of rhythm because they can't walk." Anyhow, no amount of complaining about pains in feet or legs had any effect.

Eileen insists on walking everywhere. Her mother taught her, she says. She talked all the way to the reading.
"I am holding a naked baby, almost newborn, to my chest."
"Yes," I say, exaggerating my limp.
"I go everywhere with her. We are both naked. We go shopping. The baby is talking words only I can hear. We go to the dentist together. A filling in one of my molars is loose. It falls out. What do you think it means."
"When did you last go to the dentist?"
She said nothing for the rest of the walk.
The reading room was full of old ladies, just like the old days. I looked around. Not a young woman in sight. I protested to Eileen. "I told you it was a reading to celebrate the publication of an anthology of women poets over seventy," she hissed. I looked around again. Nothing to eat. Nothing to drink. Not even wine. "I didn't realize it was only a reading," I whispered. "I feel tricked." "We're all tricked each day," Eileen replied in a loud voice, walking away, soon to return with a plate of what looked like dog biscuits. I waved them aside and looked around. Pots and aspidistras, and a glass door that seemed to lead to a brick wall. An ancient lady was standing on a dais. She looked exactly like my Aunt Helen

except Aunt Helen had a fuller moustache and no chin whiskers at all. The lady was intoning something Yeatsean, working up a thin head of steam. Aunt Helen was my father's father's brother's wife. We called her "aunt" though she wasn't, really. My father thought that her husband, Uncle Ted, who had a dry goods store upstate, had left her his money, so I and my sister (no longer with us) were forced to be nice to her when she came over for lunch every Sunday—we were living in Jersey City at the time. She always dressed in a long black gingham frock and smelled of mothballs. My father did the cooking, and there was always a lot of food. I think he was either trying to put her off guard by showing her that we didn't need her money and were only inviting her because we loved her, or else he was trying to kill her by over-feeding, especially with fat-heavy roasts. If so, he was sadly mistaken. I now think that she ate nothing all week, saving up for those Sunday lunches when she ate not only her own ample portions but whatever was left over. "Do have some more," my mother would urge, in on the plot. "Oh, no, I couldn't possibly," Aunt Helen would whimper. "I'm so full. Well, if nobody else … It's a shame to waste it." Whatever it was would soon disappear inside her gray otter whiskers, and instead of dropping dead on the rich food my father reserved for Sundays she just kept on going, mysteriously getting sleeker and thinner, her tall frame almost outlasting my father's plump form. Her fast eating did, however, have some effect on her, creating small flatulences she seemed not to notice. When the inevitable occurred, my father would mutter under his breath: "Don't tear it, lady. I'll take the whole piece." Which sent us children into giggles and banishment.

Now she floated before my eyes again, as another old lady mounted the dais. There was Aunt Helen, high buttoned collar,

black buttoned blouse, long black skirt and a black satiny straw hat. I sat remembering how when she finally did kick off she left my father only the small amount Uncle Ted had left him in his will, and which had been entrusted to Aunt Helen. The rest went to her sister in Syracuse none of us knew about. My father was furious. He wouldn't even go to the funeral.
"Do have more."
It was Eileen, shoving the dog biscuits under my nose. I hadn't realized I'd been chewing on them.
"It's a shame to waste them," I said, rising, "but I've had all I can take."
I stepped out and down the stairs, heading home, just needing to walk, even though my right leg was all pins and needles. Sometimes it happened that the best thing to do with pain is keep on right through it. But not in this case. I stopped and looked about for a cab. The podiatrist had said I was walking on the bone. That's what it felt like, in addition to the pins and needles. Nothing between bone and concrete. As I stood there I had a memory of walking by docks somewhere, maybe Korea, maybe the Philippines. They were pulling a body out of the water. In response to someone's query, the officer in charge said: Yes, we pull a number of them out each year. But then we throw them back.

*

I was late, on the way out the door for the office. A thought struck me, I turned.
"It'll soon be the anniversary of our last screw. Three years come Tuesday. Want to celebrate a little in advance?
"What?"

"Now."
"Have you noticed that when you make these exciting offers I can't refuse, the time and circumstance?"
I opened the door. She continued.
"And does it ever occur to you that the more you go on the less chance there is?"
"Maybe that's the idea," I said, covering.
"You're all talk. And as for your technique. Scottish foreplay, 'Brace yersel', lassie'."
"Think of me as a master painter at the height of his powers. In youth and middle age I was all flounces, colors, sensitivities, full of excess, no need of 'technique.' Now, a brush stroke here, a line there, they contain all. Thy slightest touch is full of essence."
"You're full of—."
But I was out the door. On the street I realized there was nobody at the office to care if I was late, so I decided I needed a trim and cheer-up at the barber's. I was spending more and more time there. Gasparo, the owner, had come as a baby from Cassino and the cutters were mostly relatives. My buddy in Korea, Lucca, had had family in Cassino. When I told Gasparo his name it turned out he was connected in some distant Italian way, so he gave me free haircuts until I put a stop to it without hurting his pride. Gasparo was in his late fifties, on the large side of small. He talked nonstop, especially about what homeless people do in the parks. "I'm not unsympathetic," he'd say. "And I'm not a *doomsayer*,"— "doomsayer" was a favorite word. "But we have to do something about it. The whole world is collapsing. Poof—." His scissors would take a wide and rapid turn through the air. Gasparo had a tendency to gloominess. When he became depressed he became unreliable with the clippers and even more dangerous with the

scissors. Today he looked a bit down so I tried to cheer him up. "I just went on a pleasure trip," I said. He bit. "Where did you go?" "I took my mother-in-law to the airport." He smiled. "Maybe I should go to Florida for a vacation. I could call my uncle, my father's brother. He lives down there. He's over eighty. He's mostly full of life but sometimes he gets depressed—it runs in the family. When he gets depressed he calls me. I can cheer him up. He's always doing something. He's not somebody who sits around and vegetated till he gets plowed under. He just bought a microwave and a van. He goes around warming up pizza, or did until the Mafia burnt him out. Luckily, he had some insurance, so he went into the novelties business. He invented what he called—pardon my Spanish—'a bullshit protector.' It's this little bit of leather that fits over the ears. He went to a novelties convention in Lake Tahoe last summer and paid his way by selling some on the way. What a world, eh?"

*

Mary is ten years younger than my wife. She is also over six feet and two-eighty. She says she weighs so much and puts on weight so fast because of a slow metabolism and because her youngest brother committed suicide after losing a football game. That was when she started eating. Mary has made herself indispensable to Eileen, carrying an umbrella over her head when it rains and sometimes when it doesn't, watching TV for her when she can't and delivering a blow by blow report over the phone the next day. These calls can last for over two hours.

Anything that needs mechanical attention, from typewriter to coffee-grinder, Eileen takes to Mary, or calls her over. They exchange dreams a lot. Eileen's voice changes on the phone.

Sometimes it becomes schoolmarm and full of sibilants. At other times it is like a little girl's voice. Mary is a junior executive at a charitable foundation. If she doesn't get her daily phone fixes with Eileen she comes running over, all thirty blocks, and mashes on the intercom. If I'm home alone I will let the thing ring until it rings itself out. She may try three or four times before she gives up. Even then, she will wait about until someone with a key arrives, and then persuade him, or her to let them in, which is against our co-op laws. Then she'll come charging out of the elevator, bawling like a sick cow for Eileen. After I'm forced to open the door before it collapses, she tumbles in and runs through the place calling Eileen's name, as if I'd secreted her somewhere. "Is she here? Is she here? Where is she? Is she sick? I thought she was sick when you didn't answer." There have been rare occasions when Eileen herself couldn't take it, especially after Mary's two recent breakdowns when she phoned repeatedly threatening to kill herself if Eileen didn't come over at once. (Luckily, she has now calmed down somewhat, being on Depo-Provera). But on those occasions we found ourselves in a darkened apartment so she couldn't see our lights from the street, TV off, crawling about on the floor telling each other to be quiet in case she was on the other side of the door, listening. Sometimes we'd find a gift hanging from the door handle. Talk about passive aggressive. But I couldn't help admiring her. She's a force of nature, something that will not go away. She has short cropped brown hair, square jaw, and little to no sense of humor that I can detect. She sometimes plays basketball in a park on Third Avenue with the local adolescents. She plays with great intensity, frequently knocking the largest youths flying. Her sharp fat elbows and massive hips are her best weapons. She scores a lot of points. Her jump shot is worth watching, and her defense is pretty good too.

*

Eileen had been attacked by a homeless man on her way to art class after Mary had dropped her off. She told me a crowd had gathered round as a man kicked her once, then, despite her cries and calls for help, kicked her again. She managed to escape into a foyer and begged the doorman to call the cops, who were soon on the scene, grabbing the guy as he was in the process of attacking another woman further down the block. They took Eileen along to identify him, but he kept denying everything until a few witnesses came forward. The guy couldn't understand all the fuss. "I thought she was my wife," he kept saying.

All this happened while I was downtown at the law courts. When I got home, Eileen, lying on the sofa, ice-pack on thigh, bottle of Advil by her side, recounted her upsetting day. When finished, I told her mine, but she dozed off. I'll tell it here anyway.

A rat was alleged to have bitten a Brooklyn woman. She was suing her corporate landlord and the hospital she was treated in. Now, I'd learned to see in rats more than one usually saw, thanks to my friend Nahtasha who had been talking of setting up an experiment in her living room designed, she explained to me, to counteract those experiments in which rats were treated inhumanely. It would go a long way to overturning the popular view of rats. She believed rats had huge potential if treated kindly, so she had devised "an experiment in kindness" for Morton ("Mort," named after a beloved uncle) and Theodore ("Tod," after her mother's favorite president). They were littermates, black and white hooded rats, "clean, affectionate and tractable in the extreme," she informed me. From my own observations I was beginning to see there might be something in what she said. When first introduced to them, however, I was not so sure. Rats do more than unsettle us. They come from the dark of the race and thrust themselves in on us. They come from a place we think we've conquered and deny us victory. They are the disfiguring disease we think we've cured. They are—but enough. Suffice to say that after a while I got on nicely with Mort and Tod and intended, if chosen for the jury, to do right by them, make a case on behalf of these much maligned animals.

Our names were called from the jury pool, and in we trooped to find three natty young lawyers, along with a rather scruffy individual. The latter went first, welcoming us unctuously, and introduced himself as one Morelli, lawyer for Mrs. Bermudez, the aggrieved party. Immediately he started in on rats. "Have you ever *seen* a rat?" he inquired. "Hey, this ain't a *dawg* we're talking about. This aint a *hamster*. This ain't a *gerbil*. This ain't even a rodent. No, this is a *rat*. And I don't mean like 'he's a dirty rat,' or a ratfink and I don't mean in the subways. I mean *personal contact* with the beast that brought the bubonic plague and the Black Death." The two corporate lawyers sighed. The hospital lawyer was beginning to look aggrieved. I suspected that they must have figured they'd let Morelli strangle himself. Morelli went on, walking about, making eye-contact. "Now, I don't mean to infer anything—." "Imply," I whispered. The taller of the corporate two smiled to me. Morelli hadn't even heard. "And," he rolled on, "I don't mean, you know, 'send the dirty rat upstate,' or 'fry the rat.' No, I mean the kind of rat who creeps into a person's bed in the middle of the night and bites—." This time he had gone too far. "Hey, hold on," said the shorter corporation. "We're not trying the case here. These facts are not established. This is only jury selection." Morelli took a deep breath. "OK," he said. "There's this hypothetical situation. Someone may have abused alcohol, and maybe even doesn't take care of herself. I'm not condoning or condemning. It's just a hypothetical. We're not here to make judgments. But *if a rat bit her*, if it would have went up to her—maybe she's sleeping it off, you know—and then her arm all swolled up—." This time the hospital lawyer protested. "OK, OK," said Morelli, "I'm just doing my job. I'm just saying, I'm not trying to influence anybody. I'm just saying that my client doesn't panhandle and doesn't live in a flophouse, and I'm assuming nobody here is prejudging anybody. We just want to start with a level playing-field." He sat down.

Then it was the hospital's turn. There was something about lost records and lost x-rays. "Can you assure me that even if no witnesses for the hospital appear that the burden of proof is on the plaintiff? Now you'll hear of alcohol abuse—." Morelli leaped to his feet. "I didn't interrupt you," said the hospital lawyer, "so don't interrupt me." "I will if you're misleading—.' "Don't tell me how to question—." "I will if—." "Let him speak," I said, looking at Morelli. All the lawyers glared at me. "Step outside," said Morelli, as if challenging the others to fisticuffs. They all trooped out. After fifteen minutes they marched back in. "I know what I'm doing," the hospital lawyer was saying. "If you knew what you were doing," Morelli replied, "you wouldn't have lost the records and x-rays." And on they went until they decided to let the judge decide their conflicts, and out they trooped again, returning after another ten minutes, talking together.

To ensure that I was chosen, if only for a break in my routine, I had meant to hold my tongue during the selection process. But

I couldn't resist expressing my feelings to a potential juror sitting beside me, a young man with a face like a chipmunk and Joe Stalin eyebrows. "I resent being treated like a moron," I confided. "Oh, I don't mind," he whispered back. I sniggered, and all three lawyers glared at me. To show I wasn't intimidated, I whispered loudly to Joe Stalin: "The jury system is a mess. Why don't lawyers give part of their fat fees to a fund that pays jurors for the time they have to take off their jobs?" More glares, so I decided to sit quietly and let things play out with people being questioned and giving up all sorts of personal information. When my turn came, I made up almost my entire bio. I suppose by then I must have realized I'd blown my chances.

Jury selection took all morning, and when it was over I was the subject of a peremptory challenge by the corporate lawyers. I went back to sit on a bench in the huge jurors' room, under a wall painting of "Primitive Indian Settlements."

*

Nahtasha was furious. The landlord had entered the apartment when she was out to check on a leak ("more like to rifle through my underwear drawer," Nahtasha snarled.) The two brother rodents had leapt out of the woodwork and bitten some exposed flesh. The landlord ran screaming from the room and headed for emergency treatment at St. Vincent's. There, he had tried to convince the young intern to send a cop to get the rats and extract their brains for rabies. When refused, bandaged, he dashed back to the apartment and tried to break down the door. Nahtasha, recently returned, had been informed by neighbors of what had transpired, so she'd double-locked and bolted it.

The following morning Nahtasha called me at the office and

asked me to stop by during my lunch break which, she'd learned, could stretch over two or three hours. When I got there, "What's the matter with people?" she said. "What is this irrational fear of rats? Don't they realize rodents can't get rabies? And there's no way my boys could have bitten that lout. Or if they did they weren't to blame. He must have frightened them, and they were only defending me and their territory." She went quiet. The apartment was preternaturally quiet. Even Roger seemed depressed and stayed in the bathroom. Roger was the Rhode Island Red rooster successor to Walter, for whom the temptation of the open window had proves too strong to resist. "If they bit him" Nahtasha continued after a while, "then it bears looking into. It might well indicate an earlier history of abuse."
"I thought you said you'd had them since they were five weeks old."
"A lot can happen in five weeks. And my boys were only defending themselves, and me. That oaf has set me back years in my experiment. He's traumatized them. I doubt they'll ever trust another human again."
"What's happened to the boys?" I asked, looking about.
"They're going into hiding, staying with a friend. I'm not telling you her name for your own safety. They'll lie low and come back when the coast's clear."
She went into the kitchen and returned with two glasses of something that looked like venous blood. She handed me one.
"What is it?" I asked.
"Beet juice. It makes you live for ever, or for a very long time. It's good for heart problems."
I took a sip. It wasn't bad.
"I've been writing this long essay, or I'm intending to—I've taken

notes—on the return of the *subject* in human/animal research. I'm planning to recreate some Skinnerian exercises without the pain-avoidance mistake. This would give me the hand's-on experience to network effectively with people doing the same kind of innovative research I intend to engage in. In fact, I was talking to Rabbi Mordechai the other day about rats and God. He agreed with me that rats, next to chickens, were the most abused of God's creatures." As she talked, she started to move her arms up and down and shake her head. The result was that her wig, her sheitel, began to slide over her brow. It had almost covered her eyes when she swept it back with an imperial thrust of her right hand. Then it started to move over her face, a blond devouring beast. Nahtasha ignored it now as she talked of turning street scales into progressive scales, of signaling languages, and a humane housing project for rats. Suddenly, Mort and Tod came charging in from the bathroom where, presumably, they had been secreted. They dashed in as if resurrected, hotly pursued by Roger, a fiery demon. Nahtasha ignored the ruckus. "Rats have very poor eyesight," she informed me as I watched them climbing the dusty old purple velvet curtains. "But," she continued, just as Mort, or Tod, lost his grip and fell to the floor, "they have excellent depth perception. I intend to simulate natural cliffs, because a cage encourages fear." I felt a sharp jab at my ankle. Roger had decided he was a woodpecker. I kicked him off. Nahtasha scowled, but continued to inform me of other concepts she was planning to incorporate into her humane housing scheme. She talked of the rats' need to burrow, their preference for sunlight and desire for running water in which to bathe every third day, full immersion. Rearranging her wig with one hand, she held a pamphlet close to my face with the other. "Experiences With the

Study of Rodents in Seminatural Enclosures," by one Hubert Fox of the University of Florida. I was about to ask a question when I was interrupted by a ruckus behind the sofa. Nahtasha leaped to her feet to separate the combatants. The stress of the last few days must have gotten to her because she snatched the *sheitel* from her head and began swatting the embattled ones with it. "Stop that! Stop that! There is no necessity for fighting! Stop, I say!" I had drawn my legs up and was in a fetal position when, out of nowhere, one of the rats, Mort, I believe, who was slightly larger than his brother, jumped out of nowhere and sank his fangs into my right earlobe. I heard a scream, but didn't realize it was mine.

*

In this state of semi-retirement I sometimes feel I could float off the planet. At night, by day, I look up and see—nothing. Going on and on. Which is why, more and more, I am staying indoors. If I look up in my study I can see a ceiling. Finitude. Even the cracks console me. There are no cracks in the sky. It is a seamless depth to drown in.

When I think too large I get confused, sometimes even terrified. In my apartment at Madison and 54th. I am going slower than Nahtasha in the Village. In the northern hemisphere, things to the north are going faster than things to the south. Even standing still in the city I am going 750 m.p.h.—why doesn't my hair stream out behind? I can't even think of things like this without everything I know being called into question. Nothing balances. In this hemisphere, everything twists to the right, aspiring to a corkscrew. I exert more weight on my right foot than my left, which may be why the heel-spurs on my right foot hurt more than my left. We are all twisting, trying to get out of the vast openness, like the seeds that hit the ground gyrating and corkscrew into the soil, digging, digging, digging, deeper and deeper, hoping to hide and grow again under better circumstances. And, of course, in the South Pacific, everything and everybody is twisting in the opposite direction. I suppose it's all meant to balance out somehow.

(ii)

Novel

In the novel I'm writing there are no people, no "characters." And if you expect a plot you'll be sorely disappointed. There's little to count on and precious little to critique. Beautiful language is absent; there is almost no language of any sort, so you won't see any reviews praising its style or humanity. In my novel, each place is the same as any other place, so there can be no confusion about where you are. The novel builds to no denouement because there is no noument. And there are no epiphanies unless the reader realizes that not having one is something of an epiphany in itself. Symbols are everywhere these days, so there are none in my novel. The storyline consists simply of turning a page, which can be thought of as a narrative in itself. If the novel has more than a page this could present something of a problem. And if you're looking for something that passes for wisdom, this isn't the place, though I do think I have retained a sense of adventure simply as a consequence of sequence. So here goes, though my novel, unlike any other novel I can think of, is very short so as not to test the reader's powers of concentration and patience. As I said, there are no characters. The world is overpopulated as it is, so why make matters worse? Perhaps I should stop right here. There may be too many people, but there are certainly too few trees.

Plot

It follows itself and has its own reasons, while underneath's a provenance safe from headlights, voices free from form, bending, summing themselves up in their own expression, no lines or limits, but plenty of leftovers and pulses like the wind, which is a way of filling things. How lively to be so exposed, staking oneself to beginnings that are in fact old and useless the way everything is at its best. The abundant is not will or idea, substance, Geist, or being. As I said once, "Lost shores are still shores," the unseen seen where things get richer, strangers to themselves so we have to ask again what air is. There's no need to pull it all together. Things break across all the time, cross and thirl and intersect and at that very point become loose again. This means you have a taste for discord. It means cures in corners and curses up close. Humiliation's its attendant in the wide where reversals and cancellations dismiss identity and work's paid in blood. Stones are stacked against us. When the horizon is so far out we can't get back then ask it for clear directions, anywhere. Ask the stone itself down there, ask the half-hidden hare, bones along the bank, the terrapin like an amulet baked in clay, the outlines like hearsay the smoke makes. They know the good dead who brought them, who direct resourceful rain, who lean on small lovely flowers to bring grief's whisper home, trying apart from yes and no to show the shape of things, though it's all a god who whistles, and birds appear who whistle and gods appear.

The Narrator

stays home with a plot revolving around domestic arrangements, all of which involve travel in the mountains by train or tram where you have to fight for a seat, and once in one you have to keep shifting and squirming to stay comfortable. The plot, it seems, also involves voyeurs, one of whom turns out to be you, and another part entails domestic arrangements that include threesomes in order to confuse any onlooker and spread the burden of performance. Another part of the plot focuses on the constant desire and struggle with the demon of self-destruction mitigated not at all by self-doubt among people who think too much. But the main plot involves the ketamine-fueled activities of a cute but aloof blonde whom the police find in a pool of blood, not dead, but unsure of her surroundings. When she recovers, it turns out that she is an Army doctor just discharged from her second tour in Afghanistan, who was hoping to start a family in the bosomy center of Silicone Valley, but this does not explain why it was later discovered that she had come under fire in the NY Supreme Court for publishing largely un-peer-reviewed articles on the causes of rape and corrective genital surgery. Her desire for "a large, fulfilling family" had to be put on indefinite hold, though to the end she still maintained God had put her on this earth to be a doctor, or something close, like the person who stands over a dead person in the middle of the street, determined to catch the criminal responsible. But she could never grasp why so often research clashes with doctrine since, in her opinion, doctrine is intrinsically wrong, and the pursuit of evidence, as she once wrote, is the most pressing moral imperative of our or any age. Above all, she believed, and still believes in her "little voice," bolstered with fact-checking. In any case, she says she's a great reader who wants to read everything she can lay her hands on, because for her reading is "a way of encountering other people" and being exposed to the variety of their motives. You tell her you read books to avoid encountering people, that you prefer books that have next to no people in them. "People confuse and annoy me. People make me jealous." "So what do you read? she asks. "Detective novels," you reply. " And sometimes a poem or two, to relax."

Style

I like to put in a lot of foreign words, if only to impress myself. Sassi, soldi, Las Trampas, Veruna, the more the better, von Phart and Chausssée d'Antin, Tahuantisuyo and Weltanchauung. I like accents such as grave, acute, circumflex, umlaut and even the hieroglyphics of anthropological linguistics that knock you about like kingpins for even daring to enter where they themselves are foreign. No real native can read them. Nobody could speak like that, or should. I also like skeletons you have to put together; "articulate" is the verb they call it. The bones speak as they move, slide into place. It is ingenious how they do it, how they "articulate." I wish "articulate" had an accent or two to make it look less functional, more exotic, the way they do with ice cream or fashion. I like to surprise, especially with words which, in themselves, are always malleable, always what someone once called "facets of copiousness." I also like words you can peel in the way that unpeeling a word is making a word, and speaking of peel, I have found that peel is often more appealing and mysterious than what has been peeled. I learned this as a child just after the deprivation of war when I joined a queue in the playground not knowing what was at the other end. It turned out to be a child distributing bits of orange peel. Since we had no idea what an orange was, that peel was it. I can still recall the whole scene. My childhood comes back as orange peel, as powerful as any orange. When I eat an orange, what I eat is orange peel.

Brian Swann

For Instance, the Glass Sponge

Repetition, inversion, variation mesh with variable articulated theme adding up to vitality of process, recurrence of all parts and the oneiric superposition that erases time, everything sharing what it contacts and is simultaneous with, the way a long life is simultaneous and parts even interchangeable when you look back at it, for it is all inherent in you; you yourself are the process, even "that reaction against your own thoughts which in itself lends life to thoughts," (E.M. Cioran). This documentary I'm making runs in all directions at once, and I always exist in a deficit relationship to it, for the world changes before us and, as I said, can be viewed only in retrospect. So how do you get ahead of yourself? Maybe it's a little like finding what you've been looking for all your life and then having no place to put it. Or, conversely, it's as if after finding it there'd be no need to find somewhere to put it, or discovering you have no need to put it anywhere and wondering why you bothered in the first place, desire drifting away, leaving you to wonder where you go from here. Hugh of St. Victor was on the right track when he said "he is perfect for whom the entire world is a foreign land." I think there are other clues to freedom in, for instance, the glass sponge, that intricate mesh of silica, invisible tactile strength and the ability to withstand all sorts of high stress and forces emanating from the alien deep it takes in, played over by the voices of singing currents, exiles motioning and shaping the strands, going anywhere and nowhere.

The Real World

> Long have I been aware of the occasional fragrance from that other world which is the real world.
> —Henry Wallace

The throb of darkness in the form of fragrance from that other world where all is rich and recurrent, inversion and variation resonant without message, is vital not in facts but processes, echoic in all parts so that if superimposed one on another there will be no time, no time-signature, or what we crudely call structure, so the now and the then, the here and the now, become not-now, not-then, not-here, not-there, the way masks are and are not, the way they put us in touch with our selves as not-selves, mysteriously absent by being present and vice versa. Even when placed in exhibition cases they only seem to be quarantined from us and themselves. They emerge through the glass as not-faces, dead-faces, faces within faces. Now this only appears to be confusing, because it is possible to get it, though you can't expect to get it just by walking along and thinking about it. It has to want you. It has to get you too, and you have to be prepared to let it, but not by allowing it to sneak up and hit you in the back of the head with a Eureka board, and not by sitting so it can see your cards in the mirror behind you because that means if it can see them then anybody can and the pack will have to be continually reshuffled, your cards continually turned over and you continually be on guard, in which case there will be no time for a game. Rather than live like that, I would prefer to run naked and barefoot in the tundra. At least there, by the synaptic northern lights or moonlit snow, in silence, exile and solitude you can draw the outline of your own body's shadow on the crust where there is the most likelihood it will endure, at least for a while, and maybe even turn into a more durable substance via

Brian Swann

an accreted remnant desire, and this will mean you won't have to burn yourself for warmth before you die stoically on the ice, and even allow you to accompany yourself in essence wherever you decide to go, for every soloist needs accompaniment, if only to help keep the beat, underline the structure of what is being played, accent the scents and tinctures of each note, and then even of itself, play what is usually considered context, continually playing, shining, wavering, beyond good or true, the aurora in the deepest part of the brain, our oldest resonant being, pulling it all together and maybe—wait for it— pulling our leg, having us on.

Two for the Road

I: House of Cards:

Cards aren't meant to make you happy. In fact, it often seems just the opposite. You can read *The Living End* as much as you want but there's no secret there for the real card-worker to learn. Sure you can "pick a card" simply by naming the card held in someone's hand, but what if you are face-down among a group of cards that are similarly oriented? It is all a question of fluid symmetry, sensing what's what. This is how one achieves authority and reputation. As for any impromptu take-a-card endings that require little or no skill, simply turning a card over will not be a sufficiently memorable conclusion. To be a myriad cardician requires demanding sleights. Close-up mysteries facilitate one's transition from pasteboard presto to impromptu self-working. This way you make a surprise impact even on yourself, becoming your own traveling ace no non-specialist can fathom. But what is revealed is no dodge, if properly understood. It is genuine mastery of the internal, executing oneself in a flawless pass, disappearing in a flicker of stratagems, all meat and no fat, a one-handed shuffle from one place to another like a flourish of fanning mirrors, a flounce off the top of the deck where all can see. This is how you give an alternative to routine with the appearance of no difficulty. You bypass the predictable, passing unreal mysteries through real holes in the universe.

II: Topit:

Your actual contribution is quite minimal. But with it you can predict a word or even a passage, even one that has been secretly selected. This can leave the foundation for learning even more sophisticated tricks, sometimes including quite large objects. Sometimes too the insides of a building can be revealed by means of psychology or good guesswork. Concomitantly, vanishing becomes resurrection inside-out. It can be done via household objects, creating a domestic eye-view of eternity that can eventually lead to a bird's eye view. Even the most insightful theoretician can never teach us how to reach into a hat and come up with anything not already in existence. Any lecture notes turn out to be hocus-pocus. But when the hocus-pocus turns out to be the main supply house, then we have the performance performing itself. So, a typical spectator is unnecessary, no more than a hypothesis when other yeasty factors are at work, the way the unseen can have spectacular unseen events. A natural bonding takes place, a self-transcendence where misdirection can take the place of real dexterity. Eventually the need for patter diminishes as the hats begin to fly with no visible means of propulsion. This is chapeaugraphy at its best and most convincing. Soon heads will fly too. This is the soul's evolving choreography. This is the topit absorbed and going without saying.

Ghosts

I: Storm:

It raged, howled, bits blown to bits, the mind growing ancient, as lights in the rented cabin flickered off and on, on and off, phone dead, and I prowled like the priest at Nemi, flashlight and candle probing squeaking corners till dawn, when I was ready to call the Society for Psychic Research or the Max Planck Institute, though by then the veil between worlds had shut, the membrane stiffened so, the phone alive again, instead I called the electric company for repairs, thinking, like Dickens, that ghosts lacked all originality, doing the same stuff and getting away with it like the Demon Drummer of Tedworth, who still, however, pounds away, and stuff still gets tossed about, feet scamper, a child screams, someone in the rafters is in two places at once like a quantum particle or flies out one window and in through another without a rocket back-pack, all charlatans, magi, composers and contrivers who lose nothing, keep everything present, reach back for the selkie, gather manifestations like flowers, trace elementals like the kelpie in the loch, time-slip tourists who will follow when we reach the dead Moon or Mars.

II: Blue Sky:

If the blue sky finds itself in me but only with what I gave it, and if what it gives back is what I took from it in the first place, and if this is what we mean by "blue sky," then we are invaded by ourselves, though at the same time we know we aren't. Things must think themselves in us so we're the animate life of the inanimate objects whose voices live in how we call them, even across great distances across which I intrigue closer by a series of sleight-of-voices so we are implicit in the deception, the only difference being that we're aware of it and they're not, though I suspect they must suspect something, the way a jellyfish must suspect it's not transparent, not just the ghost of itself.

III: Accompaniment in Search of a Theme:

In early morning, gray skeins draw down and across the sky to form a loom like the one the Tewa say this bright world is woven on. But soon it frays, threads breaking off and joining to a lovely tree flickering and unfurling, a trick of light in the ice vastness whose shadow's the world, where shadows are unreliable things, neither one thing nor another, which makes it hard to trust anything. But all is not lost, for music is shadows, reverberations, what's left floating, old shadows I sing alone in my mountain house, one light on, a fire deep in the back-log, "Derwentwater's Farewell," "Chevy Chase," "The Keach i' the Creel," "Binnorie," as another year passes, leaving fainter traits when autumn light goes round frayed at both ends until it tips over into night's mottled garden where a bird calls and I repeat it so the dog at my side whines and runs off while moonlight starts to draw across my body to make another fainter me off to the side which the dog runs into and disappears where water bends around a boulder in the stream and reunites at the other side in white, making a path I could strike along the way as a boy I set off down the passageway dug out of chalk searching for flint, the same tunnel dug out aeons ago with antler pick and auroch shoulder-blade shovel, flint I struck against flint but no spark leaped onto dry tinder, just blood from thumb or palm. I have spent a lot of time doing what doesn't need to be done.

IV: What You Think You Saw:

There is a woman, deaf, past middle age, sitting cross-legged on the floor. She is knotting and weaving string and fiber, candy wrappers, tubing, cloth strips, fibers, ribbons, all different colors, textures and materials, anything she can find, in and out, spilling over from a shopping cart which keeps moving away from her, slowly, so she has to move after it, slowly, with difficulty. When the contents are in danger of spilling over into a jumbled, tangled heap, she ties everything back in and down with more string and rope. She weaves, knots, tucks it back in. It is very hard to follow where anything begins, goes, or ends since it goes all directions, over bulges produced by internal pressure, over things crowding in, pushing out, constricted only by the cart's wire sides. She works slowly, so after a while, you don't see her any more, or notice what she's doing. What you think you saw, you didn't, a bit like as you grow older, sometimes good things don't seem so good any more, or bad things so bad.

Brian Swann

The Oral Tradition

The swallows' dives could peel eyelids back. Their glides are exact improvisings. They bank, drop, then veer off, seeing me like a stuffed traffic cop by the blood-red barn where they're hatching another generation in mud walls, turning old beams to singing trees.

The forests here are full of birds, some in disguise demanding your attention. There's a wheel-with-one-spoke bird going a mile a minim, making his universe at all places the same, then folding in on itself. In this bird's version, there is no nothing, Nothing went off, nothing hurtled into the nothing it created. His wheel continues to make it all up as it rolls on, a great storytelling, each metaphor standing for its fullest self, the same as everything else, each solipsism a joy in vast places it itself creates, the way a drumming of a woodpecker creates dawn, the way each star comes when we call it, for it is only an incandescent us.

The Director

Of one of his movies he said: *it worked like the clock of a damnable craftsman.* Salomé (in *Salomé*) could dance in his mind, but all the audience got were more like panto and coster songs, while his heroines, their happiness in ruins, raged like waterfalls in darkness. For him, changes in location were a form of speculation, mood a screen, a thin panorama like the cockamamies we used to decorate our hands with as kids, briefly vivid but erasable. He embraced simultaneity of events. Single features were syntheses and objects answered as passion by becoming gestures one had to believe in. So, for instance, every lover was a lost lexicon or a glutton for experience. His Helen (*Helen*) could make us all immortal with a kiss, but it was terror of empty space that created those livid landscapes where Cinderella and friends made sudden vanishings and night rushed in. To the end he careened across his own screen. He seduced himself, and this had consequences since events have a way of making sure they're not forgotten in interpretation. Appetite continues on its own, in spite of the person who has it, leaving traces like subtitles under the fragments and borrowed passions for those who can read them.

His career had been devoted to developing the connections between cosmic and comic for the mass market. Then one day he stumbled upon her, Dolly, trying to pry the fake gold leaf off the abandoned set of a flamboyant decade. His work suffered, but all went well until one night when Tina, his wife of thirty years, woke to find him floating sumptuously in sleep, another name on his lips, his nightclothes knotted. She intended to be epic with repercussions this time, so through mostly legal methods she hastened his entrapment. Then left. This raised possibilities in his mind. To think about them, he would spend whole mornings watching gray fog cover the plastic lotus flowers on the lake. He wondered if the rape of a clown would provide focus but gave it up as too poetic, noting, however, how the literal can be touched with new dimensions, like the white walls of his mother's boarding house in late summer. From there, the impulse was away from what he knew—tormented marriages, mistresses with criminal tendencies (the clay of comic drama)—to pure conjecture, "things that prove nothing" (Truffaut). So, caught up, he sought to capture, without capturing, the glance, say, of someone who seemed without illusions. As he walked along the lake, now empty of all save sky, he practiced his mock signature in air, all form, no substance, like a German industrialist he once knew, with his own hidden horror. When asked, he told the press he was planning to film a doorman's life.

That night, he dreamed his wife was Liv Ullmann, who, at his entreaty, gave up her career for him. When he woke, however, he thought he was Marilyn Monroe. When he looked around, there were thousands of fan letters filling the bedroom, burying the Peke. From that moment on, his career consisted mostly of inspired improvising, involving items such as a child's fringed buckskins, a mogul intent on leveling a building, and a quaint story involving a hot stove. He also began to specialize in alienating vignettes. In one tableau, for instance, the audience absent, he directed with dreamy clarity an infected employer whose customers bought almost unlimited copies of Perrault and *Wilhelm Meister*. This was followed by another of which one critic complained that fabliaux were "passé." But most of the press went wild when, in the final scene, he himself portrayed a woman on a balcony, stepping out where no one could follow.

What the audience didn't see when the curtain fell, however, was her hesitating, noticing that her hands appeared unrealistic.

So she took off her gloves. But it would have been wrong for her to have taken off her hat. In her mind, she turned to the window of her childhood home, where her father was flapping on the balcony in his flying suit, impatient and ready. Below him, a row of workers with levers stood beside a large boulder. When it was moved the men left. A small black-and-white mongrel bitch she'd never seen before ran into the room and out again through the same door. Her father readied himself for his final appearance, turning his body this way and that, somewhat reluctant, pulling his survivor's kit out of his pockets, checking the cords, studying the crowd. When the scream in the courtyard signified that the ground had risen up to meet him, she paused. Then, firmly in command, no longer dependent on mere human behavior, or what she'd read in books, thinking Stanislavsky would have been proud, at the window she toasted her liberation. She adjusted her dress. She looked down. She took off her hat. She floated down.

Back as himself, he held himself responsible for the curious illusions found in the play of children. Then, as his eightieth summer came to a close, he put his own features into a story of a supernatural beauty and her occult diary with unique powers. But before he could complete it, he felt exhausted, becoming preoccupied with exile. He had dreams of receiving telegrams from his right sleeve. They were frightening, so he left LA, alone. In the Bas-Alpes with a number of books, he tried to conceal the growing conviction that everybody's fate had been preserved only in draft form. He dreamed of leaving planes at unscheduled stops. He became less sure of what he had counted on, but he knew who'd get the role of his fifth wife. He'd seen her playing chess while he was strolling through a garden naked. He was planning to represent life as a series of confiscations, when …

In his life's sequel, there was enough light to see a man walking into the dark, exaggeratedly self-possessed. This was followed by a few shots of a woman who followed, bleeding. Some people passed by without wondering if anything was amiss. Meanwhile, everything became more and more distant, dissolving for several years, until the woman was compelled to run headlong into the audience yelling that she was still here—what did they intend to do about it? In such a situation, something was needed to help them get a fix on things, divorcing, however briefly, that shocking instant from the slow world of flickering lights and shadows they'd come to know. To help them out, they could be told the woman wasn't really there, or was having them on. That was not really her blood. Then they could safely disregard her and concentrate on the man who could be shown about to step into a bed of mined roses. Another way of getting the story across, however, might have been a long shot, hoping for the best, using whatever drifted into the lens. But since, presumably, precision still counts for something, that might not have worked. So, in view of the audience's continual loss of memory, they might have had to go too. But before that happened, the woman had adapted to her situation. The man was forced to make a choice. But the high wind that had arisen will continue to push him backward, into the field of trampled flowers. Will anyone try to save him? The woman? The audience, if it were permitted to remain, would it leap ahead or adapt the story to its own ends? Or will the audience finally have had enough and heave a rock at the screen, collapse the whole set, silhouettes flapping free of the cave wall, and will that be worth watching too?

Snow in June, or Why I Hate Actors

I am my remembering self, and the experiencing self, who does my living, is like a stranger to me.
—Daniel Kehneman, *Thinking, Fast and Slow*.

That tall Philistine headdress crossing a Tuscan back road could be a porcupine caught in my headlights, lit from within. Those girls on a Watteau lawn might well be made of light, while down cathedral steps shadows creep from the mouth of stone lions. Things you forgot or forgot you forgot ring like buoys signaling the hidden, or signs marking where you can be lowered into a pit in order to be raised and draped in a technicolor coat. So go the rocks, so goes the sun and the world of many colors turning into the shirt of Nessus that eats you up in flame before you have a chance to know what it's all about, consuming you in a shower of sparks, flowers and flurry of fire to the descants of the dying, brightness that blinds where the steps have been worn down and shadows thick as snow take what's left, creeping across green expanses, down into deep places, up again like smoke so nothing is wasted while everything is pretending to be itself which is why I hate actors; you never know where they are, going or coming, being or not-being. Where should you go if you look to them? Why indeed do we look to them who are always someone else? If you are, where are you? Who and what would you look like here? A focused illusion, a divination of time present only in the divining? In this time and place other selves break and bury to revive as shards of a morning always snowing yet always June. And still, with only words to try to look through, strangers, we are trying to see beyond our lives.

Brian Swann

The Theater

> *The whole world ministers to you as the theater of your love.... Life without objects is sensible emptiness, and that is a greater misery than death or nothing.*
> —Thomas Traherne, "Meditation 65"

I: The Brink

The water stopped. Flowers quit at the first sign of snow, which rocks now breach like dolphins. Brightness hangs in the branches overhead that line the sandy path shiny with frost. A bluejay calls, two sharps, rough spondees that open the trees to where the ocean moves slowly, saving all it can, giving up only a stone or two, a shell, smooth pebbles which I will find transcendent with sea-sheen, as if they were all versions of themselves and each other, while waves push up as far as they can, withdraw, return, reveal, cover up, give, take away, always on the brink, the cusp, the edge.

II: Coherent

It could just be a trick of leaves and flowers that gleam and glint, but I know objects want me as much as I want them, since they're more than surface, more than moment. I could play the game of mirrors, me within me, but this would not shock me awake. So I catch as I can, let it go, let me go, and the world's weight climbs back up to where it is unbroken as song, tall as a falcon, coherent as rain.

The Cyclist

As I pushed down the chain snapped. I found a bike shop where the owner removed and held up the severed links, shaking his head. He handed them to me and went into the back of his shop, returning with a smooth band of black cloth like a yoga belt. "This should do the trick," he said. "Everybody's using them now." He looped it round the two gear wheels and, handing over the cash, I rolled the bike out. But when I hopped on board and pushed down on the pedals they just spun round and round and the bike didn't move. I got off and saw the problem: There were no links in the band for the teeth to engage. I should have returned and demanded my money back, or at least requested the return of my original, if useless, chain. Instead, I remounted and started pedaling as if nothing was wrong. I didn't want to draw attention to myself, especially since people were already starting to stop and look at me. I decided to make the best of things by acting normally.

I kept this up for some time, looking straight ahead to make sure I was going in the right direction, looking about to ensure I would not be sideswiped or bumped from behind. I began to relax, to feel at ease; things were going well. The city ceased to be a dangerous blur and I took the time to observe what was going on about me, observe the faces of people in taxis or on buses until after a while I thought people were looking at me in a new way. From time to time, a group would form on the sidewalk and stand silent as I pedaled fast, as if I was catching up with myself. Soon, I began to imagine myself as The Man Riding a Bike and even see myself in the eyes of the onlookers as The Man Riding a Bike. In this way, I was doing us all a service. I had a role. I was pushing on, showing the way, improvising in a straight line. The plate-glass window to my left, when not blocked by people passing in front like Plato's shadows, afforded me some assistance in that I could orient myself in it, check to make sure I was not leaning too far out or too far in, in danger of losing my balance and falling over. As I sat on my leather saddle I began to recall happy hours spent on my new green Raleigh riding through villages and beside fields on my way to pick plums in orchards or blackberries and filberts from hedgerows. Such reverie, however, was not without its perils. The *Pequod*'s mast-top came to mind as I rocked a bit.

As time went by, when I glanced over it seemed the onlookers had gone quiet or had lost interest, but when I looked closer they were standing still because they were absorbed and transfixed, the way that staring at a color too long will make you hallucinate. I wondered if they had begun to doubt not only what they were seeing but who they were, the way a word repeated too often loses its meaning. Whenever I found myself thinking what they were thinking or feeling, I had to ring my bell to clear the way, remind myself that I was only riding a bike, with nothing to prove; that, as the young people used to say, I needed to get with the program. I needed to be the bike. "Be the bike," I'd mutter, by which I think I meant what an actor once told me: I can play all characters because I have none. Be that as it may, as dusk fell I found myself slowing down since I didn't want to bump into something or fall off and hurt myself. But decelerating too fast to let another cyclist pass, I wobbled and, as I struggled to regain my equilibrium, a memory came out of nowhere, one I hadn't known before and so could not vouch for. I was about three or four, sleeping in an enormous bed in the house where I was born, I woke to a light coming through the open door and family sounds floating up from downstairs. I was aware I was alone. I looked into the large mirror at the foot of the bed and saw a face. Not me. Gray. Me. I cried out, tried to run away but fell onto the floor and could not move.…....

Balance

I: Emptiness

An echo is a diminished thing, yet still its journey adds a dimension even if it is the dimension of the diminished. It incorporates emptiness until emptiness is its voice. But just what is that emptiness, that space or sound so full of the void? Is it a kind of dream inside the dream, a kind of music; articulation, not assertion? For articulated objects can move in many directions, in many tenses. The mind never lets anything go; it articulates eternity, it lives in fantastical shapes of emptiness and has done so from our beginnings. Around fifty thousand years ago, Neanderthals brought into their caves at Aray-sur-Cure two lumps of roundish iron pyrites, the cast of a large spiral gastropod shell and a spherical polyparium. This was the first sign of human fascination with the fantastical in nature, which is the fantastical in our own nature, empty, waiting to be full, even with nothing.

II: Silence

The fantastical and the symmetrical balance, in silence. In silence everything is equal. Here I try to balance everything I've known with everything I haven't known in order to know what I know more completely. I try to hear the true dimension of the echo. But protection against stimuli is almost as important as receptivity. So I try to imagine a prehistoric silence where silence overflows, buzzing at the edges, a constant cascade. Yes, I am *appentitor silentii*, seeker of silence; I envy them all, those Continental Quietists, the Seekers, Irish peregrinati, those desert dwellers at the top of pillars, St. Francis in his barren solitude at La Verna, Saints Cuthbert and Aiden on my native wild Northumbrian shores. They all experienced something I never shall, a conscious silence in which they could hear themselves, the echo of the self that's part of the vastness around it, full as a raincloud.

Monarch

Quietism might be thought of as its own worst enemy since it runs away from itself only to be transported into itself in an effort to get beyond itself. Even death is no barrier. It likes where it is, but there's no knowing really where that might be, though it believes it is eternal. And that's why it is so important, a kind of transport into essence where there is no tension to resolve, no burden to slough. In the quiet there is, however, a sense that something is following you, something pushing you from behind but you don't know what or where. It's not a house or a horse, it's more a wind or a winged flyer. It seems to move into your hands, tingle down your fingers and all you can do is wait, hoping to discover where you are going by where you've been. But as you watch, your hands disappear like smoke, salt melting back into the Dead Sea, breath of migrated monarchs freezing them from inside as they rise en masse from oyamel fir and pine to mate in crystal air only to fall back and shatter, gorgeous stained-glass shards on the silent wing-strewn floor of the Sierra Madre.

Reflective

To imagine a language is to imagine a form of life, so I'd imagine a life of quotes since there is no new thing under the sun, so how does it matter much if dying's only a quote, a turn with words, part of an order which is only a paradigm of thought, of numbers, a world of ranked earth, water and sky with all sorts of helpers in the after-world, androgynes with wings, others with a hand for a tail and so on, analogies and recombinations in a world I just read about held up by trees, one to a corner, for words are the pleasure of what you imagine so you can then believe and then choose to spend your time in, for example, sporting in the Gardens of the Sun, sipping flowers, or—there are too many alternatives to count, but we know the way to make everything cohere into coherent mirrors and better ways of going into the dark so vivid it can be thought of as light, so bright it cancels itself out the way soul can be thought of as excess of being and the dark itself excess of light, a blinding blackness, vastness moving into vastness, the dark beat of *el oscuro corazon* where stars swim and the moon reflects and we measure time with fictive music since earth's so much of the things we are and the self self-consumed is trapped behind glass like a sunflower crazed with light, when the iridescent peacock-blue flowers of the magnolia hang over euphoria hanging over the gulf and shining back on us with some heat, for how can one be warm alone, defective and unrhymed?

Phrases are included from, in order:
—Ludwig Wittgenstein, *Philosophical Investigations*, 19, p8e.
—*Ecclesiastes*, 9.
—J.M. Coetzee, "On Zeno," *Diary of a Bad Year*: "The order we see in the universe may not reside in the universe at all, but in the paradigm of thought we bring to it. The mathematics we have invented (in some accounts) or

discovered (in others) which we believe and hope to be a key to the structure of the universe, may equally be a private language ... with which we doodle on the walls of our cave."
—Wallace Stevens, "To the One of Fictive Music."
—Ibid.
—Eugenio Montale, "*Portami il Girasole.*"
—*Ecclesiastes*, 4.

The Best of It

I wake scared. I have always woken scared, even now, stomach a pit. My earliest memory is of waking in my mother's bed, light just failing, and finding myself staring into the vanity mirror at the foot, seeing nothing, just an emptiness that seemed to go on forever. My cries and screams brought the household running. This feeling persisted and at age 15 drove me into the arms of Jesus where I was born again on February 13, 1955, and admitted to "the Order of Crusader Knighthood," where Wesley's hymn "Jesus, lover of my soul" resonated with its call to be hidden and safe, not left alone and defenseless. A year or so later, however, my fear was still extreme at waking, rising to a kind of dread; religion provided no haven or solace. Perhaps I was suffering from something in the blood, since my Anglo-Saxon ancestors had a word, *uhtcearu*, which meant dawn sorrow, anxiety, "care" at waking. Be that as it may, for a while my solution was to delay waking as long as possible, but this presented its own problems. It did nothing to alleviate the fear which, as I lengthened sleep, was allowed its own sphere to play in, conjuring intense shapes, confused and fractured stories. But what was this fear? What is this fear, for it persists even, or perhaps more intensely, today? I could say the usual: fear of dying, loneliness, helplessness in the face of time—with time, you can't win. When I was in hospital recently, time was the healer, but at the same time it was making me older and weaker. My body was improving and deteriorating at the same time. The reasons pile up: a failed life and perpetual fear of failure, of being found out, the shame of old age, its pains, all these and more would be true but not sufficient to account for a sensation as palpable and immediate as sweat, producing the desire not to wake, to stay in the unconscious, despite the pitfalls and largely unravelable complications, one of which is the fact

Brian Swann

that the unconscious has its own unconscious, and if it listens it could hear me coming, but if when the time comes it just lies there, doing nothing, pretending not to be or something else, or even protecting itself like a camouflaged snake or poisonous sea anemone, or letting someone else do the work, if work is what you call it, if this is so I may have found ways around the problem, though none truly solve it, in fact they avoid it and so leave it as it was, or, by avoiding it make it even worse off, though I hope it realizes its narrow escape from being meddled with, and that will make all the difference, if difference is the right word to describe something that has remained the same for years with whatever name it chooses to call itself, since it prefers name to actual so the idea of risk to itself will be reduced and it can claim that since it is just a word, and only in that nominal sense liable, existing as a kind of fiction with an escape clause, a trapdoor of emptiness behind it, it is therefore beyond quantifiable and so doesn't really exist and can do nothing on its own though at a pinch, at the first sign of danger, it can pretend to be anything it wants, even pull back inside itself like a turtle and just sit there inside itself, a stone, for as long as it pleases, and so virtually out of sight and not worth bothering about, which was perhaps its point from the start, so even if it doesn't listen, hears or hears me or not, it is free to do as it pleases, evade, escape, or just lie there in plain sight, invisible for anyone who cares to notice, along the lines of a spider-web, "tight, transparent, concentric," spun from air, drawing in creatures so we struggle and concede, becoming part of it, our only evidence of existence a shiver in the web so we and it are neither here nor there, a rhythm, a pattern whose sole purpose is itself, space filled by ellipsis, for here there is no end or beginning just pieces of the middle going round so whatever else it was you were looking for you won't find, and though imaginings can get you somewhere, and information impel, it's misdirection that will do the trick, a few steps backward and to the left and then the left again, and more improvising as a way to camouflage, escape and fulfill your potential, the way Poulenc said that pattern should be played "very blurred" for full effect. The opposite of this, of course, is to go straight to the heart of the matter, to its very core and guts, by the most direct and unironic path possible, the way adopted by St. Martin of Tours who, with a narrative absolute in focus, driven by the articulation of a straight line, exorcised a man by thrusting his arm directly down his gullet and out the poor fellow's anus. I'm sure the saint took no pleasure in this, and it should be said that it must have taken great self-control for him to have resisted wiggling his fingers out the poor man's bum-hole if only to prove (a) it was a real hand and not a stage prop or (b) to elicit a laugh or round of applause. The aim of his action was to demonstrate to demons that no place is safe for them, but a presumably unintended consequence was to show that there is no place to hide for anyone or anything, not even from ourselves not even if, like me you are a recluse, a hermit, making ourselves as small as possible. Fortunate demons, I muse, who can command bodily ingress and egress *ad libitum*, the risk of St. Martin sojourning in the vicinity being very small. The body's very design, open at both ends, played into their hands, making it vulnerable and open for invasion. But the best irony is that we who possess these bodies do so from the outside; they persist, as it were, without us, afford us little relief for refuge from the world or self, allow us to feel that there exists what Gaston Bachelard called "a corner" where we can "withdraw." Yes, life is still the way Seneca saw it in his "Moral Epistle to Lucilius," a sad thing where "we believe we have an impregnable interior, a place where we are defended, where we can steel ourselves, but then it turns out that even we ourselves cannot get in." There is no place to withdraw, no place to hide. The best we can do is to make the best of it, though we don't know what the best is as we try to catch and weave back in all the loose ends, snag threads and trace the dark, all the time enduring something like the middle of the night when the AC cuts out or breaks down and the silence heats up as we, exhausted, sleep on in the sweat and swelter, thrashing about, or just lie there, eyes open, wiped out.

PART FIVE

No Conclusion

To strive, to seek, to find, and not to yield.

Bleared shadows in the Ukraine or Ur of the Chaldees from the wooden porch where I rest my oar and look out to one tree in the distance, "Oak," I say out loud though I know it's not, and beyond that a mud flat, "Beautiful sand," I say though it isn't; there's just tree, mud, no more, and as far as I can tell it's not even the Ukraine, or Ur, for that matter; I just said what I said because I knew someone was listening, remembering how I was tricked one May morn waking to find snow all over that turned out to be cottonwood. Yes, you have to be careful, so when I hear someone say the tree is worthless, "bare," I recognize the subterfuge. No, I say, there's a bird on a branch, "beautiful," and might have said more but I hear cries for help from a child below in the water and rush down, becoming hero of the hour since no one can swim, honored with sweet black wine, almonds, and choice cuts of roast meat. What more can you do? they ask, as I am about to take my oar and head out into the night. From my sack I take a mirror and paper on which I trace the reflected outline of a star overhead, then I copy likewise tree and mud flat until it stretches to the very edge and seems to fall over, while the sky goes out backward and upside down, as if coming to no conclusion.

Brian Swann

IN XOCHIQUETZAL'S GARDEN

Obviously to describe the shape of the world the first thing to do is to establish my position.
—Italo Calvino, "From the Opaque"

I shall then show that a human being likes to 'withdraw into his corner'…
—Gaston Bachelard, *The Poetics of Space*

I place a car-key compass in the book to keep my place and am about to close it up when I notice for the first time that my window desk points south, due south; so, I think, this is how it feels to be *located*. But it doesn't last. To be in one place means you can't be in others. So I take the compass out of the book and shake it up. Again, unsurprisingly, one hand points south. I close the book and spin my swivel-chair. Where it stops, that's where I move my desk, sit down, open the book and come across boys who sit as birds and fluff their feathers out in the tree in Xochiquetzal's garden, preen while inhaling blossoms that are her virgin vulva, washed and odorous, sip with butterflies her deep nectar, play pipes and whistles, make birdcalls while avoiding toy darts from toy blowguns, watched by the goddess herself and people who dance festooned with flowers, all the visible parts of articulate desire, conjured from the iron core of things, and read the Origin Myth from the *Florentine Codex*, bk. 10, ch. 29, where a boy found good maguey that his mother, Mayahuel, made into good aguamiel. She also found firewater; Johnny Walker, it was called, Dimple, Pinch, Cutty Sark. Cuextecatl the tlatoani drank it. He wouldn't share. He asked for more, and more, until he stood up, tore off his breechcloth, took out his "divinity" and waved it about like a prayer-stick, so the elders expelled him and his wife Mayahuel and his whole family, so he drank a lot and never again wore breechclouts, even in bed, just pyjama tops, no bottoms, so his divinity swung before him for all to see and they all had to worship his divinity, and his wife became addicted to enemas and netti pots, and his daughter cut herself, but his son was afraid and for a present made up a box of songs for his father. "Wake," said one, "the flames have risen. Dawn is here. The flame-colored pheasant is calling, the flame-colored swallow is flying, and the flame butterfly is passing by." But his father tore it open, then threw it across the floor. "I thought it was a box of cigars," he said. And the son in piety bled onto paper and burned it. But when his father started to stick hairpins and knife-blades into his ears and squeeze his nose red and pull out his eyelashes, when his eyes turned puffy, teeth gray, wattles like a turkey, the son made a polished mirror and held it to his father Cuextecatl's face. But he knocked it aside and made his own mask of turquoise snake teeth and quetzal feathers, and caught the train for the city, promising to return. And the son also left, for months living on gray-green buttons in deep caves, in reflected sunlight that feinted across sun-soaked plazas where air buckled, and below that he lived in vivid flowers on vivid walls, white flowers carved to thick froth, where he told a two-headed deer who was the woman he'd followed to that place that he loved her, as she leaped like a shadow against the wall of the turquoise enclave while quetzal plumes rained down, but she said: "No, it was these intoxicating flowers, not me, these songs in the house of the green-swan cacao flowers or golden-flower bell-rattle hummingbirds, the dancing transvestites with bird masks, they brought you. I was never here, let alone a deer." She laughed and was gone into the dark, into the eye's shadow, the tear, but not before he learned her song that said everything is something else, and can be anything, as he listened to the cricket repeating the same lonely phrase with no reply over and over under his window, watched a hummingbird too fast for its own shadow that lingered over a young girl in a shawl sitting on the sidewalk selling lizards, while over her head ripening fruits were light taken in and shaped to fit their shadows. Beside him, trancelike flowers, yellow, red and white, mottled like the thighs of the divine mother for whom men still dance in feathers, then turn to deer which go to live on the high barren plain whose music is echoic over the hubbub, postcards and avocados, above the cathedral's sacked temple, and he thinks of a self spread out, flayed thin, for him to live and dream in, making a close rhythm beaten out of the bloody flower of the sun itself while a woman poked about in the pile with a stick, turning over a radio's entrails while her son sat and played with the frayed edges of her shawl. The day before, he saw an eagle land on the stinking ash and refuse pile to which the blind were driven, left, and picked up late. They were attracted by the firelight that somehow got through or was reflected off the windows of new high-rises, reaching higher and fading, building upward as if they knew what was on the other side. He picked up some dry petals and a twig as the sun began to set over Montaña Humiante and its shrines to the Virgin, Mujer Blanca, over the magueys and Indian villages, their toasted beans and caged toucans, their silver that bruised everything it touched. He looked up at Chapultepec, which gave its porphyry to the statue in the plaza with the broken hands. The wind evaporated on the full black braids of whispering women. He could ask them where to find some flowers for his room, huge flowers of the sun, the shield-flower, *chimalxochitl*, beautiful fragrant flowers. But he might as well have asked the green flash of hummingbirds, the evanescence of the tiny *pajaro mosca*, for as he approached, the women kept moving away through broken blue-green laurels and scrub the color of llamas, kicking up dust and the odd sparrow, all that was left of Cuauhtemoc and his men who at death turned to birds of rich plumage and went behind the sun to live in its wide fields of flowers, forever.

+

In the Museo Nacional de Antropologia, the knife sleek as a mirror, still sharper than his new razor, looked hungry just lying there on its bed, *feed me, feed me,* the obsidian knife, the eternal child, *tecpatl*, son of Cihuacoatl, *Lady of the Snake Skirt,* mother of all, who opened her womb and dropped him from the sky, and when he got lazy she herself came and walked among the people dressed all in white with him swaddled on her back until she left him in the market place where a woman would find him crusted with gore and get the message and rush him to the emperor who knew what needed to be done and soon the twin staircases sang with repaid blood, the world righted and the skull-rack swollen, and he kept looking through the glass at it, glass itself, through his own reflected face to it, and when he got home he took from its dried-out cardboard box his pocketknife of best Sheffield steel with mother-of-pearl handle, reclining unused on its brittle cottonwool bed, the only thing worth having his father ever gave him, and which his father had probably given him, a fetish he took everywhere he went, to no end that he could see, while through his window el Grito de Dolores rang from the balcony of the National Palace, beamed everywhere, the cry of Independence. *Ah,* cry the peasants, let us leave these small plots, these ejidos, and head north, braving coyotes, desert and thirst for the fields of California and the meat-packing plants of Iowa, and *suck, suck* go the Indian babies at the breasts of their barefooted mothers on Calle Cinco de Mayo and the flanged twig brooms go *swish, swish* along the Calle Insurgentes, sweeping the library steps, and his gas-heater, his *calentador*, got too hot for its own good and exploded *pop, pop* like the wooden guns of Subcomandante Marcos rising out of the Chiapas forests as in the National Palace Diego Rivera's mural of a utopia waved bravely from its wall and peeled and he was trying to read months' notes on the meaning of sacrifice as the Grito de Dolores poured out of the radio and *La Jornada* open on the table praised the Zapatistas and cursed him and his.

+

Where's the past? I'm thinking. Here or nowhere, I decide as the Indian waiter turns to fire that flowers and disappears into a monarch butterfly making its way across the clatter of dishes into sunlight prowling like a jaguar through the sunflowers, under the calla lilies and bougainvilleas until a brief shower brings quetzal flowers falling on stunted junipers, and when it stops the fire-serpent swallows it again, and the green jay's call vanishes into the indigo mockingbird, into day's smoking mirrors, and I forget who I am and vanish into the still-beating heart of a chili-red flower near which hangs Huitzilopochtli, arms and thighs blue, face crimson, ready to plunge into the flower's heart his sharp obsidian beak for new fire to take back to the sun, over the broken bottles under the magueys, over the motorcycle crash and taxi pile-up, over the Mazahua beggar and old women down from the hills with multicolored fruit, past the codices still burning in government offices, over the flag of the republic toward Popocatepetl, across the lake we float on, float on where we cannot be reached, but yes, he's still there as I'm crossing the

canal that leads to the brackish lagoon, rain stippling the surface
a few marigold petals shiver on, and a boat came from the other
side luminous as a monarch butterfly while the festival behind lit
fire after fire so the whole place burned like an unhealed wound
and as we passed we said nothing for he was a washed-out specter,
I too, both older than the surrounding mountains, father and
son, and as I turned around to see him go, I saw something like
thread pulled from a spool, unraveling, so I couldn't move until
he did, and then the track on the water was the frayed cord of
the phone on which he'd called to tell me to go to hell which
is where I went and found him again where one man, yellow
and red, tasseled hat, green skirt ringed with seashells, flayed skin
draped over him, the face way down his back, genitals round his
neck, was leading the other, chalk-white, tipsy, shorn head under
plumed headdress, hand in hand, "father" and "son," captor and
captive, both the same age, and one will tear out the other's heart,
and start a fire in his chest and it will be beautiful, the world
renewed, fresh fire in the blood, carried everywhere to destroy the
old, and the son will live in the Sun's retinue as he flies down the
steps to be gathered by the father, boiled and eaten with squash
flowers, finger-bones ringing like gourd rattles, head-nerve
singing, thighs planted firmly in the pot, a flower-tree, the flower,
ciucatl, the song, *xochitl,* flowers everywhere, delicious flowers,
palms, hip bones, ribs, forearm bones, soles of the feet, select
parts for the gods and select friends, torches to light the world
and the sun itself, fathers and sons all illuminated from within
where everything is at stake and there is more than one winner,
though you wonder if the sons know that.

+

Last night, in the smoke, the moon had a seizure, wobbling so you couldn't understand it. Now flowers on the hillsides are still confused, flying off in the remaining wind while peasants are following a funeral, heading for the horizon lost in blue lightning. The dead man's feet point backward to the maize fields where he was born. A dog gnaws a bone in the dirt. No sign of *policia*. Later in the cafe, Ignazio the organizer, tells me he'd read in an old book about a fountain in the rocks where the water pours out and becomes green, and about a turquoise spring that sings between pebbles and the bell-bird responds. The song of the water, he says, sounds like tambourines. "Where is this place?" I ask. "Nowhere," he says. "It's called Tonacatlalpan." Only for princes, owners of the world, a world only for princes, nothing for the common folk, those who suffer torment and misfortune here on earth." Another procession passes, this time a wedding and the air is suddenly clear as glass. I recall Ignazio's mother telling me that Motecuhzoma had many mirrors in his palaces, so he was everywhere and nowhere, exaggerated, diminished, getting lost in them, in himself, and the mirrors broke, and he was scattered in little pieces.

+

Over a large square table covered with a white cloth an anonymous flag flutters like a Chichimec paper-bark banner stuck between rocks. Rubble from the quake still litters the street but the café is crowded as the waiter escorts past our table a woman with hair the color of onyx, wearing a skirt of appliquéd seashells. When I look over for my wife she's gone. Have you seen her? I ask the waiter, who looks puzzled and walks off. I think of "the opaque obsidian mirror with its riddling dark reflections." That night it's hard to sleep, down with heron and duck, oriole and troupial, in an underworld of mud, layer on layer, age on age, silent as a junk shop shut up for the night. I wake with the sun among my shells' clapped-out carillons saved from the rust ocean, waterlogged fruit, and the doll with her appliquéd shell skirt reflected back and forth in the mirror where our photo keeps coming at me as if quoted and going back as if living deepest is living elsewhere, someone else, lost. Next morning I order another mescal, and another. "*Para todo mal,*" says the waiter. I look around. It always seems I'd never seen this place before. Pepper trees by Goya, an iron cross a magpie sits on, tomatoes' beating hearts piled up on blankets, drums moving shuffling girls down the hill, dogs arguing over a chicken foot, and behind them the city squatting like a comic-book drawing of a city. I watch a plane far off head out as if for it the world is always far off. I think of the American girl I'd seen lifting her skirt near the Templo Mayor before she was my wife, before we crossed the canal that led to the brackish lagoon in which they'd drowned girls. Rain stippled the surface a few marigold petals shivered on. A boat luminous as a monarch butterfly came from the other side where the festival continued fire after fire, the whole place burning. No one was in the boat, as if we all cease to exist as persons, as if what we become is no one's business, as if solitude and absence alone can make love possible.

+

The craftsmen picked a feather carefully and placed it, from green birds, yellow birds, from jade brought out the jade, from gold the gold, bejeweled the sun, wove the glow of brittle jade, from the flower brought out the flower, turned flayed skin to flowers where now mothers sit in rebozos, babies at the breast, among child beggars, parrot-colored taxis, black armored vans, pink crosses on black telephone poles until the wailing around midnight, the moon out in back streets where a veiled woman in white walks beside girls who'd wept while priests cut their throats and laid their bodies in the lake's whirlpool that swirled the blood with jewels, stones, gold before people in silence returned to the city with its rubble from the quake still lying on streets, where a young girl in a shawl sits on the sidewalk selling lizards beside me as I read the book Homero gave me years ago, *Poesia Indigena*, where beings and things diffuse, blood and beauty fuse, while over my head ripening fruits are light taken in and shaped to fit their own shadows falling over me with trancelike flowers at my feet, yellow, red and white, mottled like the thighs of the divine mother who was painted with chalk and fed deer hearts, for whom men danced in feathers then turned to deer that went to live on the high barren plain whose music is echoic so I can still hear it over the postcards and the ransacked temple now cathedral, and I think of how it was to be flayed, others in my skin that never really fitted anyhow, or me wearing another's like the bloody flower of the sun itself while maquiladoras and factories wail to the north, along the border, drawing in women and girls with ill-fitting black tunics, heir to broken, scattered bodies left along the border, piling up. And I keep going until I see a plane buzzing a burned-out gas station where a man is dismantling what's left, watched by a magpie sitting on a fence, that's unlucky, a solitary magpie, and an Indian girl on a racing bike darts by leaving a trail of perfume, followed by five young Indian men in a pick-up truck, whooping and laughing as they force me into a ditch where an old black dog finds me. Her massive head sways from side to side as she leads me out of the ditch and into the pueblo, stopping from time to time to listen, check I'm still there. When she turns her head into the sun I see her eyes are all gray.

Tequila Sunset

... for the beaked bird/of maguey is on the wing ...
—Malcolm Lowry, "For Under the Volcano"

I have shrunk into a bottle with girls naked as fuchsias, smooth as cornsilk. Here I am magnified, rhyming with myself, with women, bodies fragrant as milk-corn, flesh the kiss of tequila, and I close my eyes.

*

He's in for life, I should say "Let him out. He's been in long enough. At least give him parole." And I do, but he himself won't budge. There he sits in a child-size steel chair bolted to the floor, in cuffs and leg irons. I read his lips through plate-glass. *Innocent.* Oh, sure, I mouth back. We're in this together. Be back tomorrow. *Take your time*, he says. *You always do.*

*

Time's a trap, I tell them. Shut yours, they say (in Spanish). So through barred windows I watch flowers, I watch pigeons fly on and off a statue that has never been identified other than by its shattered head.

*

Out I go again where light bangs about and arteries spurt. A jaguar leaps, falls back. Above the stars and smog, day is forming serpents, skulls, huge plants that could eat you down to feet and fingernails. Slowly, a stain creeps over everything, hanging like a purple arras, and Aztec angels hold in each hand an orb heavy as a tumor, throbbing like a heart. As I stand on the steps of the Templo Mayor a pack of urchins yells at me: *pinche gabacho, pinche puto gabacho, pinche puto pendejo gabacho.*

*

Last night, over the steps, a comet opened and closed. Space makes you think of eternity, that it's in your power to believe nothing changes, so I looked as usual into my bottle-mirror and was shocked to see puffy eyes and sunken sockets, jowls and wattles, and remembered in the museum a mask of turquoise, snake teeth, quetzal feathers, and when that failed I walked into the water and vanished. They can wait a long time, I thought, but I won't come back.

Brian Swann

Mirrors

The god of duality is at work,/creator of men,/mirror which illuminates things.

I: The Measurer's Choice

Not quite zero. The wind manages to clear the mountains over which the moon is sharp stone. Snow glitters over the crust and the whole world is open straight out into space in all directions. More snow falls out of nowhere, and smoke keeps curling in curlicues and codicils that swirl over the roof. In the thick of things I am a high-wire act trying to keep my balance on a string stretched from pole to pole, confused because space is curved or flat depending on the choice of measurement, and we can tell nothing about its curvature, and I know only what we can get from the results of experiments, so making decisions based on their results is embracing scribbling on walls that flop or fly off, and the sliding night of sleep fades into ditches, takes root and fires up, steering the future like a snake looking straight at you but going backward like something out of a medieval bestiary. So I look down through the snow and see the dreaming head beside the abandoned building plot with to its left or right, depending on how you measure space, warm shadows rippling in antiphony and a laurel tree sniffing the air of its own being and pronouncing itself satisfied, or so it seems to me as I forget the sub-zero cold and circle the sun in a no-man's-land where empty space may be devoid of matter but not properties, and where space is curved or flat depending on the measurer's choice.

II: A Pair of Mirrors

The age of the universe, they say, is ten to the power of thirty-nine, off the charts, ungraspable, so old the idea of age is meaningless, but they also say the universe is a self-excited system brought into being by self-reference, which is something we can relate to, since it's like us going about our days as collaborators in a participatory universe which gives birth to consciousness, which gives meaning to the universe, which is an endless series of receding reflections in a pair of facing mirrors each taking from the other what it's taking from itself.

III: Impersonation

> *Anda vestido de la piel humana*
> —Homero Aridjis

When day ends depends on the shadows, and where you've been depends on words almost too quick to be thought but which you grasp to crawl inside and wear the way Aztecs wore their enemies and then who's the real and who's the impersonator and who's impersonating who?

IV: Man in the Mirror

> *… there where your shadowless soul shall pass*
> —Isaac Rosenberg, "The Mirror"

Here's the mirror again, condescending, mocking familiar who greets me each morning as if it's glad to see me, as it slowly draws everything into it, sucking it all in, into its shiny emptiness, void as water to fall out its back where I leave without maps, no history, just the necessities someone else would take, even though it's too late.

V: The Mirror

> *The thinking of pre-literate antiquity was radical like the body of the sea-urchin or the star-fish.*
> —André Leroi-Gourhan, *Gesture and Speech*

I need some relief so consult the mirror and decide to split, travel on as someone else, taking just the necessities someone else would take.

It is early morning, but soon I stumble across evening about to swallow a few old fishing shacks, long mud flats and a sea like a badly wound demo tape skipping patches and playing itself out. What look like body parts have washed up. Recognizing some, I feel a compulsion to collect them into neat piles the way they do in fairy tales, hoping something might happen, though I know there's no guarantee the right parts will find each other, but so what? Then I glimpse multiple magi hurrying along the sand like crab-bubbles. As the tide swings out, I'm sure I can see the ocean's underpinnings, sense how it all hangs together and plays out. The sea-bed is bright but grows darker as I decide to walk out on its mirror which is the sky's mirror, walk among stars and starfish, a spatial flow existing for itself, always open to revision, the way the I is saturated with limitless blue, the way fish rise from its depths, silver scales flashing like cymbals, the body of stars swimming in night sky, refreshed, here where the myriad soul can feel secure, and at home.

Perder el Hilo

No one here had ever heard of him or his poems, not even the elderly blind gent in a gray suit I met at Café 991 on Calle México who thought that maybe the title foreigner in "The Foreigner Who Died in Juchitán" could have been Pancho Nacar himself, or perhaps it even referred to me.

"After all, you're a foreigner, and this is Juchitán."

"But I'm not dead. I just translated him and want to know him better."

"In Nice, I met a man from Harlem who was retracing the steps of Ricardo Wright across Europe. He carried with him everywhere a huge solid oak table, which he said he couldn't write without."

"And what had he written?"

"Nothing."

With elegant finger-tips he traced the contours of the table.

"He gave my father, the schoolteacher, an inscribed copy of his famous book."

We discussed it, but he remembered a very different book from the one I'd read. I told him so.

"Exactly," he said. "Now, how does your poem end?"

"'When people of pure soul visit the dead,/ They'll leave him flowers of cordoncillo.'"

"Future tense, so he's not dead yet."

"Maybe I made a mistake."

"No, I like it. Ah, cordoncillo, it used to grow around here. You know '*nacer*' means 'to be born'."

"It's 'Nacar,'"

"I have never seen the name 'Nacar.' 'Nacarea' it is 'mother-of-pearl.' 'Cordoncillo' is 'bread', no, *como*, what I do with the thread, not 'bread' but—."

"Braid," I said. "As with hair or thread."

"You know the phrase *'perder el hilo'*?"

"To lose the thread."

"Yes, and to lose the thread is to remember the thread. That's a Juchitán saying. Do you recall Valéry longed for a literature of no dates, no names, no places, and so on, one created in the same spirit as the Holy Ghost?"

"Well ..."

"It is quite possible Nacar, or Nacer, was from here. But it's also even possible that you wrote the poem to follow it here, to the exotic Juchitán where you would meet me and even, metaphorically speaking, find your own death, *une géographie secrète*. You must remember De Chirico saying that a painter must never show his brushstrokes."

"No, but Borges said that memory is a rubbish heap of inventions."

"Exactly. So forget Nacar, for in all likelihood he has forgotten you, or is buried in you and you in him."

Balanced in the Backflow

The wreck wouldn't start again and then I lost my key. So I set off under a sky saturated blue, passing a few skinny trees with white flowers so delicate they looked contrived, pressing on past lizard and snake until halted by loose barbed wire strands nailed to bleached posts across which has fallen a dead saguaro. Over its outstretched arms someone had fitted a stained and tattered shirt. I pressed on hoping I knew where I was going.

*

I kept trying to balance a coin on edge. Outside the paneless window of the shack, the sea shivered. In the sink was a small fish I bought but didn't know what to do with. I also kept a desert plant in a can. When it thundered, the locals said it was angels or spirits or something else passing by. A pipe through the desert brought water too hot to drink. By day I sat in the surf and paid a boy to bring me a bottle of pop now and then. They said the locals had no word for time, but down the dirt road someone was putting up a hotel bigger than this entire place. A few years from now, I will read in the papers how it was blown up with sacks of fertilizer.

*

Despite what I tell myself, there never was a time when I could pull down the sky and put another up, be headlong in love with anything, no questions asked, and so on. I lied to myself then as now, and sometimes feel I should drag myself out for a good beating. I've always dodged the truth and no one really knew, I think, except the little capuchin my favorite uncle Len brought back from the oil-fields of Abadan when I was a kid. Every time he saw me, he screamed like a demon, leaped onto the mantel, shat into his hand and, without aiming, hit me every time. Grandfather always thought this a good joke. When he died he left me only these: Never trust a small-eyed horse, never go down the mines, always watch out for my grandmother. I got what I stole: A pearl-handled knife he used to slice apples for the rescued canary/finch, (the "mule"), and the silver cap for his bull-headed meerschaum ("keeps out the rain"), both of which I lost when someone who knew his way down a chimney ransacked my flat.

*

The snow builds up, silent inch by silent inch. You hope it knows when to stop, but if it doesn't you could imagine a cult springing up, white its sacred color, its litany based on the memory of bird calls, saving by silence, a language so pure it seems echoes, solid in that it's all of what's not there, a creed where reflections are the same as substance, salvation the same as accident, and where you know where you are, where you've been and where you're going by holding up a mirror and watching behind and all around the enveloping episteme of white, while waiting for spring when the stream in spate from wild and quarried heights snags on itself, hurls spray up and off, a basket gathering, letting fall, balancing in the backflow, checking what it lets through, an ever new way through an old physics.

A Fantastic Roman Opera

Un sueño musical...
—Rafael Alberti, *Roma, peligro para caminantes*

(for Masolino D'Amico)

Don Tordo Sassello finally steps out. Spring's limelight had not been incentive enough, but now with his entry, Act I of the immortal *Bellissima* comes alive. He opens his mouth: "*Hah! che tempo!*" His notes carry far and wide, bright as the tips of waves falling over a dark green sea, over a dark green shoreline. They cut through the "Knifegrinding Song" of the People of Acciappamosche, who keep at it in the background until they've ground the blades to dust. Don Tordo struts about in his new costume, back-lit with pastel filters, elegiac in his gray, mottled waistcoat, cravat and skin-tight breeches. He has all the aplomb and cachet of a well-traveled troubadour, some latter-day Tristan, slayer of dragons and worms, lover, musician, while over his sunburnt visage falls his long Mozartian locks. Chest swelling, he breaks into the lovely aria "*Stavo a ppisscià.*" "*Stavo a ppisscià,*" he sings in his lyric tenor, "*jjerzera llì a lo scuro.*" Humming, he strolls along one of the backstreets of old Rome, Roma Sparita, the Via Cappocciotto nel Ghetto, greeting people against a backdrop by Roesler Franz. He is looking for something, as he notes in "*L'anime cosa so?*" In Act II, Don Tordo meets his rival Don Merlo, who we first encounter lounging along the shaft of his empty cart, whistling softly as he watches a young girl in a blue dress walking along, steadying on her head a basket of fresh fish with a folded red parasol on top. This is the heroine, Airone, coloratura, surprising for one so young, who will later sing the delightful aria "*Lo pijo in quello largo e in quello stretto,*" as she walks under the Portico d' Ottavia out onto the cobbled streets near where I live, just around the corner on the Via del Tempio, top floor. I have the non-singing part of the critic who is always observing things from his balcony and commenting recitativo and obligato in my thin tenor on, e.g., the fishmongers with fish laid out on slabs, chickens pecking about, the cries of vendors and the breeze that catches long loops of cloth women are holding up—oh, there's Federico Fellini coming from lunch at Da Giggetto, where to implement my meager income I sometimes help out in the kitchen, slicing baccalà or tossing ice cubes into the boiling olive oil used for carciofi alla guidea. Then, from the direction of the Arco delle Azimelle, out of the shadows steps the villain, Baron Corvo, in black satin, growling a few bars basso profundo, his shining vest trembling, his skinny legs poking out of his frock coat like sticks. He's joined by his co-conspirator in a russet shirt, who goes by a nom de plume, "*L'Americano.*" He's nervous. It's all about turf. He sees danger everywhere and, basso buffo, keeps repeating one line like a fist while the Chorus taunts him to the strains of "*Matrimonio Fallito.*" In order to effect his nefarious ends, which include the downfall of Airone, he pretends to be a heroic fireman, but fools no one. There are no fires. Until in strides Prof. Desmondo, *poeta irlandese*, tipsy counter-tenor, dressed as one of the wild swans of Coole, determined to start one and have something to write about. But his matches fizzle, and besides he's wandered onto the wrong set. Protesting, he's escorted out. As he leaves, the orchestra, thinking it's the end of Act III, begins to leave, followed by the audience, to the recorded sound of water falling in fountains and evening birdsong.

Quotes from G.G. Belli, *Sonetti*).
    "*Hah …*": "What a perfect day."
    "*Stava …*": "I was pissing last night, there in the darkness".
    "*L'anime …*": "Souls, what are they?"
    "*Lo pijo …*": "I take it in the wide and narrow."

Imagine

Imagine a monologue between two people. You can't do it, right, not really, it's not logical, so I free you from the burden of even trying, though, as I say, you can do it, sort of. At least, you can sense it. Hence the problem of the enigma, which is something like the problem of mathematical platonism where it is claimed that mathematical ideas exist independent of the human mind, though it's the human mind that is conscious of it. On the other hand, a great body of mathematics has been developed without any reference to physical reality, motivated by the narrative of mathematics itself, seemingly independent of the mind's construct. This is what interests me since it could lead to the idea of a narrative developed out of its own needs, for instance, Swift's experiment to write upon nothing, or body artists maiming themselves and so becoming self-consuming art objects to the point of suicide— Whoops. Here is a point where my narrative disappears down a wormhole in the text to reappear on board the largely empty *Queen Mary*, bound for New York, mostly empty except for me and Traffic of "John Barleycorn" fame: Steve Winwood, Dave Mason, John Capoldi, Chris Wood. Bored with First Class, they've come down to my level and spend their time getting stroppy, sloshed at the bar, making the bartender hate them so much he feeds them foul pink concoctions which they are too drunk to notice, and— Whoops, down the hatch with that too and probably out into the Atlantic. The past is a far country, and so is the present, but at least it's a bit clearer, though it too takes odd turns. As someone once said, time forks continuously in, for example, memory, for, as Pavese said, "the richness of life lies in memories we have forgotten," a phrase that hovers over me like the face of Kalypso, the Hidden One, the Death goddess with the veil over her face, descendant of the Paleolithic veiled Venus of Willendorf and Dolni Ventonice, Kalypso who lived in a cave on the island of Ogygia, "navel of the sea," who wanted Odysseus, "The Sufferer," to drink her ambrosial nectar to become immortal. This is how the ancients thought, in mythic narrative, where time and memory are so intertwined they hardly exist, which is why Plato wanted poets, descendants of these primitives, to be expelled, for not thinking "rationally," in discrete entities. Me, I prefer thinking like a chrysalis, growing into gorgeous unknowing until it bursts and flies away as lights in life, tangles of fire, which must have been something like the consciousness of humans long before the Greeks, way back into the Paleolithic, about the time some 50,000 years ago when Neanderthals brought into their caves at Aray-sur-Cure two lumps of roundish iron pyrites, the cast of a large spiral gastropod shell, and a spherical polyparium to think with. This was the first sign of human fascination with the fantastical in nature, our nature.

Whoops!

Dogs on the Roof

I thought of telling Curto that Tamburro was lying to get the day off, that her grandmother had in fact been dead for some time. Instead I simply told him that Tamburro just wanted the day off to visit the Villa Giulia and the newly discovered Laocoön. "In that case," said Curto, looking past Tamburro, who was glaring at me, and out the window at what I was now sure were dogs, "in that case, give my regards to your grandfather. Yours too," he said to me. "You can go too, Michael." I looked around for Michael. Oh, he meant me. I was about to thank him when he stood up and, his back to us and face to the wall, started moving slowly round his desk. "*I, seguerre, puellas,*" he hummed. "That's Virgil." Tamburro walked over to my desk. "You know," she said, "you don't know everything. I'm not going to the museum. I've given up that kind of thing." "Since when?" I asked. "Yesterday," she said. "I'm going to the mosque, if you must know." "The mosque? I was wondering about that outfit you're wearing. A bit severe. And why are you looking so miserable?" "It's not an 'outfit'," she replied. "And I'm not miserable. I just never smile any more, that's all. Shafiq said 'He who fears God never smiles.' I shall never smile again." She sat down. I went to the bathroom. When I returned, I looked over to Tamburro to ask if she'd given up wine and sex, but she wasn't at her desk. Just a pocketbook that lay open on a chair. Inside I could see a pot of honey, a half-eaten rusk, and a large black book which I took to be the Koran. When she returned from wherever she'd been I pointed out the window. "There are dogs on the roof," I said. "Impossible," she sniffed. "Dogs are disgusting and unclean. Those are pigeons." "Did I ever tell you," I asked Tamburro, "that in Ceylon once I put a snake's head in my mouth?" But she had left again, and I didn't intend to tell her that the snake was dead. There was no one else to talk to. The others were hunched over graphs and numbers, or dozing. They didn't like me anyway, I don't know why. Maybe they thought I was a HQ spy. So I went over to the door frame and did ten chin-ups to strengthen my rock-climbing grip. Then I sat down again at my desk and flipped through the pamphlet Curto had given me, "Advice for Trainee Salesmen." My attention was caught by advice on how to break down the resistance of people who were reluctant to buy what you were selling. This is what it said:

1/ *Compliment him on his achievements.*
2/ *Discuss his interests.*

Under these headings, scenarios unfolded involving a Noren, a Sitka, an Alex Ferman, and others, men of non-specific nationalities as befitted our multinational corporation that specialized in lubricants. Before her conversion, the word "lubricant" would have set Tamburro off into gales of uncontrollable laughter. Until today, she could have been heard at her desk or in the Ladies' Room, or just about anywhere, singing or humming "*Bella Ciaou*" or "*Bandiera Rossa*" or even a stornello or two. "*Ali-mo e taci-tu*" was a favorite. She also had a taste for dirty jokes which as often as not seemed to involve a Russian ballet dancer on a plane with a squirrel stuffed down his trousers which he fed through the fly with bananas. Curto called me into his office. "What's with Tamburro?" he asked. "She just told me that if you love Allah you love destruction. Wasn't that what the Young Turks said when the Commission of Union and Progress planned to blow up Hagia Sofia?" "You're asking the wrong person," I replied. "How so? I thought you went to college. Anyhow, she's making me nervous. She just said there was no god but Allah. She's giving me the trots, *la caccarella*.

Dogs on the Roof

Nun dico bene?" Recently, he'd taken to quoting Belli, though he was from Genova. "Oh, yes," I said. "Look," he continued, "I'm a humanitarian, but enough is enough. Live and let live, but I'll have to fire her if this goes on. Want to hear a joke?" "Sure." Who doesn't? Sucking up never hurt. "What do you call people who eat people?" "I don't know. Cannibals?" I volunteered. "No—Humanitarians!" he bellowed. "You know," I said, "there are dogs on the roof." "Doesn't surprise me," said Curto. "Doesn't surprise me at all. Dogs, you say?"

Silence and Nothing

In the outdoor café, she sat at one side of the glass-topped metal table, I at the other. I drew a finger through a coffee stain, she adjusted her big hat. I tried thinking her thoughts and didn't like what I thought. I had been avoiding this, wanting to do it, not wanting. I knew if I asked she'd say yes, so I didn't ask. Instead I rose and left, and almost at once regretted it. I missed her, as usually happened. I needed to get away, at least for a while. I got up, sat down, got up. Left.

George met me at the airport and asked if I'd like to go with him to an open house and concert. "But I'm in these old wrinkled smelly clothes," I replied. "I haven't had time to change." "You can do that later," he said. "Take your baggage with you." "I only have a carry-on. But OK." I hadn't seen George for some time. Though I'd known him for nearly thirty years, only recently had it occurred to me that I didn't really know that much about him. The week before, I had been reading a book on nineteenth-century art and come across a famous artist by the name of Sir George Hayter, Queen Victoria's Principal Painter in Ordinary. Casually, as we chatted in the limo, I asked George, who bore exactly the same name, if he was any relation to the illustrious portrait painter. "Great-grandfather," said George. "And here we are." The driver pulled up at the front door of a place that looked like Roedean, a distinguished academy for young ladies. We got out and found ourselves in an elegant crowd walking into a magnificent building. "All this goes," I muttered to George, "and everyone in it when I'm Socialist King." "Socialists don't do that," he replied. "They spread the butter thin. Or margarine." We moved around in the massive loggia, George greeting people, I looking at the paintings, mostly portraits going back to Queen Anne, some seeming to stretch almost from floor to ceiling. George had been invited to give a lecture on his work as curator and restorer, so we went into a classroom filled with girls chatting and giggling. Their teacher tried to quiet them, but the noise didn't bother George who found an antique chair and tried to hoist his 6'6" frame up onto it. It wobbled, and he had to come down. Through the doorless arch of a side room full of odds and ends, I spotted a low, heavy table. He and I went over, tipped off books and ornaments, and carried it out into the classroom. George climbed onto it and began his talk, while the teacher prompted her charges with "You remember, girls, how we discussed this last week," or "You remember how we touched on that topic yesterday," and so on. I got bored, and, hoping George wouldn't notice, wandered off. A small group was walking along the corridor, and I thought a woman called out my name, or maybe mentioned it in conversation. How did she know my name? Maybe it wasn't exactly my name. I continued on to the portrait-lined great gallery with a ceiling of Tiepolo clouds. In this place it wasn't so much the paintings, drapes, tapestries, carpets and the rest that were on show so much as the air that had been allowed in and distributed for us to breathe and enjoy, shared tastefully and generously for no other reason than that it was possible to do so. Even the brightness of the light had been controlled and distributed to us. George joined me after his talk. "Go well?" "No." We walked outside onto a gravel path under pollarded trees, by topiaried bushes, beside articulated flower-beds, skirting the maze. Talking of old times, we joined up with some people going into what looked like a chapel. "Where we going?" I asked. "Concert," George replied. "Of what?" I persisted. "You'll see." We sat on stone steps around an amphitheater. On the wall across from us were paintings and photos of Stonehenge. The audience slowly went quiet, but no musicians had yet appeared, no podium had been set up, no chairs or music stands. "What are we waiting for?" I whispered. "Silence," said George. "Oh." I shut up. Minutes went by. "Well?" I queried. Then, "What's the concert?" "Silence," George whispered in the silence. I looked around. "What?" I repeated. "Nothing," said George. I sat quietly, until after a while I began to hum a tune in my head, a melody I had just invented right there. While humming, I was trying to remember it for later. Maybe other people might like it. But then I realized anyone can make up a tune. It's the harmonics, the orchestration, the bass line and the rest that's the hard part, not to mention that the business end would present problems. And the fact that I can't write music. Still, I enjoyed my concert for as long as I could, then, "See you later," I sotto-vocced to George. "I need to change. I've got to change."

Out I stepped, back across the garden into the mansion where, after a little difficulty, I located the side room where I had stashed my carry-on bag. The place was still full of bric-à-brac, with the aromatic addition of leftovers from some sort of reception. Since there was no door I had to act fast. I opened up the bag, took off my sweaty shirt, stripped down to my underwear. But standing there in my socks, I got sidetracked by my reflection in a dusty, cracked mirror atop a chiffonier to my right. Suddenly, I was aware of a woman in a big hat who came through the doorway, stopped, turned away, turned back, looked at the mirror, looked at me, turned away, left. I heard her laugh, then whisper to someone, but all I could hear was "nothing."

The Tree

"Let's go visit Milton's mulberry," I say. "What do you mean?" she replies. "He planted it, I tell her, "when he was a fourteen-year-old undergrad at Christ's and then wrote 'Lycidas' under it." "How is that possible?" she says. "Mm," I say. "Hadn't thought of that. They also say he planted it in the year of his birth, 1608." "That makes even less sense," she says. "Do you think it's still there?" And it is, in a corner of the Fellows' Garden, half buried in an earth mound, branches supported by props and a lead sheet wound half way around the trunk, which is rotting and filled with decay and duff and cool mosses deep. "That must be it," she says. "Rather disappointing." "I doubt that's the original," I tell her. "I bet it's an offset." "How much?" she asks. "How much what?" "The bet." "You don't bet on such things. Even if Milton didn't plant it, he did sit underneath it. I'm prepared to believe that. He was a genius. The universe went right through him, like the tree of life, axis mundi. Everything was made clear to him as he sat under this tree. The plan to justify the ways of God to man was already playing in his mind, about to bear fruit." "He should have planted an apple tree," she mused. "The tree of the knowledge of good and evil was an apple. Plus he could have beaten Newton to gravity. Was this a black or white mulberry?" "What does it matter?" "The book says white were planted for silk worms. Or maybe it was black. I'm not sure. In any case," she continues, "if you have to justify the ways of God to man that means those ways are in need of justification; something's wrong with them." "I guess. Here, you want a puff?" "You know, this tree's in such a mess it might as well not be here. I could push it over and all that would be left would be stories. It could be a fake." "Maybe." "How much do you want to bet?" "You and your bets. Stop trying to benefit from uncertainty. God does not play chess." "Wanna bet?" "I'm too tired to argue." Just then a breath of wind shifts the tree a bit, and its leaves whiffle like tissue paper. Then it shifts again, as if trying to get comfortable, find something to lean on. I feel like sticking out a hand but that wouldn't be right. "I thought I saw a snake, over there," she says. "Anyway, I'll catch you later. There must be *something* to see in this town that hasn't collapsed or is in danger of collapsing." She turns. "Enough of poets," she says. "Facts, I need facts. I'm going to see Newton. That's where I'm going. Trinity, right? Then see you back." "Darwin was also here at Christ's," I reply, but she's gone. I sit down under the tree, take one last drag and decide not to lean against the trunk, since I doubt it would bear the weight, but as I look up into it there seems more tree, thicker, denser in the languid air of the fens. I feel a bit dizzy and sleepy, like one of Tennyson's lotus-eaters. Suddenly a sparrow dashes in with a sharp chirp, but, unlike Bede's sparrow, it does not fly out. It is followed by a small flock whose shadows are soon absorbed by the leaves. I hear their little voices drifting like downward smoke spreading wider and wider as if underwater until there's almost not enough light to go round. I feel I should help out but I can't move. I could, for example, give the sun a boost up and tell the moon to hang on a bit while I replace the planets in their slots or even ease a few out of orbit just for fun or to amuse the children bright as berries who are climbing here and there in the tree, dancing about it singing "Here we go round the mulberry bush, mulberry bush, mulberry bush," miming how they wash their hands, wash their clothes, put them on, take them off, flitting round and round, in and out, round and round.

Dog

Until today, I hadn't paid much attention to the stuffed pooch with floppy ears and a large black nose, big or bigger than a real dog such as Beethoven. Just now, however, he happened to catch my eye as he sprawled on the sofa beside the bookshelf. Actually, it wasn't the dog who caught my eye but the silver crown on his head that said "Birthday Girl," because I'd always assumed the dog was male, but no big deal. Words can change things, tell you what is and what isn't. So I inspected more closely, and still didn't look like a girl-dog to me, not like my childhood border collie True, whose name was originally Cambo, from the place where we found her as a lost pup. We later changed her name to True, the name of a hound in the pack of the famous nineteenth-century huntsman John Peel, after my grandmother discovered we were related to him, even though it turned out that the original True was a boy and our True was a girl. "If ever you get lost on the fells at night," my grandmother told me, "make sure she's with you. She'll lie across you to keep you warm until help arrives." (She also said that if you keep flowers in your bedroom at night they'll poison you). I never put either of these to the test but I often woke with True/Cambo lying on top of me so I could hardly breathe.

Now, sitting in the armchair across from the dog, I was beginning to think about dogs in general and related topics. Why do they come when you call? What is it that comes when you call? What is it that comes when you don't call, that comes without your calling? Where does it come from and what should I call it when it arrives? I could call it something arbitrary, something that would not normally apply, but this runs the risk of confusing everyone concerned, including myself, which means I will have given myself over to it as the source of my confusion, contributing to a sense of being redundant. If you can't call something by its real name what can you call it? It will elude you and always be gone, taking you with it, forever following, till you are lost. But the real name is hard to find, as many fairy-tales can attest to. However, once "it" arrives, there's a good chance we can sit down like civilized beings and talk, even if I might be talking or negotiating from a position of weakness. I've noticed, interestingly enough, that once engaged, the weakness and nervousness often pass into the excitement of distortion and subterfuge. How we both cheat and distort! How we pretend, each to have authority to say what is or what isn't. We do not forget to use the element of vagueness, the allure of fog. Everything is possible, once you engage. Thinking which, I returned to the dog across from me. She looked thoughtful, though her thoughts were probably just sensations, precise, if vague intuitions, a kind of shaped scent. It's anybody's guess, but she seemed relaxed in her canine surety. You certainly got the sense she knew your every move, even when you were not there. I wondered if she knew she had that silly crown on her head. Probably not, since if she did she might well have taken it off. But there again she might have left it on to confuse me to keep me off balance, keep me guessing and so retain her independence and my deference. In any case, she certainly looked pretty with it on and, as she sprawled on the sofa, eyes fixed on me, I could imagine her keeping me warm on a bleak moor at night. She looked confident and capable. I wondered if she thought I was too.

Argentina

We sat on a long wooden bench. When I turned my head, I noticed the joints in the wall's sheetrock had been clumsily taped and painted over. I wondered if anything would fall off onto me and kept looking behind or reaching back to touch the edges to check until I felt a pain in my arm. "Leave them alone," she said. The first thing I'd noticed about her as she walked in, quick as a bird, was that she was smaller than I remembered and that her once-luxuriant chestnut hair was now gray, though still held in place on the left by a snap. I never could recall her face so there was nothing to compare it to, though, so far as I could tell, it looked right. "I like your scent. Floral," I said. "I'm not wearing any," she replied. "I never wear perfume." We sat quietly in the large lecture room at the Center, desks strewn with what appeared to be lecture notes. The sheet in front of me had "quantum entanglements" at the top, and scrawls underneath. A young man came by and handed her a sheet of paper with a Latin sentence. She took a ballpoint pen and quickly sketched out the sentence structure, then translated it first into English, then Spanish, then, surprisingly, German. Was it possible that her family was part of the German (Nazi?) exodus? Was she Catholic? How did she feel about the new pope who had never been part of the vocal opposition to dictatorship in Argentina and did she think washing the feet of the poor was enough? Did— "All done," she said, handing the paper back. We continued to sit rather rigidly side by side. Slowly I felt her leaning into me. I wanted to kiss her but was unable. Instead, I gently touched her nose. "Why did you agree to meet me?" I asked. "I was going to be here," she replied. "I have to drive back soon," I said, "to clean up the mess. Lots of water. Muddy as hell in the basement still. Would you like to come?" "I can't," she said. "Then will you be here when

I get back?" "I don't think so." I pulled out an eyelash and bit it in half. Then I pulled a hair from my right eyebrow, and bit that in half too. I began to sweat. "Do you still like horses?" I asked, hesitantly. "Cattle," she replied. "I breed them. In Madariaga." "Cattle?" "Horses too." I thought of Boudicca, and as we sat in silence I began tracing shadows and images on the white wall. Horses figured largely. Images, I thought, how they arise from other images, and if you're lucky they make beautiful lasting forms for the unknowable deep meanings without words, the way the Minoan double axe represented the epiphany of the Goddess since she assumed the shape of a butterfly rising from the horns of a bull. Meaning flows into meaning until, perhaps, there's nothing left, or what there is bears little relationship to what you started with.... When I came to she'd gone. I went to look for her, finding her at a public phone in the lobby. She was speaking rapid Spanish. From the little I could make out, it seemed one of her students at UBA had been shot, or a cow had aborted, something of the sort. I sat down on a hard wooden chair. "I should have kept her in the lasting condition of an abstraction," I thought, "kept her *lointaine*. I should have left things alone. I'm ridiculous. When you live long enough, people you've known or think you've known become characters in a story whose plot is your life. Everything becomes you. And people aren't people anyway, nor things things. They're ideas. Yes, I should have let sleeping dogs lie instead of keep poking and waking them up as if repetition made things true." I decided to wait for her to finish her call. The minutes crept by so I went outside to stretch my legs. When I got back there was just the phone sitting in its cradle. Perhaps, I thought, she was staying here at the conference center, so I set off to check out the old mansion, opening any unlocked doors and peeking inside. No luck. I decided to wait in my room in case she phoned, but I forgot the number and all the rooms looked the same. I noticed two men in hotel livery following me. I explained my dilemma. "Let us help," said the younger. "What is your number?" asked the older. I told him my problem. "Your key?" Same problem. "Perhaps it's on the top floor," he said, pointing to the elevator. I thanked him, walked over and pushed the button on the wall. When it arrived, I stepped inside and the thing shook. Steadying myself, I pushed the button and waited. I pushed again. Slowly, we had lift-off. The contraption began to move, creaking and shuddering. It reminded me of my old cage-like lift in Rome with its fit-like ascension and appetite for five-lire coins. I found myself urging the thing upward, so by the time I got to the top floor and stepped out I was pretty well winded. I managed to locate what I thought was my room. The door was unlocked. I pushed it open to find a number of suitcases on end. I kicked one and it fell over, opened up, empty. I turned to find the two men behind me. "Is this the room?" one asked. "I don't think so," I said. I went from room to room on the top floor, but all I found were open, empty suitcases. By this time my hip was playing up, titanium or no titanium. I heard music coming from down the corridor. There they were again, leaning against the wall, smoking, and listening to a small radio. To be friendly, "Del Shannon?" I said. "Runaway?" Who?" said the younger. I repeated myself. "Who's he when he's at home?" said the elder, turning the music off and putting out his cigarette on the wall. "Are you a guest here, sir." "Sort of," I replied. "I was told I could leave my stuff in a room until I came back." "And when did you say that would be?" he asked. "Didn't you say you were looking for a lady?" the young one said. "Lady, yes. Case."

"Perhaps you only thought you left it here," he continued. "Or her," said the elder." "It had important stuff in it," I added. "Then how did you get by without it?" "I don't know," I replied. "But I do *know* I left it here." Then, "Do you know," I said, to break the tension, "Marcel Duchamp once said that when people say 'I know,' they really don't know. They believe." I sat down. The men left. Hell, I thought, I do *know*. But if that's so everything should be where I remembered. How many of me are there? *The first time I saw myself in a mirror I was sure the person in the mirror was as astonished to see me as I was him.* "What did you say, sir?" I looked up. There they were again. "I said that Alice fell through the looking-glass because of curiosity. She couldn't see all the corners of her room and leaned in too far and got more than she bargained for. A bit like me. Curiosity killed the cat." "What cat?" said the younger man. "Have you lost a cat?" "Cats aren't allowed," the older man reminded him.

    Unable to let go, I'd tried many times in various ways over the years to contact her, using whatever meager leads I had, but with no reply. Perhaps, I thought, she's dead. But in that case, I told myself, I'd have heard from her. Could I have done something to her? I finally decided she'd flown off as planned for Argentina at what happened to be the time of Perón's return, the military coup of 1976 and the dirty war with its "disappeared." We'd met by chance at a party and I'd only known her for a few hours overnight when most of the time I was unconscious, so she was in effect an abstraction, though one with garlic on her breath. What I remembered from that cold December night in the city was that she was tall, statuesque even, and was from Ohio, I think, and very young, much younger than I. I remembered her scent, her blue panties with lace tops, a blouse held together with a large safety pin and her saying "I've never woken up in such a lovely way before." I also remembered her panic at not finding the green contact lenses I'd removed to safety the night before and her announcing "I'm going back to Argentina come hell or high water." I also seem to recall that she asked if I wanted her to be the mother of my children, but maybe she was having me on. Whatever, I hoped she'd avoided both hell and high water for, despite my efforts over the years, as I said, I'd not been able to find her and had largely given up, deciding that even if she survived she'd probably married and changed her name, maybe more than once. Then, decades later, one winter evening, having read for the umpteenth time "Math, the son of Mathonwy," with its story of flower-faced Blodeuwedd who turned into a bird (owl, actually), on top of *The Golden Bough*, I laid down my treasured pocket-size green cloth copy of *The Mabinogion* by Lady Charlotte Guest, with "J.G. Frazer, Trinity College, Cambridge, October 1906" neatly handwritten on the inside cover, which I had picked many years ago for 6d from Heffer's outside bookstall on Petty Cury. I got to my feet and put out Gretchen the cat, who didn't want to go out, poked the sleeping Argus to go and do his business, but he growled, so I let him be and poured another generous shot of Irish whiskey into my coffee. Soon I was drifting about in Google tasting this, testing that, and absently typed her name. As usual, I got: a realtor, a managing cosmetologist and an actress/rock star who had appeared in *Penthouse*'s "The Great Pet Hunt, Part 2." I was about to quit when the computer crashed, as it often did. When it came back up, I decided to give it one final try, and then let go my obsession, which had done enough tsuris. But in my haste before the computer nosedived again, I made a number of typos, maybe even misspelled her name—who knows what I typed? The result was—"There! That's her!" As I read, it all hung together. There were even photos of what I assumed she might well look like. There was even an e-mail address.

How the West Was Won

The girl in the cable-stitch sweater is on the way to feature in the spaghetti western *The Marriage of the Trapper in the Open Air* and is complaining to the milord and his lady, on their way to the same set, of having to be smeared with cochineal for the part of Pocahontas. They are all waiting at the Missouri as the brass band plays "Shenandoah," and the milord gives the finger with right hand and the V-sign with his left to the rude locals to show "he's not to be trifled with." His bride squints to look up at the station clock and then down the tracks to look for the westbound train, the "gravy train" as the rude mechanicals call it, but the eastbound comes slightly ahead. Across the muddy road in the obsolete open-sided crematorium, four bodies are waiting to be loaded along with a number of wooden crates headed back to Washington filled with all sorts of items including various animals, whole and in part, plus a collection of Ghost Dance shirts and deerskin dresses stained and pierced with bullet holes, as well as fringed saddle decorations carefully made from pudenda cut out and stretched, along with a few choice tobacco pouches made from savage scrotums. Meanwhile, at the other end of town, a young man in a puffy red jacket who had insisted on going to the football game in high heels has encountered some difficulties in a bar and he has had to fight his way out, in the process discovering that running in pumps presents its own set of problems, while in another flashback FBI agents interrogate wedding guests and in another the groom in Vienna, Indiana, puts on the turntable Franz Lehar waltzes but it refuses to turn until he kicks it so everyone in period costume begins to dance to the strict time-signature except for the bride-to-be who is sulking because she is getting married to a trapper in the morning without benefit of her lucky cable-stitch cardigan, which her mother has told her she has to take off before she arrives at the station in St. Louis where she hopes he has improved his wardrobe since she doesn't take kindly to his choice of a puffy red jacket for the ceremony, especially in midsummer heat, but he isn't thinking of marriage as he hightails it out of the fight in the bar, thinking it will never work out because all he wants is to be himself, and what does that say about modern marriage? he thinks as both trains arrive almost simultaneously and the dead are bundled aboard along with crates and all sorts of stuff, and people pile into the coaches without checking they're going in the right direction, and the Viennese orchestra begins to play as if it was in Act Two of *The Cherry Orchard*, and the sound almost drowns out a noise like sunbathers on beaches right round the country who are captured by *New Yorker* cartoonists who have words for the kind of thing where people keep heading west, across the wide Missouri, land where the sun never sets and is there for the taking before bouncing back like a tsunami.

The Usual

I:

Looking closer, dogs on the roof again. I stood up from my desk, knocking the journal of Colonel George Chicken to the floor, just at the point where he was being fanned by the Cherokee in 1725. It landed on top of William Bartram's account of winsome Cherokee maidens, "innocently jocund nymphs," with whom he was sharing a basket of strawberries they'd picked in 1775. I'd knocked that volume off my desk the last time I saw dogs on the roof, about an hour ago. Kotzwinkle's voice intruded on my reverie. Once again he was trying to convince the chief librarian he needed a day off. "My grandmother is—." Not that again. The old man wouldn't buy it. Kotzwinkle had already told me and I'd told the boss that he wanted the day off to go apartment hunting with his latest conquest, Pol Hering ("Red Herring" on account of her hair), who worked in Archives. I looked out again. The dogs were still there, on the roof. When I passed the desk of Miss Rubenstein I saw her slip a pat of butter into her compact case. Inside her open pocketbook I could see a pot of honey and a half-eaten rusk. I pointed to the dogs. She thought they were pigeons. "What would dogs be doing up there?" she asked. "Did you know Muriel's just had a stroke?" "Just to attract attention again," I said, but that sounded harsh, so, "She's a well-meaning woman," I continued, "decent in most respects, and I suppose if she'd thought about it maybe she wouldn't have had a stroke." Miss Rubenstein stared at me and stood up, closing her compact case with a snap. I'd clearly said the wrong thing, though the night before I'd read the latest *Time* synopsis on new discoveries about the nature of women. Much good it did me. I was going to go over and tell the boss about the dogs, but decided against it. I picked up Colonel Chicken and William Bartram and put them on my desk. I'd catalogue them tomorrow.

II:

On the way home there was a small fire under the hood of my new Chevy Celebrity. Squirrels had stashed away burlap in the air intake. The cops pulled me over and gave me a ticket. This was my reward for planning to drop by and visit cousin Frank in the hospital where he had been working installing a newfangled magnetic thing. By a strange coincidence, it was the same hospital where I visited my mother on a regular basis. Magnetic Resonance Imager, I think that's what it was called. Frank was helping install it in a converted semitrailer for use as a mobile diagnostic center. The thing was packed with powerful magnetism and when they turned it on it smashed into a nearby forklift. Two steel tines, eighty pounds each, came flying off the forklift and knocked Frank twenty feet. When a paramedic rushed over to cut off his pants the scissors flew out of his hands and stabbed a bystander. Another poor fellow had many bones broken. He had to have a metal rod inserted in each leg and a metal plate put in the bones of each arm. I hope he requested non-magnetic metal. A cop had his gun pulled out of his holster. Later, rescuers discovered all their magnetic bank cards had been erased. And all this had been caused simply by turning the MRI on to make adjustments to the cooling system (it was cooled by liquid helium).

III:

I didn't think the car would make it to the hospital so I drove home at twenty mph with smoke drifting over the windscreen. I parked, went into the kitchen for a drink and a sandwich. The bat was still there, hanging upside down, dead, gripping the insect-screen from inside. The window was closed. How the bat got between window and screen was a mystery. It made me lose my appetite. I pushed the window open and tried to pry it off the screen with the very same pair of Regency sugar tongs left me by my aunt, Miss Martha LaBelle, and which she had used to fend off a robber who yanked her from her wheelchair by her hair and attempted to relieve her of her artificial limb. I soon gave up, tossing the tongs and closing the window. The bat would have to wait. But my appetite returned, so I decided to leave the car still smoldering and walk to Goldie's Diner. On a whim, I followed a bird's call, a bird I'd never heard before, which conveniently was coming from the direction I was planning to go anyway. So I headed upstream along tire-encumbered banks, past a landmark, one of the trees the Cherokee had bent, a "marker tree". There are still a few remaining, some of which I used when putting together my catalogue of the genus names of aphids which can be found in "Special Collections," under "*Sur Les Traces de la Langue Mère,*" subsection "The Cultural Significance of Trees." Lewis and Clark are said to have come this way. They didn't, but William Bartram did. I don't know about Colonel Chicken. When I reached Goldie's (open 24/7), I saw the woman who comes in at the same time each Tuesday. She had high cheekbones and worked in the plastic tomahawk factory that supplied the Braves. She came over with her coffee cup and sat by me at the counter, asking if I'd like to share a hot dog. I declined. "You look foreign," she remarked, not for the first time. "Somebody said you'd drowned." The other diners ignored us, looking as if they'd rather not be there, a demolition team, sitting together, silent. They'd have enough work to last a lifetime. The woman went over to join them. Behind me the mirror had disappeared, all steamed over. It was raining now. Through the window I thought I heard that same bird again, but it could have been a stump-grinder. I ordered the usual. Fried chicken, gravy, no peas, followed by pecan pie à la mode. Hold the ice cream.

Home Sweet Home

Beside the river, a guinea pig grazing with chickens and wild game. The traveler shook the iron gate of the mission. No one answered, so he gave a push. The heavy metal resisted, then relented slowly. Inside, he stopped and stared. Behind some trees he could make out the heads of buffalos. As he crept closer he could see human legs underneath.

Paine had planned to travel and vindicate the national character, its manners and institutions against the aspersions of unfriendly travelers, mostly foreign. Dr. Tennille, brother to the Georgia Secretary of State, had referred to John Ross for information about his people's early history. He was especially interested in manuscripts, letters, and treaties. He had been surprised by what he had already discovered about the system pursued by agents of our government, so he had turned to Paine when he learned of his travel plans. Paine agreed. As he wrote to a friend: "I thought if the real position of the question were once understood by our own country and its rulers, their ends would be sought by different and unexceptional means."

The traveler walked carefully through the courtyard and soon found himself where the buffalo had been. He continued until he saw a tunnel, which he entered with some trepidation because it was so dark. As his eyes opened, he was aware of something close by. On either side of him were ranks of buffalo-men. Some were in handcuffs. Some were red, some were black. None said a word, but stared straight ahead, not even seeing him, it seemed. He walked faster, and emerged out of the other end.

Paine had studied hard before his trip, both European literature and his own country's early history. Once embarked, he wrote letters back home regularly. In these letters his disappointment soon became clear. But he reported honestly what he saw, or so he told himself. In addition, he sent back articles to eastern newspapers and began collecting materials for Dr. Tennille. He even made a visit to John Ross on his behalf, garnering some interesting pages. In his articles he was particularly critical of the Georgia Guard, whom he described as more like banditti than soldiers, and more than once told the story of an Indian who had hanged himself rather than fall into their hands. Most of these articles were never printed. They were found long after his death among his private papers. Where we also find letters to his old friend, the Rev. Schermerhorn, telling him of other incidents regarding the Guard, such as when they broke into Ross' cabin with bayonets, dirks and pistols. A Sergeant Young struck Paine across the mouth and shoulder when he remonstrated. Then said Young rode off into a storm, his escorts whipping their horses and singing obscene songs. To comfort himself, Paine had hummed "Home Sweet Home." Ross asked him to hum it again.

As he came out of the dark, he found himself facing the façade of a lovely baroque church. He put his shoulder to the heavy oak door and winced with pain. But the door gave, and he found himself in a library that seemed much too large for the building. He stared into the fragrant dark. All the books were bound in steel, "to keep out unwanted eyes," said a voice behind him. "Our task is made no easier by the intrusion of the parsimonious who would seek to reduce the possibilities of God's plenty." The traveler backed out, shivering. He soon found himself in a more respectable tavern where he found a tattered copy of the *Western Songster*. Flipping through its pages he found "Home! Sweet Home!" He had pointed out to the landlord, one Captain Nelson of the Georgia Guard, as they were talking about matters literary, that the song's author and he shared names. The captain looked at the paper held before him, called Paine a damned liar and kicked him in the shin. The captain was not an uneducated man. In fact, just before the unfortunate incident described above, they had been discussing the nature of idealism. As Paine bent to rub his ankle, as if nothing had happened, Captain Nelson continued the conversation. "Reckon you've heard tell of Marryboy?" he inquired. "His system of nater? Morabeau. Him and Tom Paine were— here, he any relative of yourn?"

The traveler backed out, then retraced his steps across the courtyard, back through the tunnel, now empty, through the house and out the door, across the courtyard, through the heavy gates until he reached the river and the grazing animals. There were fewer than before. But he was soon apprehended.

As reward for his answer to Captain Nelson's query, he found himself in prison, which consisted of a log hut, bunk bed of boards and straw, with one tattered blanket. There were poles overhead with old coats and shirts strung over them. In the gloom he could make out another figure at the other end of the room. He walked over, and was astonished to find a chained Indian, who said his name was Chained Indian, son of Speaker Going Snake. He had refused to speak to the U.S. census taker. He refused to talk any more with Paine, but from time to time would sing "Jenny will your dog bite?/ No, sir, no." Then lapse into long silences. That night Paine was visited with troubling dreams, and would often wake confused. After a few days, the jailer, one Stoop, befriended him, and allowed him out to sit beside him at his tobacco and liquor-soaked desk. He brought him up to date with the local news. "Some beautiful slicking done last night," he'd say. "First one timber fell, then another, and the whole family tumbled out on their knees. And the little ones squalled Mammy, Mammy." Paine remonstrated, to no avail. Didn't Stoop know the Constitution was sacred? "Pook," said Stoop. "You a 'bolitionist? I once shaved a fellow's ear off with this yer razor. You? He went deef."

When his time was up, Paine went back to the mission. Inside the gates, handcuffed men were working on buffalo heads, fitting them with what seemed mechanical devices. Entities should not be multiplied unnecessarily, the traveler said to himself. What's the point? He stood and watched, feeling vulnerable. His father floated into his mind, holding a cutthroat razor with which he had once shaved his son's head. That's what happens to atheists, he'd said. Tyrant, the young Paine had screamed into his mind.

He sat on an oriental-looking sofa, looking out of the window. He was surprised to see two men on horseback ride in. The door opened and someone who introduced himself as Colonel Bishop bounced in. He was a little man. He introduced his friend, Dr. Farmer. "*Parlez-vous français, monsieur?*" Dr Farmer asked. "*Oui,*" Paine replied. "*Mais je suis américain.*" "You're a damned French abolitionist!" screamed Colonel Bishop. "Insurrections of negroes and Indians! Where's that Saint Helena that Kill Blast belonged to?" "I'm from New York." "Where's that?" asked Stoop. "England, ain't it? There's no use in it at all because there's two ways to spell everything." Paine excused himself and was about to withdraw when he realized he had nowhere to withdraw to. Instead he let them talk and planned to take a dose of salts in the morning, before returning north. He told himself to remember to pick up his small trunk of clothes. He had hidden some documents for Dr. Tennille among the garments. Stoop had kindly stored it for him, "in a safe place."

American Sounds

I think of American sounds...
    —Theodore Roethke

Now, in this silence, mountains will slowly return, and birds, perhaps. Weekend gone, they're gone, leaving their noise like a bruise, streams dammed, holes dug, planks over mud they made and up in the ancient appletree. Blackberry bushes taller than a man have been cut and crushed for bike and four-wheeler trails for him and her and two screaming kids, a boy, a girl, helmets on, visors down, and a yelping dog oblivious to their *Invisible Fence*, round and round and round, with wheelies, sun and shine, dawn to dusk. All day he's yelling things the others cannot hear over power drill and chainsaw, weedwacker, mower, miniature tractor, two cars and a truck so they never have to walk, and even an outboard motor for the canoe on their half-acre pond they skim around with life jackets on. But they're cramped on ten acres, so they've bought ten more each side where a bulldozer's driving a road up through stone walls built almost two centuries ago when settlers felled and stripped the hemlocks, scaring souls away. It winds up a quarter mile into a hayfield where they're building a bigger house, the latest to rise. Soon trucks will arrive to dump traprock that sounds like mountains falling. Then phone and electric companies will dig trenches, lay wires, erect poles. Oh for the quiet of late fall, when it's mostly hunters blasting away, or winter when it's only snowmobiles shattering the silence, and probably that donkey who's been roaring all year at the end of the valley like a soul in hell, or Bottom waking up.

*

Brian Swann

In the spring melt, the rails fell into the creek and stayed there, so I guess you could say that was the end of the line, though now there's a Railway Museum nearby, meaning a dude ranch "under indigo mountains." All the seasons are brutal here in this country where a dozen families gave everywhere their own names or where they were from, this Hollow, this or that Corner. Here they'd stripped bark from hemlock to tan hides, then stripped the mountains. Beauty came much later, just before the railroad, after everything that could be carted off was. And beauty paid. Tonight there's a ghostly feathering in the air, a lantern lit and flickering, to go with the hum just below everything, a low groan that's always here, day and night, summer and winter. In California it could be tectonic, a prelude, here it's anybody's guess, though no one seems to notice, not even after the new hotel burned down "in suspicious circumstances," though the city owner had painted Buddha eyes on the revamped silo he incorporated into his spa, and although on the golf course he carved out of the mountainside in anticipation of an Indian casino he'd put a massive Buddhist statue like the one the Taliban blew up, and though, to keep the locals happy, across the road from the First Old School Baptist Church (1856) "available for weddings and funerals" and the shack with a large flag that housed the Veterans of Foreign Wars, he erected a giant trout standing on its tail that, unfortunately, from across the street and in a certain light or haze looked like a statue of the Virgin Mary.

*

You might say everything's here for a reason because it needs to be here though how it arrived isn't always clear. Sometimes you don't know what you want until you find it. Other times unless you know what to look for you won't even see it. Or you can see it but not know what it is. Chrysophyte, for instance, the ice-flower, one only, way in the corner where the land rises to caves and foothills. You'd need a book to tell you it exists, but it's there, where even flies don't go, relic of the tundra. And then it's the other stuff nobody wants, roof tiles and engine blocks, ovens and old cans, a wonky trike: mixen, pelf. But there's a catalpa too, roots deeper than the dross, a tulip tree and sycamine whose berries shine even at night when, as everywhere, the Pleiades swing naked and frore like trapeze artists. If you stand on that toilet bowl you might be able to touch them. Certainly, a Gaugin could come here and choose his *vahine*, have his way and leave her isolate as Tlingit, talking to herself. Sure, there's a price to pay for all this. The odor, for one, pyretic and sickening, that could, I'm sure from time to time melt the polar icecaps. But the moon is unaffected, and the dog, part-coyote, and in habits at least part pi-dog, his head on my knee, takes it all in as patchouli. This was a quarry once. A city was built from its bluestone. You can still see rusted machinery. Sometimes kids play on it now the gates are down and warning signs peppered with buckshot. Paper drifts about over everything we once wanted and now don't, like that ladder. It's new. How did it get here? What's its story? How high'll it go? This place is prone to stars, though they look like broken glass. Sometimes something explodes. So watch out. Fires run underground. There's something for everyone. You can't make this stuff up. But it's tired. I'm tired too. From time to time trucks rumble in with dirt. That's how they deal with all this. It isn't here. Never was. Flattened, filled. Gone, trove and trope. Later, they'll stick up a few signs saying something could be hazardous.

*

"Clear off my land!" I yell. They look around, then stomp off over the rise where they wang a bluejay to pieces. Everything is theirs. They have inherited the earth, even the insides of my cabin which they once strewed under pines and tossed into the old quarry among tiles, broken glass, tires, and old bedsteads. This land's been cleared more than once. Clear-cuts and blasting powder took of mountain tops, wedges along bluestone lifts turned pre-Devonian seas to right angles. But at night sometimes there's fur along the cabin's sides, great galaxies howling overhead, stars diving over earth like birds, and in the mornings I can feel my skin close round boulders smooth as apples, watch shadows and images across snow-fields, companions, analogies.

*

I meet him on my walk. I'd never seen him before, so I stop to chat of this and that comfortably. I get expansive and remark on the marvels of nature. He says little while I tell him I've been reading how everything is just a rearrangement of molecules and genes. "It seems we're all the same," I say. "Makes sense," he says finally. "That's how you can put fish genes into tomatoes, pigs' genes into whatever and god knows what into cows to increase the milk, and why not, if, as you say, we're all the same which, incidentally, I do not believe, I mean, it's ridiculous, just look at monkeys and then look at us. Still, if we can do something then I believe we should, like going to the moon, if we really did, it's crazy, but all done for a purpose." "Yes," I continue, taking a deep breath, "chains of molecules stretching all round, taking different forms." He turns, grunts a goodbye, but "By the way," I say, "do you know anything about that guy who has a cabin somewhere over that stone wall in the woods? He hammers all morning and blasts away all afternoon. I hear he used to be a Jersey cop who came up after 9/11. He must be getting ready for terrorists. Boom-boom-boom, exactly two minutes apart, as if they'd come at him in two-minute intervals!" "You think it's funny?" he says. "You think you're safe? Good fences make good neighbors." He walks off, over the wall, into the woods.

*

Behind the rusted run of three-strand wire strung on bent steel poles he dips water from the trough and tosses it in arcs over his head. He shakes some off. Down by the gulch someone is singing a simple song over and over. Across stripped and trampled banks where willow, rose and snowberry once grew a light staggers. Nothing moves in this cow-burned land. He leans against a broken binder, hoping he'll still be here when something happens. But now there's just crickets in dry patches of bunchgrass, or just one cricket: impulse, fade. He listens to the cricket he can't see. Wet, he heads back in, reminded of his mothers' old white dog shaking off water from a pond that July 4 when the band played and fireworks fizzled in the unexpected storm that made the front of the ranch house fly up like a tent flap, and above it all one cricket calling, a dry run of syllables between flashes saying something that made him sad, its pyrrhic trills speaking the stony land and a couple of flinty stars that stretched to mountains from which thunder rolled with the weight of old machines, while the radio crackled out a long sad song until drowned out, then wandered back again.

*

Spray hangs in the air, and waves the size of men roll in on top of one another. There is a steeple, a fire-station and a lifeboat shed. Houses crouch down, back to the sea. Out of nowhere, birds flock in and settle on roofs, on dwarfed trees. It sounds like the crackling of a huge fire. Some of the men get guns, some whistles, others stones. They yell and bark and fire until the heavy cloth rises, fraying at the edges, bits falling off. It wheels above the tolling bell and as the birds cross the empty airstrip they block the falling sun. They could now be anything. Nobody knows what they are. The important thing is they're gone. As the men high-five, a dog sniffs a pile of bloody feathers. Someone toes it aside, wipes his shoes on the grass.

*

History passes on until it's safe to tell the story of the hole in that starry Ghost Dance dress, that slashed and blood-stained shirt. History says, Look, we have come through, and the wings of the museum stretch to enfold the frisson of color, order, organization and information, such sadness, such triumph. There is a cost of admission but what is the price for your pudenda cut out, stretched and stitched into a fringed saddle decoration, your balls and ball-bag cut off and made into a tobacco pouch, your children shot, for nits make lice?

Pioneers, O Pioneers

I still don't know why you want me to go, I said. We just thought you might like to, Mike said. But I'm afraid of heights, I said. I get a funny feeling between my legs. In the prostate.

Don't worry about that, said June. I do too. But why me? I said. If it's PR you want, Allen Ginsberg's your man. He couldn't make it, Mike said. Ah well, I said, in that case I suppose I could go. But I still don't know how to repair things. Leave that to us, they said. It's only two days at the station anyway. We'll be back before you can say Yuri Gagarin. But I still wasn't sure I liked the idea, especially since I'd just had breakfast and had heard about the bathroom facilities up there. Well, OK, I said. But first I have to check with the wife. OK, they said. But be quick. We leave soon. Just like I thought, she didn't go for it. How about I wave to you? I said. Well, OK, she said. But make sure you do. So I know you're all right. And write. I was still debating with myself when the limo arrived. Soon I was walking around the rocket's cabin wondering what I'd write about. Actually, it seemed pretty obvious; wonder, for one, and, well, more wonder, I guess. Why didn't you ask Robert Frost? He's dead, said Mike, our pilot. Oh well, then how about James Dickey? Ditto, said June, our navigator. Besides, I don't like him.

Mucho macho. We want wide appeal. I hated his "Falling," said Mike. Hated it, said June, adjusting his seat belt. Do I have to wear this seat belt? I asked. I feel constricted. Up to you, said Mike. Just don't look down if you've got that prostate problem. I know exactly how it feels, said June. Hang on.

The Governor

I believe in God, though, of course, he knows nothing about it. I also suffer from thoughts picked up here and there like viruses, though, of course, he knows nothing about that either. But he may. It is not wise to overstate a case. Your health and emotional balance depend on it, as they do on not over-eating or over-exercising. Nothing in excess, as the Greeks used to say. I was thinking these thoughts yesterday when I suddenly realized I could believe anything. Anyone can. You name it, someone somewhere believes it. This gives me hope for humanity which is, as someone famous said, everywhere creative. If we'd all just believe this, in the words of the song, "what a wonderful world this would be." Believing is easy. It's not believing that's hard. It's such an effort. You need proof. Much better, if you have doubts, about God, for instance, is to hedge your bets and do what the emperor Hadrian did and build your own Pantheon. Open the sky and let all the gods in. Well, that's what I was thinking yesterday: believe anything you want. Today I decided to put the thoughts into practice. Luckily, I didn't have to wait long. As I walked in the Village, two bearded gentleman stopped me. "Are you Jewish?" one asked. Now, I'm not a racist, but I'm six six, blond, blue-eyed, with a small nose. "Yes," I replied, and not only because I have found this to be the most polite word to use when responding to most queries. As he made a move toward me, hand full of pamphlets, I saw his bus behind him with large letters on its side announcing the Messiah's arrival. Almost simultaneously I was startled by a blast of music like a demented hora. I decided I wasn't ready for the Rapture. "At least," I said, "I may be. We all may be. I have to go," and I took off, but, unfortunately, only to encounter round the corner on Bleeker a group of Hare Krishnas. Side-stepping them, I ran smack into a group of men and women whose leader asked me if I'd accepted Jesus into my life. "Are you Jews for Jesus?" I replied politely, which seemed to offend him. "Do I look like a Jew?" he said. Because of his attitude I did not provide an answer, which would, of course, have been "yes." But then I relented. "Did you know," I said, "that 'Christ' is a Greek word? So is 'Jesus'." "So what?" said a sidekick. "Do you want your sins forgiven or not?" I didn't like his looks. "Let me get back to you on that," I said. "In a bit of a rush right now." And it was true. I had arranged to visit a friend in Jersey and had rented a car to pick up at a certain time.

Once out of the tunnel and in Verona, I parked the car outside my friend's modest house and beeped the horn. Nothing. I beeped again, expecting him to come out, but he didn't. So I tapped the horn again but the only person to put in an appearance was an irate neighbor who yelled at me. I would have liked to explain that in New Mexico, where I'm from, it was considered impolite in the pueblos to knock on someone's door. You just waited outside until someone noticed you were there and came out. Or not, as the case might be. Of course, you don't beep your horn, but this was New Jersey, not New Mexico. Anyway, as I sat, there was a tap on my window. I rolled it down and recognized him immediately. I'd seen him on TV putting everybody in their place, comforting those who needed it, telling everybody what was what; nobody messed with him. He was almost godlike, someone I could believe in, twice the size of anybody else. Fittingly, he went by the same name twice, anointed twice with the same brush, so to speak, perhaps for emphasis, so nobody could forget. It reminded me of Jimmy James, the old comedian my father never forgot who, as he talked, blew cigarette smoke out of both sides of his mouth almost simultaneously. (He had a sidekick named Eli who kept jumping off piers into the mud left by the receded tide.) "How are you?" he said, and it seemed to me he really wanted to know. Fine, I said, and told him my name. I congratulated him on his lap band and laparoscopic surgery. "I hear you, Peter," he said. "It's been a blessing. You have a good day, now." I said I would and watched him as he walked away. I was surprised to notice that he was the same weight and appearance as before the surgery. From behind he looked like a pair of huge legs protruding from a large bottom. He didn't appear to have much above the waist, as if what he had was an afterthought. But he seemed to be a very nice man, an impression confirmed when, an hour or so later, realizing my friend wasn't at home or, if he was, he wasn't coming out, I decided to drive back to the city. But I got lost almost at once, so I pulled over, cut the engine, and had just taken out my map when someone stepped off the sidewalk, waving to me. It was the Governor again. I rolled the window down. "Why the map?" he asked. "Are you lost?" "I am," I said. "Well, now you're found. I live just here. Come on in." He turned and pointed to a huge thatched house a bit like a picture of Ann Hathaway's cottage I'd seen on a calendar. "Well, thank you," I said, getting out. "That's a lovely house you have there, but they're very hard to maintain." "Tell me about it," he said. "And there is always a fire risk," I continued, "from all that dry straw, not to mention the birds, rats and mice that nest in it." "True," he said, walking up the garden path, "but I'm not worried. I have a large family. All's well. Come on in. Dinner is already under way." He ushered me into a room the size of a baronial hall. What looked like a Thanksgiving dinner was in full swing with lots of people round a massive, groaning board. He noticed my surprise. "There's room for everyone at my table," he said. "And I like to get an early start on things." He waved me to one end where a boy, mouth full of stuffing, stood up. I apologized to him but he ignored me. "Are you the Good One or the Bad One?" I said, not knowing what else to say. "The Bad One." He glared at me and walked up the palatial staircase. I sat in his place and looked around, catching the Governor waving at me. I waved back. He waved again and I realized he wanted to talk to me, so I got up and walked to the head of the table. "Sorry to ask this right now," he said, "but could you lend me a buck twenty?" "S-sure," I stammered, a bit taken aback, and dug into my pants pocket. "Here," I said, handing over a dollar bill and two dimes. "No," he said, smiling. "I mean one hundred and twenty. And it's not for me. It's for Paul over there. I owe him. I'll get it back to you very soon." "But I don't have …" "No mind," he said. "I'll catch you later. He can wait. Enjoy your meal." But there was nothing I could eat. No vegetables at all as far as I could see. The turkeys all seemed undone and oozed blood when sliced. I commented on this to a neighbor, who told me that the Governor preferred them that way. I would have liked to have asked the Governor if this was true. I also would have liked to ask him how it felt to be such a large man in such a small state, the most densely populated in the union, so many towns crowded together, the one with the misleading moniker of "Garden State," not to mention a very low bond rating. It can't be easy for him, I thought, but when I looked in his direction, he seemed perfectly happy. Catching my eye, he smiled and waved a turkey leg. I thought he looked a bit like Charles Laughton as Henry VIII, Defender of the Faith, Governor of New Jersey, the Garden State.

Brian Swann

BEING THERE

We heard the President today on TV say—well, what did he say? I forget. But he has such a nice voice, manly. And we thanked him kindly. My husband said he seems to wear a mask, smiling all the time, but I find it fetching, although it's true it does make it look as if he's gone away from time to time. But he's a nice man, so they say. Nice, like us. Not like them. He gives us what we want, or think we want, or what we ought to want. Great things are astir, he said. We thank him for this, and for warming that lonely office, sacrificing his own peace of mind for us. It must be exhausting. He must need a rest—Hey, Mr. President, come stay with us a bit, play with our children, go to our church, swim in our pool! Barbecue! With you in our house we won't grow old, or not as fast.I can't believe it! He's come! Just a break, he says, from affairs of state. How's the golf hereabouts? Kind of you folks to ask me. He sends his bodyguards home, then bends to pat our dog and kiss young Jess. Nice dog, he says. He drives our truck and station wagon. He knows a lot about football but less about soccer. He helps me put the groceries in the car. He even helps me undress and wash my undies with Joy. Oh, joy! To have the President ("call me Joe") at breakfast praising my pancakes, helping me serve—"I serve at the peoples' pleasure," he says. Each day he says, "You can have it all. Eat up. More?" Each day he slaps my husband on the back as he ushers him out the door to work. "You can be great," he says. "Don't look back. Onward! The future is always bright." Even my husband likes him, and he likes nobody. Last Friday night I even found them practicing cheers together. Such short skirts! What nice legs the President has. Just fancy, he's blue blood but thinks nothing of talking shop and asking our opinion. They say he's related to the Queen of England. I feel quite singled out. We all do.

Dogs on the Roof

It's all we can talk about at the mall. Should I have curtsied? It's as if we've split him up—a clone?—and each has taken him back home, like some sci-fi movie I saw. It's all a bit like the movies, really. He plays the Prez and we play us. It would look good as a TV series. Since I know him so well now, I could play his part—anyone can be President, right? Isn't that what we're told, or is it you have nothing to fear but fear itself? Anyhow, I'd be him. But I'm not sure I'd spend so much time with folk like us. There's a country to be run, and anyway, Hollywood, that's where it's at. And to be President you need mucho moolah. If you get enough you can be President for life, like what's his name in, you know—or was he the one who was shot?

Optimisme

This morning I spent ten minutes looking for my gloves until I realized I was wearing them, on my head, under my beanie. Then, walking through the park on my way to Chelsea's Spalding Fine Art, I kicked a gray tree root that turned out to be a frozen dead squirrel. I found a tear sliding down my cheek. It must have been the cold. In my effort to get any leverage at all on things, for some time I have been dropping into galleries where confusion is given some sort of shape, however unsatisfactory. For instance, last week I happened upon a hybrid painting and slideshow where eleven flat-screen monitors lay on their sides, sound on, being used as canvases with dribbled brush strokes while a cable TV show was playing over them. In the background a body-artist was maiming himself on the way to becoming a self-consuming art object, all the way down to his shadow. Despite myself, I found this spectacle rather encouraging, though on the way home I kept hearing behind me in sync with my footsteps a scuffling noise like cloth rubbing against the sidewalk. Thinking it was the back of my cuffs, I hoisted my trousers up without breaking stride. But when the sound continued I paused, gave a sharp tug, and continued on my way. Still the rhythmic rasping persisted, even got louder, so, coming to a full stop, I yanked my trousers up so vigorously I almost castrated myself, just as an old lady shuffled by in floppy house slippers.

    Given my emotional situation, I should have been in analysis years ago. And in fact I was, once. But it didn't fly. It didn't even get off the ground. What secrets I had I didn't want to give up or even acknowledge so, in effect, I had none. But, confidentially, my biggest secret is that I am afraid of being alone, not afraid of solitude, but of loneliness, a kind of living death since without a witness you do not exist. Being your own witness does not count, and you know it. But it's not really your own death you fear, for what can you know of that? It's the death of a loved one. That's where you experience the nothing of your own death. And that is where you mourn for yourself.

My favorite novelist, Thomas Hardy, once wrote that if mankind was given the choice of a God who existed solely to torment him and a God that did not exist at all, he'd choose the former. I wrote that down in my journal when I was eighteen and ever since have struggled with its implications. For a while, I took refuge in the idea that God had to exist because he was a mathematician and numbers were a constant in everything, seeming to compose every star and constellation, every leaf and earthworm. But then I found out that a great deal of mathematics has been developed for itself without reference to physical reality, motivated by problems within the narrative of mathematics itself, and that upset me. Was God this kind of mathematician, a gamer? Fact is, there is no refuge.

But why be morbid? As the years have slogged by, my sharp edges may have blunted, or fallen off, or just got bent out of shape. Bumps and cuts have deepened and scabbed over, screams turned dull de facto routine, while blows and bangs have turned blue, bruised and numb. At best, losses grew new skin over an emptiness, like balloons, slowly deflating. In short, I adapted and the adaptation became me. Yes, I also grew a crust; I became crusty, kind of kin to a Crusty, one of those filthy creatures who frequent the streets and squats of my East Village, complete with pit bulls as a kind of protective skin with teeth. But I'm not a Crusty. I keep myself clean to the point of obsession in order to hold things together and not give in, get some sort of leverage, slip through the air and create some sort of space and shape to move around in, my own shadow.

Someone once said "I sell the shadow to support the substance," but I prefer to do the opposite. The shadow is what animates. The past is all shadow, as someone wrote, adding that the richness of life lies in memories we have forgotten. We live in time, but time itself is not what it seems. It forks from countless pasts into countless futures, and all the time it is layered so you can fall though and keep falling. Nothing is what it seems, I think, as I think about typing this up on my ancient Olivetti, snowbound. Then, looking up, I recall how Descartes, snowbound too, with nothing to do, decided to think the opposite of what he had thought before, not even trusting the senses but he did believe that certain things were beyond doubt. As an example, he gave the madman who was wrong to think that his head was a gourd or made of clay and that his body was made of glass. But, as I looked out over the snow, I saw nothing crazy in this. Such perceptions seemed a reasonable response to the self. Maybe Descartes was the crazy one, trying to fill absence with reason. For me, absences struggle to leave themselves and if they succeed absences return as presences return. When they return, however, they have nothing to say, so they say it, and leave. I've always known my body was made of glass and my head a lump of clay, but I also know I am a set of precise chaotic processes, a fractal infinite in my indents, getting smaller and smaller but never quite disappearing. But who knows? I can't count on always feeling the same. Right now, for instance, I feel like part of a favorite Sandro Penna poem ("*I colloqui*"):

> "*Non vivo. Solo, gelido, in disparte*
> *Sorrido e guardo vivere me stesso.*"

("I don't live. Alone, cold, apart,/I smile and watch myself living.")

I get up and look at the mirror to see if I'm still there. A Jabès aphorism comes to mind: "The face reflected in the mirror does not wipe out the previous one." Slowly, I see faces and a red balloon like the one in the movie. I hear the clatter of keys in my head, the old-fashioned kind that embody their force, make words with heft so everything rings. I pick up my battered brown cardboard suitcase and set out from my sublet. But when I arrive at her apartment in the Marais I realize I don't have the case. I must have put it down somewhere. So I retrace my steps, but when I cannot find it I feel a sense of relief. The case had been my father's and was practically empty. And I am starting a new life. So back at her place I walk up the three flights and knock on her door. Again and again. No response. So, tired, I risk the descent via the rickety old elevator cage that shakes and groans like a human catastrophe as it drops. No matter which button you press it chooses itself when to stop. So, closing my eyes, I pull open the cage door, close it behind me, press a button. The contraption shudders and shivers, begins its slow descent, finally shuddering to a stop at what I assume is the ground floor. It isn't. The thing has gone half way into the basement and quit. No matter what I push, it will not budge, so I decide to haul myself up to the ground floor. I force the door open, only to find myself face to face with a pair of ladies' black woven leather shoes. "I like your shoes," I say, though of course she can not hear me. Suddenly, without warning, the monster shoots upward and stops at the ground floor. I step out and stand beside her. "I like your shoes," I say, warily, as if on a first date. "You're late," she replies. "Where are your things?" I shrug. "I like your smell," I say. "What?" she says. "Smell. Not your scent. I like the way you smell." "I'm an atheist," she says. "I know," I say. "Me too," she says. "Let's see how all this works out. You smell good too." I know I'm late. I'm always late. But we did work out, for almost forty years, though I wouldn't be late for her funeral, as she had predicted. She also predicted I would be late for my own. We'll see.

Now I watch myself trying to live without her, my life cardboard. I can't even say I'm made of glass. I can't see out, you can't see in and there's a don't-touch sign stuck to me. My genomes fly out the window, party balloons. So I follow the sound of typewriter keys back to where time forked, as it does perpetually, into countless futures in most of which we do not exist, though in some she exists but not me, and in others I exist but not her, and in others where we both exist. Now neither of us exists anywhere though as I bang this out I fall through layers and scramble to my feet in Iraklion, August 15, 1974, 6:25 p.m., where I first happened to run into her, literally, at the sign-in desk of the Knossos Hotel. Actually, she stepped backward and fell over my case. I helped her to her feet and managed to persuade her to have dinner with me. So we are sitting at a table in a taverna, me with my execrable French, Amélie with her adequate English. She takes a pen from her bag and, on the basis of a few hours' acquaintance, writes my horoscope on a FIX Hellas paper napkin: "*équilibre, harmonie, sociable, ésprit abstrait. Fantasie. Humour. Indépendance. Non-conformisme. Optimisme.*" This piece of optimistic stained paper is what I have in my hand now, holding it lightly by the tips of my fingers, which I always took for the beginning of her hair. I wear my hands on my head and my heart on my sleeve. I hang on by my fingertips. I keep going.

Floaters

As I was walking home yesterday, I saw a squirrel run down a tree and tear at a plastic bag on the ground. After a while, he began pat-patting it the same as when they bury a nut and tamp the earth down over it. Then he shot back up the tree. I walked over and saw that the bag contained dog poop. As I stood there, my mind idling in neutral, something rose like an old carp from a muddy pond, a quote from Doughty's *Arabia Deserta*, to the effect that the foreheads of the ancient Semites touched heaven but their feet were stuck in excrement. Or something like that. My mind is always slipping gears, always idling, but it does work. It works in order to try to find others, though mostly it ends up chasing its own tail. It aims to get to the bottom of things but if it does there is only a trapdoor. So it attempts to join things. Since things fly off easily, it seeks to tie them in, join them by their edges. The result is a fabric of edges. Who knows what's in between? Who knows what's inside. Perhaps nothing. Perhaps poop. Which reminds me of Dean Swift's "excremental vision," Swift who wanted to conduct an experiment "to write upon nothing," something I do all the whole time, but I'm still here, though when I walk I'm never quite sure of the direction, something like those "primitive" cultures where the past is in front, the future behind. Moreover, time flows in different directions in a number of ways, like motives. For instance, I was walking down the street recently when I saw a man in an old gray suit carrying a pail of yogurt, very like the yogurt-sellers when I was a kid in Kanlica, on the Bosphorus. I ran after him, calling out that I needed yogurt, though I didn't. He broke into a trot. When I caught up with him, I'd like to buy your yogurt, I said. It's already spoken for, he wheezed, out of breath. But then he said, OK, I can spare this much, and he drew a none-too-clean index finger across the creamy crust. All the way to the bottom? I asked. He looked puzzled. How, I explained, how can you translate your horizontal line into a vertical volume? OK, he huffed, in that case and on second thoughts I need it all. I can't spare any. It's all or nothing. All right, I said, I'll take it all, though I don't know what I'll do with it. He looked offended again. In that case, he said, you can't have any, and continued on his way. I was thinking about all this as I sat at my desk this morning thinking how George Eliot and other nineteenth-century novelists would have dealt with such a situation in their detailed and firm way of impressing themselves upon the world, phrasing and shaping it in language sound and entire. Their worlds were solid as anything, I thought, still watching the man and his yogurt in my mind's eye, solid, yes, even at a time when their world was losing God, certainties and shapes. The phone rang. It was my accountant, Steve, asking me if I wanted him as usual to file tax returns for my mother-in-law, who had just died penniless, assisted living and nursing homes having eaten up all her savings, what she called her "legacy." I covered the receiver and repeated his question to my wife. "Idiot," she muttered. "Of course not. What's the point in dying?" I conveyed the decision to Steve, hung up and returned to my desk, where I sat looking out the window where my floating reflection looked back. Yes, I decided again, I was indeed an idler, living in shadows, even if the shadows were those I cast. Shadows, I thought; who was it said, "I sell the shadow to support the substance?" I don't know, but I do know that I sell nothing. My last book sold two hundred copies. All at once, out of nowhere, I felt my heart racing, playing havoc with its stents, beating as fast as a shrew's heart, which, if you could hear it, would sound like a finger running through a comb. (Since a shrew's metabolism is so high, if it can't eat crossing a road, it dies). I took off my reading glasses and ran to the kitchen, grabbed a hunk of cheddar, returned and noticed a piece of yellowish paper at the back of my desk among bills under a bag of mixed nuts. I pulled it out carefully and found, in my handwriting, a quote from Jacques Maritain in whose study at 26 Linden Lane I used to live, among his books, papers and letters left behind after his death. I still remember many letters for help and advice, soulful, even desperate appeals from all sorts of people. One letter in particular stands out, from Henry Rago—but I digress. I unfolded the brittle sheet carefully and began to read about the soul searching for "a compensating victory, an illusionary eternity in the region of surfaces unfailingly arranged." I crumpled it up. What did "unfailingly arranged" mean if it all fails? What's the point? And as for eternity, it's just another form of the future which, as we saw above, is in the past. I didn't get the great Thomist then and I don't get him now. I don't get philosophy and I don't get theology. They miss so much, like economics. I sat back. My heart had slowed, but now floaters were crossing my eyes and I had heartburn. I tried to follow them in their meandering journeys, their wanderings. I tried to hold them in some shape, put them in a bag, but couldn't. They drifted all over the place, unpredictably. Perhaps, I thought, an algorithm could make sense of them, do for them what our ancestors did for the night skies. I took off my glasses again, closed my eyes and enjoyed the spectacle.

WHOLENESS

As I waited to cross 14th Street at Avenue C, I rolled around in my mouth the word "diplodocus," a word I'd loved since childhood. I looked about at the elevated FDR, the giant Con Ed power plant that exploded in Hurricane Sandy, the apartment buildings that were swamped in the same storm that pushed my parked car up 20th Street to 1st Avenue. All this, I mused, was once protective marshland, lovely fields of reeds and swaths of meadow grass, home for duck and deer, bear and cormorant, not yet covered by garbage and sunk under landfill. I could have wandered happily here, I thought, looking inland where, among tall trees, were fields where the three sisters thrived, corn, squash, beans, fields belonging to Shepmoes, the village at 14th and 2nd where the spring still flows, but now into the sewage system. I was woken from this nostalgic reverie: first, by the sudden realization that I was having a nostalgic reverie; second, by the fact that "nostalgia" involves pain (*algos*, pain), then, more violently, by the pain itself when one of the two wooden planks carried over his shoulders by a burly red-haired Con Ed worker hit me in the back. Oblivious, he walked on, looking, I thought, like Odysseus setting off across the mountains of Epirus with an oar over his shoulder, just before he stepped into the street against the light and narrowly avoided being hit by one of his own trucks. "What a comedian," I muttered under my breath. "What's the rush?" I was about to continue my monologue when I realized that crossing against the light was something I too did all the time even knowing it was a stupid thing to do, especially since I'd been hit more than once. It was as if one me knew it was wrong, while another me said what the fuck. How many of me were there? How many mes were there? Which one kept getting hit and not learning from the experience? All things resemble each other, said a poet, and he should know. Maybe I should try to find my own resemblances and use them as replacements or metaphors for the me which is increasingly pissing me off, me doing, me reacting, me screwing up, opposite mes, contradictory mes, mes feeding off a guilty conscience for all the stupid things other mes do, even mes who try to find new nourishment from gaps and fissures instead of stepping over them, mes who give up, mes who don't. In this welter, I certainly live with a lot of second guessing and guilt. But didn't Jacques Ellul say a bad conscience was inseparable from freedom? So does guilt make you free? But how do you achieve that freedom from the me that caused the problem in the first place, especially since we are continually manufacturing more tension and conflict in order to push ourselves forward into more potential, more experience, greed being the human motor? Sometimes I think I would like to make amends to myself by creating reprisals against myself and that way continue to haunt myself like a cop to keep myself in line, or some of my selves in line, just one would be a start in pulling myself together. "Pull yourself together!" my father kept telling me. If only I could manage this I might be able to change the way I live, change the environment I live in, since everything, including pain, takes place in the mind, even things that aren't there, like missing limbs, or even missing beings. When I look in the mirror at different times of the day I am shocked to see different faces, some from years back, and many that really scare me from the future. I've even caught people I don't even know peeking out through my eyes. But for the most part the face is a mask that cannot stop the skin from drooping, the cheeks from sagging. I must be somewhere in there, maybe in the gap between each face, the bits slipping off to the side. The same kind of thing happens when I leave the mirror, sit down, calm down, idly rest my eyes on my hands, but they are not my hands, or if they are they're more like the shadow of what's there. I don't want to see the rest of my body, wherever and whoever's it is, and pretend it's not there until a crisis (such as being hit by a truck) forces me to think otherwise. If I could, I'd say it's someone else's body, that mine lies in another dimension, somewhere in the minds behind the faces in the mirror.

*

At home that evening, I was considering downing a cold beer and watching TV, something I seldom do, when my hand happened to reach up to the bookshelf and came down with *The Encyclopedia of Ignorance.* Hoping I might at least learn something helpful from ignorance, I leafed through the brittle pages and discovered an essay somebody had marked up and underlined phrases from a distinguished Princeton physicist whose essay seemed to be about the idea that quantum theory promotes observer to participant. I browsed, and discovered that the topic interested me. I forgot all about beer and TV and dug in. The essay, I think, suggested that one can be actively involved in one's own being, not just get hit by things, so to speak. I was rather shocked by this idea, as I should have been, since I went on to read that Niels Bohr once said that "if you are not shocked by quantum theory you don't understand it." The professor said that quantum theory joins the particular with the system in what he calls "wholeness," a "non-separability quite different from classical physics." I didn't have a clue about classical physics, but I took his word for it, especially when he went on to say that there is no universe "out there" that can be observed safely from behind a plate-glass window, as it were. So we have to ask what it is we want to know and what we think we're looking at and to that degree change the universe. Wow, I thought. Wholeness, yes. My new "I" would give the world the power to come into being through the very act of giving meaning to that world and in so doing give meaning to myself as part of that world. What a wonderful idea! Now I didn't need to deal with identity at all. I existed. I was everywhere in all my sinewy nakedness. I leapt to my feet and summoned my wife, told her we were going to change everything, starting with my wardrobe, all of which she'd bought for me and which she was continually trying to get me to refresh and update. After all, it was Thanksgiving, the day before Black Friday when shops try to get an extra step up on the competition. So, despite the fact that I hated shopping, off we trotted. Sadly, however, most shops were closed, but not Forever 21 on Union Square, where I saw a t-shirt with NO PAST NO FUTURE across the front and wanted to buy it but my wife said it was poor quality. "They trot out all the rubbish," she said. "They try to convince the consumer they're getting a bargain." "The consumer consumed," I observed wittily. So we walked over to 5th Avenue. Again, most stores were closed but not The Gap. It was wide open and we fell into it. The place was almost empty except for signs announcing SALE and various percentages off each item until it seemed they were giving the stuff away. There were cartloads arranged to trap and catch you, come at you enticingly, seduce you into buying what you didn't want, in all directions, make you over, piles of clothes I could see little difference between. I was getting hot, things leaping out at me, "Buy me! Buy me!" I wanted to take off my puffy coat and leave it somewhere but it might get stolen or bought, so much choice, so little choice, I started to lose control, felt nausea rising, started to panic and ran out for air, pursued by a security guard but I outran him, didn't recognize where I was and ended up in another store across the street, losing my wife in the flight. Luckily, she ran after the guard and caught a glimpse of my panic-stricken face peering out from behind the glass door across the street. After she calmed me down, we went home, where I tried to regain my grasp on things by sitting down and thinking how a glass of cold beer would do the trick, until I remembered I didn't drink. So I reached up into the bookshelf and came down with a book I didn't even know was there. I leafed through it and saw it was something to do with anthropology, flipped through until I came to a chapter on the language of a people called the Fish-People. I was struck by the description of how the language fixed physical space and objects ("home," "hill," and so on) only in terms of human presence, with values dependent on human presence, on the person experiencing, a phenomenon the Princeton physics prof has termed "non-separability." For instance, something is described (in one word) as extending toward or away from the speaker, not, for instance, "on the road," but "on-the-road-toward-(or away-from)-here." Space, I read, is active for the speakers of this language; a thing is the perception of a movement's direction, extension, orientation, so the thing and its surrounding space are given its structure and expressed in one fused, pliable word. For example, in English, "field" is a specific area in a specific place, a "noun." But with the Fish-People the notion of "field" is conveyed by a verb root, "-*btlvuf*-," telling how an open area lies and extends. "Field," I read, is a "dynamic phenomenon", not a static object. It could be translated as "where-it-fields-away," or "where-it-fields-toward-here." I sat back, imagining, from where I stood near the East

River this morning, how, four hundred years ago, I would have told someone where the fields with corn, squash and beans were situated if I didn't know the language that used to be spoken round here which was, interestingly enough, I discovered in a footnote, in the same language family as the tongue spoken by the Fish-People. I took a yellow pad and copied out some of the ideas, including the following:

FMPNBTLVUFL: "where-a-field-stretches-out."
(Pron. *Fump-noobtl-vufl*)
XFDLVXBTLVULF: "where-it-fields-toward-here."
(Pron. *Chufdl-vchbtl-vulf*).

Eureka! I thought quietly, so as not to disturb my wife who was probably taking a bath. That's it! Now, where should I start, revise my language or the universe, which, in essence so I had learned, are the same? I could lose myself, my self, in this; my odyssey would be over as I rested safely in the arms of an idea, no more wandering about, lost in fields that aren't even there, not really. Of course, there were a few problems. The speakers of this language are unaware of its stupendous implications, but no more than most speakers of any language are aware of the language they use. They just speak it and go about their business. I doubted the structure of their language influences how they act or how they are in this world. I was pretty sure they don't know how dynamic their world is. Luckily for them, I did. I had the advantage of now being conscious of what for them was/is just habit. As I explicate it for them they can in a way, of course, live in it through me. All I have to do is figure out how to turn this information into practice, make my world less thing and more me, me everywhere, in everything, nothing alien to me, even a humble field, a field of being. With discipline and dedication

I believe I can do this. The world, the universe, will cooperate since that is its natural innate nature, its inherent structure, its "wholeness". In my excitement, I called out again to my wife, but she didn't seem to be around.

WILD JUSTICE

The material world is uncontrollable, so it controls us. It gets inside, the way noise invades, gets to our mind and stirs anxiety, a tightening in the chest. I don't need an explosion to prove this. Something like the thump of heavy feet overhead will do, like the Devil in clogs. It makes me nervous as a herring out of water, creates angst, can drive you mad. Why the constant movement? I think. Nothing moves constantly, except the sea, and that's scary the way it stirs up the depths, bringing to the surface what should stay below, pushing down what should stay on the top, roiling, repeating. So how is one to become indifferent to this? Refusal would not be true to the experience since refusal is just a kind of rage internalized—how angry was Bartleby? It's a jumping up and down inside oneself where no one can see until it crests like a wave and falls over, dense, intense, full of trapped air, falling it knows not where.

I could elaborate on this, could, in fact turn what actually happened into a story, disguising it and thus affording me a back door out, the way a child tells a fantastic tale only to end it with "and then I woke up." No, this time it will be "a true history of fact," as the author of *Robinson Crusoe* announces at the very outset before going on to cobble together for his hero a life with what could be salvaged from the wreck of the ship he arrived in, stuck on rocks just offshore. Actually, it did all happen exactly as I am about to set out. I'm not making this up out of nothing which would be impossible anyway since nothing comes of nothing which, of course, is not true since everything comes from nothing, or what will become nothing via entropy, as the latest theory of the universe announces. The universe, they say, as I understand it, (and I read a lot), came from nothing, and the nothing that came before that became the nothing we know and can measure. It was smaller than the smallest thing you can imagine and yet it contained everything, so all history as it goes on is just variation using a few components and combining them in an almost infinite number of ways, perhaps out of a sense of boredom for as one gets older boredom becomes a form of entertainment, and perhaps because all the big things have already been made and there is no alternative but miniaturization which means eventually you end up with is what we call nothing or it gets so small it has to expand, and off we go again into the nothing we call eternity. So boredom spills out in all directions, babbling along. It goes wherever it likes because it has no preference, which is why it is bored in the first places. Did the Big Bang have a preference? No, it only preferred to be itself which it could only express in an explosion. It was so bored, the density was denser than anything you can imagine. Its lack of preference was so intense it shot about white-hot in all directions except, of course, there were no directions which is why it created them as it went along and that is why today direction is so attractive, for to have direction is a great thing, an aim, a purpose, a passion. But things still eventually got so boring for the universe that it all slowed down again and that is about where we are today with the cosmos at the tipping point, about to reverse direction the way, on a smaller scale, the earth's poles have done more than once, and return whence it came, the cosmos, or would if it weren't so bored, unless it decides stasis is the best option given the state of things and stops dead in its tracks. That's it. I may decide to follow suit since everything in our lives depends on precedent, which is itself a kind of comfort, a kind of direction.

But before I ground to a halt, I decided to do something about something that has been making me distinctly uncomfortable for so long. I would make one last effort to counter the nausea. So, emptying my pockets of all the lucky pennies I'd picked up over the last month or so—they only work for one day anyway— I went up to the floor above via the emergency stairs. For years I had put up with that woman, her banging feet and all the rest which I will detail later. When she didn't answer my knocking and bell-ringing and door-kicking, well, read on. It would be largely pointless to detail all the circumstances and events that had led to this moment of existential crisis, though I will mention someone using a phone rendered redundant by a foreign voice so loud through an open window it could have reached the moon. Someone, this same lady, or someone else, I'm not sure, had also taken to washing clothes all day and night in a bathtub as if she were pounding them beside the Ganges or Brahmaputra. The sloshing was accompanied by much yelling and singing. More than once her tub overflowed, collapsing my bathroom ceiling, swamping my apartment. But did I lose it, did I complain? Apart from a mild note slipped under her door, I did not. I swallowed my anger and put it all down to the price of city living, living on top of one another, anonymously. Did I complain at the constant banging and crashing of feet at all hours, up and down, up and down for years and years? Did I get angry and protest at all the yelling, screaming and arguing in different voices, the dropping of heavy objects, rolling them about like bowling balls, Rip Van Winkle's, scraping of furniture, intense vacuuming that could have sucked said furniture up into itself, screams and yells like "Murders in the Rue Morgue," the deep, long peeing like a man? I did not, except for more letters slipped under the door, carefully composed letters written on my old company letterhead, letters that were never acknowledged, though I gave my home phone number, and which had no effect. Sure, sometimes things would quieten down for a day or two, but then they'd start up again with even more force, tuning me up, as if the time had been used to gather strength, put me in my place, test my manhood. I did call management now and again but by the time security arrived and knocked at the door the inhabitants had hunkered down and lapsed into silence. All I got from the security detail were hard looks and the announcement that next time I should not wait, but call as soon as the problem started. It was pointless to tell them I had done just that but they had taken their sweet time responding. Eventually I got a notice from their office advising me to stop wasting their time.

This whole matter is embarrassing on a number of levels. Sometimes, things got so confusing I even found myself following the footsteps around like a dog, nose in the air, wondering what they were doing and where they were going. Sometimes, when they were absent, I almost missed them and strained to hear them. At other times, as an intellectual exercise, I would try to distinguish intent from accident, actual from imaginary, but with no luck. I have even found myself wondering if what I heard was like a ghost-image, an after-image, a residue of something that was once there. But that made me feel lonely, so I quit. Worse was trying to anticipate when and where a noise would start up, or where, when and where it would end. It made me very on edge, like continually waiting for the other shoe to drop, which sometimes it did not, confusing me even more. Or I'd be lying in bed and hear her phone ringing and think it was mine, which sometimes it was. As for the sounds skittering and clattering up and down the hallway, there are times when I can't tell if they're in the hallway or in my head, especially when they turn into my bedroom, closer and closer, or go in the opposite direction, farther and farther.

Occasionally I thought I wasn't even sure there was anyone in the apartment, though there was a name on the door, "D R PATEL." Were those initials or profession, male or female? I had never seen this woman (if it was a woman). I might even have had a case like "Psycho" on my hands, and everyone I'd heard could in fact have been her. Anyhow, as I said above, I took the emergency stairs, closing the heavy door quietly behind me. For some reason, Heraclitus' "the way up and the way down are the same" came into my head as I put my ear to the door of 9B. Nothing. I rang the bell, waited. Nothing. She could have been asleep, but that was a risk I was prepared to take. The miserable cur next door was barking. I'd take care of it later. Taking a step back, I gave the door a startling kick with my right foot. It barely moved. So I took a run at it and hit it with both booted feet. It shuddered, but didn't open. The third time did the trick. The door flew open. I stood and listened. Even the dog had shut up. I looked about. The layout was identical to my own apartment. I moved carefully, poking into cupboards and closets, pulling out drawers. There were no carpets and no slippers, which meant that the occupant was in violation of the contract of occupancy. There were few clothes, and I couldn't really tell if they were male or female, which is not unusual these days. All right. I stomped up and down in my L.L. Bean boots, slammed doors, toppled over everything I could lay my hands on, opened the window, picked up the phone and yelled into it, yammered in tongues, scraped furniture along the floor, banged the walls. Finally, I ran into the bathroom and turned on the faucets, hot and cold. I stood back, watching with satisfaction as the tub overflowed and ran onto the floor which would soon buckle and cave in. That should do it, that's how I'd get my own back, the whole floor collapsing, a Niagara ensuing. That would give her a taste of her own medicine and balance things out. That would let her know the kind of man she was dealing with.

Discourse on Method

The storm had closed the office. Snowbound all day, I'd been indulging my hobby of philosophy by re-reading the masters, Descartes mostly. Finally, tired, I put him down, and, after gazing out the window a while, decided, like him to rightly conduct my reason, and "earnestly and freely" apply myself once more "to the general overthrow of all my former beliefs." After a while, however, I realized they had all been overthrown many years ago and I didn't have the energy to find and overthrow their replacements, even if I could since, we all agree, it is hard to know the truth. I am made aware of this every time I look at the Franz Hals portrait of Descartes that hangs in my study since I learned that the original in the Louvre was not by Hals and we don't know who the artist was, or even if the man in the painting is Descartes, or if it looks anything like him. Be that as it may, I thought I still might still be able to continue my notes for something I called "The Teleology of Teleology," even if we don't know what can we truly know and believe, and if things are tending anywhere at all. Events at best reveal their full meaning only with time's perspective, but more often time renders them useless to a mind grown exhausted in the pursuit. Ideally, time should cover events so they shine clearer, the way water splashed on a mosaic's tesserae reveals vivid colors that had faded, patterns that had paled. Unfortunately, however, everything usually everything ends up cracked and covered with a thick layer of dust. And we can't expect our senses to help us tell what is and what isn't for, as Descartes stated, we can't rely on obtaining "absolute confidence" from the senses especially when there's no way to distinguish the state of waking from "a vivid dream of ordinary life," (in fact he almost persuaded himself that he was dreaming while he sat there writing). So what can we rely on, what control? I started to lever myself up from my captain's chair, but plopped down again. I'd been sitting so long my legs just gave way. How long had I been sitting, what time was it?—not that it mattered. I recall someone once saying that time forks perpetually into countless futures in most of which we do not exist. The same could be said of the present, which goes up in smoke each moment of each moment, a phenomenon scientists call "singularity," the first known example of which was the Big Bang itself, which created time and sent it and us hurtling toward an End present in everything. So, as I just said, what does it matter, since even "the richness of life lies in the memories we have forgotten"(Pavese wrote that just before topping himself over some young American actress). What a luxury to forget memories and at the same time remember we have forgotten them! Ah, the pleasure of paradox, the creation of a field of force which, while reconciling opposites, keeps them apart! We exist in paradox, all our life. I remember one of my ex-wives' small daughters, mid-tantrum, screaming "if I can think of it, it isn't what I want." How true. We truly want what we cannot even conceive of. We don't exactly cancel out, but we do sort of disappear in the process which, as I understand it, is what the Persian proverb could mean when it says: "I am there from where no news even of myself ever reaches me." Lost, we are complete.

 I pulled myself together after these deep thoughts and levered myself up once again. I looked over the desk to the windowsill where, in a fit of unusual fit of optimism, I had planted three packets of basil seeds I found in our laundry room a year ago: Siam Queen, Purple Petra and Italian Genovese. I leaned closer and saw that seedlings were pushing up through soil littered with the tiny silver segmented egg-casings of tiny flies that were flitting about just over the soil. The plants seemed none the worse. Perhaps they and the flies were symbiotic. Opposites are often symbiotic, just look at— Enough! I said out loud, startling the ancient cat and knocking Descartes to the floor. You have to draw a line somewhere, a line that is not manufactured the way we manufacture a retrospective plot for our life ("every plot is an exercise in optimism," said Pavese). As I stood, I sensed the onset of an ocular migraine, shining geometric figures slowly starting to drift across my sight, so I stared fixedly out the window, hoping they'd come to a stop, and disappear. But they didn't. Instead I saw my late mother, whose faience bowls I had just polished and left on the living-room table before walking back to the kitchen where she was sitting on a high three-legged stool. She looked tired, though she was much younger than I am now. In fact, she even looked like someone I'd like to date. "It's hard just to raise my right arm," she said." It's an accomplishment just to know it's still there." With her other arm she pointed to the thick leaves of a tall rubber plant and I noticed that she had dusted as far as she could reach. There was a clear line dividing dusted and dusty, clearer than the line between known and unknown, living and dead. Did she expect me to finish the job?

*

Next day, life slowly began again after the streets had been plowed. My life as an actuary could restart, though for some time I had felt I had been losing control, that I could count on very little, that nothing made much sense. I had first become aware of this sensation toward the end of my most recent marriage, during which time my wife was becoming increasingly tenuous, constantly accusing me of being "emotionally distant," when in fact I was simply thinking how I could go on. One August day stood out when she'd said she didn't want to go to the garden party in the Berkshires which we had agreed to attend. Then she changed her mind, and said she did want to go. And then she changed again and said she didn't. Tired of her games, I drove to Chatham by myself, though in truth I didn't want to go either. When I got there the party was as tedious as I imagined, so I took a glass of wine and wandered off through the English-style garden, past a man-made pond and through trees where a path opened out onto a charming clearing, complete with swimming pool, pool-house and patio. There was a chaise with someone asleep in it. So as not to disturb, I crept up quietly and discovered the person was a woman in a bathing-suit, deeply tanned, lying on a blue-striped towel, eyes closed, absolutely still. As I got closer, I thought her face looked like my wife's and I wondered whom she had driven up with behind my back. I whispered her name. Not a muscle stirred. Then I found myself close enough to touch her, so, reaching out to her left leg—ahh! I pulled my hand away fast. Burned! I touched her right leg—aah, hot! I touched again and pressed down. Metal. And then I saw on the inside of her left arm a tab: SCULPTURE PLACEMENT INC. WASHINGTON, DC.

*

Whatever, as the kids say today. As I noted earlier, for some time I've been feeling my life seeping out the edges, eluding me, so recently I decided to do something about it, starting small by creating a game of intrinsic teleology for my walk to work—I already had some largely ineffectual rules for home, and I worked with rules all day in my office, but the passage between was unpredictable, something of a no-man's-land. So this game constituted my peripatetic game theory of strategic decision-making, a method by which I hope to ensure that my gains were more than my losses. And on the whole that's how it turned out, even if it meant I had to fudge the mixed-strategy equilibrium to produce what I called my "theory and practice of expected utility." It went like this: Each morning on my way to work I allowed myself to collect ten women, with only one swap-out allowed, so I had to choose wisely and carefully. If I didn't reach ten I lost them all, so the impulse was toward generosity. Today, with roads cleared of snow, there were more people about, hence more opportunity. Things, however, had not gone too well. I was being particularly picky and had only collected seven by the time I got down 1st Avenue and turned onto 7th Street, and I was conflicted about one woman who seemed to be walking with her daughter. If I did not take them I would only have five. I'd picked them both up a few days ago before the storm and wasn't sure if I was allowed to use them twice, a latitude I had allowed myself when playing a previous game which had consisted of cars. If at any time I saw two BMWs, for example, I took them both because, not being much of a car man, I couldn't really tell if they were the same year or model. I decided to add both women again because time was getting on, and who could question my decision? But that still left me short near journey's end as I trudged down 7th Street, snow piled up to my left, burying cars and garbage bags. I was getting downhearted. Three still to go and nothing in sight. Suddenly I was aware of a shadow other than my own cast by the morning sun behind me. I could tell by the quick tapping of the footfalls that it belonged to a woman. I got my hopes up and was rewarded with a woman whose thick brown hair fell from a ski hat over a faux (I hoped) fur collar. Two to go. I could hardly believe it when the same thing happened almost at once. This time the woman had thick black hair but not as long, and no fur collar or hat. Just half a block to go. I looked about, expectant, but my luck seemed to have run out, and I started to walk much slower, hoping against hope. I needed one more, but even at my slow pace I soon found myself with one foot inside the revolving door. I was contemplating the desperate move of going round the block when I glimpsed a woman about to cross 4th Avenue. Just at that moment, however, someone pushed the door from the other side catching me up so I staggered into the building. The doorman looked at my quizzically as I stood there, not sure what to do. Did she count, and make up my ten, or not? After much soul-searching I decided rules were rules. She would not count, which left me one short of my quota, and rather disheartened. As I stood by the elevator I looked up at the clock. Nine on the dot. I looked down at my watch. Two minutes past. That was when I decided that, at the start of all this, although part of one of my legs had entered the building, the vast bulk of my body had remained outside so I was strictly speaking, en route. Moreover, there had been no volition in my entry. I was swept up, I was a victim of someone pushing the revolving door so it had set in motion an action which was the opposite of my will. Therefore, I ruled, the lady on 4th should count. Things had worked out, as planned.

Smoke up the Skirt

The fool up a ways scares me from my nightmares. It goes on all night, explosions lighting up the sky. Drunken whoops and whistles. Next morning, bleary-eyed, I wander into the garage. In a corner I notice some spots of blood and five pink blobs that on closer inspection turn out to be five newborn pups. I must have forgotten to put the door down last night. I call her, but she's cleaning her teeth. I call again, but she must be cleaning her teeth again. A hundred strokes up, a hundred down. I call again but she must be washing her face. And cleaning her teeth again. Putting up her hair. She kills me. "Come *now!*" Eventually she comes down. "You're so impatient. Give me a break," I think she says. "Where would you like it?" I say, not for the first time. Just then, the coyote mother returns and pushes by. "Not a coyote. Coydog," I say to no one in particular. Just then there's a knock on the front door, so I go back up and open it. The local policeman, putting on an English accent. Too much TV. "Do you by any chance know anyone in this vicinity by the name of Mr. Rimbo?" he asks. I know he's trying to trick me. "Rimbo? Rimbord? How do you spell it?" "R-i-m-b-a-u-d." "Oh, you mean Rimbaud." "If you say so, sir. Do you know where he is?" "Six feet under, I imagine. He's a famous French poet. Deceased." "What makes you think I'm not aware of that, sir?" Then it hit me. Rambo. That's why they called him 'Rambo' in the movie. The poet as hero. The poet as avenger. "That's why I killed her," I blurt out. "Killed whom, sir?" He doesn't trip me up that easily. But there's no point in making a run for it. "I'll need you to come to the station with me," he says, in a tone that reminds me of my father who used to say things like "Stop blowing smoke up your skirt," or "blow it out your ear," at a time when I had no prospects and needed encouragement, wanting to make a name for myself as a writer, and for a while even holding down a position as signpainter until I forgot to write backward on a glass window so it could be read from the outside. Anyhow, looking back, all this Rambo business was a bit strange because the only writer I'd ever liked even a bit was Rimbaud, and that was probably because he died so young. I could have identified with him, maybe even internalized him. I wonder, is that how you blow smoke up your skirt?

WALT WHITMAN ON THE ROOF

As you age, you realize something is always coming down the pike at you, and they come, one after the other, excruciating as kidney stones, sneaky as cancer. Not long ago, as I started to cross Lafayette I was hit by a double-parked delivery van that suddenly shot backward, breaking my right arm and affecting my speech, despite always being on the watch for the unexpected, in particular for things going backward. Hummingbirds are no problem, since that's what they do in the natural course of events, but pigeons, I watch out for those, and for unpredictable squirrels. Sometimes, inexplicable, I see a cloud go in reverse. I know such things are possible because I myself flew backward, so now, crossing a street, I don't watch for what's coming at me, but what isn't. In particular, I keep an eye out for anything parked. Even a tree can get my attention. And I stay away from circuses. Elephants, as someone said, are confusing. They look just about the same coming and going, especially from a distance.

All this is a bit disturbing since I myself tend to do things if not backward, then in reverse. For instance, I was approaching old age when I bought my first house, a time when I should have been concentrating on my eternal, not my temporal, resting place. I remember the house well even though when I went to move in all my furniture was missing and the house was empty. I returned to school, but by the time I got to the classroom all the students had gone, leaving a beer bottle on the floor like the Lost Colony. When I looked out the window I could see them sneaking off into the woods just as a hawk swooped down from behind, silent, onto the back of a raccoon but came off second best, dragging a broken right wing. I felt sorry for it, the way I'd have felt sorry for the raccoon if the owl had sunk its talons into it. It's a little discombobulating, especially since I am thin-skinned and emotionally vulnerable; certainly not, as my wife claimed at the divorce proceedings, "emotionally flat."

My hat that renders the wearer invisible also does its best to warn me to watch out for things coming at me, from any direction. Today it warned me of a middle-aged woman whizzing along the sidewalk toward me on a high-tech scooter. How old did she think she was? Ten? Pretty soon I was dodging a fleet of them, not one under fifty and not a kid in sight. I almost got run over, barely making it to the gym in one piece, where the janitor in a baseball cap was sitting behind his desk outside the Men's changing room. He had left the corridor in front of the swimming pool with ponds of standing water, relying on a small sign that said Floor Slippery When Wet and a large one that rhymed: *CUIDADO: PISO MOJADO*. I tried informing him about the danger but he ignored me, concentrating on blowing hard into a recorder and making all sorts of squeaks and whistles. I tried again, but it was like talking to a brick wall. I changed, worked out, and he was still blowing away when I left limping from my fall in the changing room.

That evening, my hat warned me not to go to the party Hamish was having on his roof, but I ignored it since I had a question I wanted to ask him ever since we'd worked together as hospital orderlies ("porters") in London a few years back but never had the courage in case I was misunderstood. The story was this: He'd taken the dirty laundry down to the burly Scottish washerwomen and they'd raped him. This didn't stop him doing his job, however. He kept delivering and they kept raping. But was this true? I can't remember who told me this. I doubt it was Hamish himself, though he may have had reasons for putting it about, and it certainly wasn't the women, at least I don't think it was. It even crossed my mind that it could have welled out of my own Freudian mire. But I was reluctant to ask Hamish in case I phrased my question wrong or was misunderstood and got an answer which had no relation to my query, whether by accident or design, and which did not even interest me though, of course, it could have revealed something about the person who gave me the answer and even something about the person who was asking it. Also, there was the danger, often experienced, that when I wanted to know something I would get sidetracked in my thoughts, or expressing my thoughts, and I have been known to ask a question which had no relation to what I really wanted to know, perhaps in order not to appear impolite or over-inquisitive. However, in the case under review, my chance to ask Hamish came when, despite misgivings based on previous gatherings on the roof, I decided to go to his rooftop party. I tried to ignore the fact that I was afraid of heights and the sky makes me feel vulnerable and unprotected. Look up, and there's nothing to hang into and there are things that could come crashing down. In fact, the whole thing could collapse. In any case, once I got there I couldn't find Hamish so I occupied myself knocking back cheap white wine and watching the pigeons, most of whom were flying more or less in a forward direction, until a woman came over, the same one I'd seen on the elevator that morning and who had almost knocked me over on her scooter. She was nibbling at a limp shrimp in one hand and sipping from a cup in the other. She at once assumed familiarity, informing me that, like Garbo, she was allergic to shellfish. "But that's—," I said. She continued to inform me that she never took a bath because she didn't want to retain water. I wondered if she could fly if I threw her off the roof, but managed to slip away when I spotted Hamish explaining what a sporran was to a group of young women. I went over, but after saying hello I forgot what it was I wanted to ask him. It was beyond the obvious, I knew that. It was coming back, and I'd started to phrase it in my head, when the woman pushed in. "Did you know," she said, "that she went to bed at nine each night, hugged trees and covered her paintings with cheesecloth when she was away?" Questions, questions, always questions, never answers."Did you know she allowed no photos on the wall and no flowers anywhere?" She was still asking questions when I found myself sitting on the top stair staring at the peeling wall, a brick wall once whitewashed but now peeling and crumbling. And as I sat, a story came to mind about how Bodhidharma attained enlightenment by staring at a blank wall. I felt more like banging my head against this one, but decided to give it a shot. I sat and stared. But the more I stared the more the wall seemed to come at me, come off itself, even, full of things, unconnected occurrences and effects, flashing images going in all directions. It took all my strength to tear myself away. It would have been very easy to have been overwhelmed and have the wall fall on top of me.

While thinking these thoughts, I was watching the pigeons and wondering if the shape of their wings could have provided the idea for angel wings. In the Middle East they'd started out as rock doves. Then I sense I was being watched and, turning, was aware of a lion staring at me through the mist. Next to it was another lion. Ham claimed to be have been a safari guide in Africa so maybe, I thought, these were his stuffed trophies. I went over and stroked a head, but received a splinter for my pains. Maybe they were one of his carpentry projects. Ham saw my confusion and wandered over. "Aye, laddie," he said, "I used to hunt but now I call myself an animal lover. I won't even run over a rabbit or a hare though I'll still shoot one," and he left.

I sat on the tar beach and slowly became aware there was a woman trying to sit on my knee. She had green hair speckled with red spikes of blazing stars poking through, and the odd bluet. Giving up, she rose, lifting the hem of her dress just as a pigeon dove off the railing and into the maelstrom beneath. I got to my feet, spilling my wine, and looked over. Birds like Mother Carey's chicks drifted over dark waves of people in swells and crests. I was tempted to float down when I heard Ham telling his favorite old jokes to the lady with green hair. "People who eat vegetables are vegetarians, so people who eat people are humanitarians," he announced before beginning his slurred version of "Loch Lomond." It was just at that point when I saw Walt Whitman on the roof, walking in a field of erotic potential, and decided things were not at all as they seemed.

Period Piece

Here across from the unused New York Central elevated tracks, in the basement of a house built for those fleeing lower Manhattan's yellow fever, below ground level, where a now-blocked tunnel once went from my flimsy door under nubbly Belgian cobbles to the river, through rubble-fill dumped on top of reeds and mudflats, with the Old Homestead restaurant just up a ways not far from the flattened Zantberg, and the meat market named for Melville's Gansevoort grandfather, where Herman worked as an outdoors customs inspector for nineteen years hunting his whale, here, a stone's throw from Sapokanikan where tobacco grew, and the path started that brought from across Mahicanituk waters hides and pelts, and from across the island, from Montauk, Sewanakie, across her body whose flesh was corn, and breath, tobacco, her love turned smoke, from long before Adam whose flesh was a pound of loam, a pound of fire his blood, tears a pound of salt, sweat a pound of rain, eyes a pound of steel, thoughts an unstable pound of cloud and a pound of cold wind his breath, sewn in belts and straps, worked white columellae of the whelk and quahog purple, here outside Brecht Jr.'s house on the corner of Bethune where I didn't dream the dead horse I fell over one night late but which wasn't there next morning, nor the naked drugged-out tranny hookers, "Sweet Chocolate" and the rest, as they checked out their make-up in the side-mirrors of trucks squeaking on their springs before climbing in the back while the pushcart seller did a brisk trade in KY jelly, coffee and tissues, here where on the barricaded piers signs were up again after someone else had fallen through and another body found near the Mine Shaft, the Anvil, the Hellfire Club, the Hell Hole and I didn't imagine one morning waking to thick black smoke of tar and creosote filling my basement as another pier was going up and maybe the house, hell smoke roiling in coils and twists so even my cat coughed, nor the banging at the door already weak with break-ins and a woman there I'd just met in Westbeth across the road. Hold me, she said, later telling me both her parents had died in fires, before informing me she hated men, and was "androgent," so when she left I didn't call and soon the poison letters arrived with threats informing me I'd been had and used the way men use women, and maybe it was the times but women were more confusing then than usual, coming in all sorts of combinations, like Judy, ex-*Playboy* centerfold and exotic dancer who said she had two vaginas and made out with her twin sister so it was hard to tell, she said, where one body ended and another began. "A mirror made me pregnant. Everything I own I stole." At a bar a woman told her, "Your mother wants you to return to your roots." She cried a lot and wouldn't let me touch her, but kept returning, asking to be hurt, here below ground where I'd hidden a former student who'd blown up ROTC buildings at Old Nassau even though he'd failed my Public Speaking course because he said actions speak louder than words, here, where small barred windows were covered with gold velvet curtains bought in a Pennsylvania warehouse where they said the curtains came from a New Orleans whorehouse, so I matched them with red plush sofa and chairs, an aspidistra in a brass pot, an antimacassar tossed over a coffin-size book box that had crossed the Atlantic four times with me, a Victorian oak table, expanding everything with mirrors along the brick walls, laid down imitation Turkish carpets, and imitation logs from Gristede's for the non-working wood fire, beside which would sit, e.g., an idealistic woman Weatherman who would later do time for blowing up the Merrill townhouse on 12th and whose book I read when she got out but all I remember is that the male revolutionaries like to fuck the female revolutionaries in the ass, and where would stand the six six poet from California, father of six, who at first I didn't recognize when he dropped by and asked to stay while he expressed his new gay necklaced, chain-draped, bell-bottomed self and who for a week regaled me with tales from the bathhouses— but why go on. Here, one day, all was gone, starting when my anesthesiologist friend from the Sansone Gym learned he had something I didn't know existed, "gay flu," and threw himself off his roof, and some piers burnt down to the waterline or turned to family-friendly parks, and the Mine Shaft became a Chinese restaurant, and the meat market with its carcass-luggers for Adolf Kusy Co. Fine Pork and Provisions and others was made over by Stella McCartney, Theory and Pastis, Richard Meier, and Diane von Furstenberg.

 And me? What me? For some time I've been saying like Rip Van Winkle, "I'm not myself. I'm somebody else."

Out of It

My car went into the ditch after turning over and over before it settled and burst into flames. I watched from space through the smoke, beautiful, the infinite purposelessness of beauty, time stopped, consumed as flaring flowers, clamor of butterfly wings, before righting itself while windows cracked and tires exploded, and August whipped stones so they too caught fire, and I flew off, over it all, my husk discarded, a cicada's, and I climbed like smoke, away, out of sight, out of it, with no leftovers, regrets, bygones, no tuning fork to fit it all together again, obstructions not even diversions for this wind filling the incomplete, raising the useless and shaking it off, staking everything on itself, no hedging, resolving the uprooted, the unseen, shaking itself from shadows, driving the discarded back into itself, beyond whys and wherefores, beyond various, beyond what can be seen where it slides into its own slipstream, distance no object, heading on out, climbing like smoke away, out of sight, out of it.

Brian Swann

WAITING FOR THE TOW TRUCK

They said the motor was broken. That was as technical as they got. The talk was all "capitalist accumulation." Eike upbraided the wipers. Andreas was hugging a knee, quoting Lukács, Adorno and others in the Frankfurt School, all the while thinking how to get a hand up Janine's skirt. A fly sighed in the rare silence. *Machinery has greatly increased the number of well-to-do-idlers—* Marx washed up from the boatwreck just offshore while on either side of us islands faded to gardenia petals, the rain stopped and a rock in the water snagged a wave.

"The revolution in permanence!" called Bogdan from his hip flask, just back from a hunting lodge in Bosnia. He wiggled the stick in its loose socket. Janine gave him a look. There we sat like a snapshot of saints while under the hood who knew. I wiped a steamed window as a light brimmed over the road. We hoped it was the tow-truck we had forgotten to call.

Morning

I wash to vanish, to varnish, shine air, cleanse the air, expand the weather, let go what I don't want, to signal, to prepare, to expect, to agree to tell my body to be again, to pose, to pause, to be attentive, gather sweetness for those who look and who might also want to touch, to share, to touch, touch, to achieve the clean strength of horses, to be clear as libation, to sip another sharper self, to grace this self, to face the world full for it belongs to you, you do not belong to it, to wash mortality the way a watchman goes out into the dark with his light so for that while, he shines.

Bio Note No. 2

Poem and Prose Poem: Ancient and Wild

(I) Poetry:
**

At Cambridge in the early '60s, my poetry curriculum began in the eighth and ended, for the most part, in the early nineteenth century. But when I was about seventeen, in high school I'd happened upon William Empson's *Seven Types of Ambiguity*, along with the poetry of Thomas Hardy and Robert Graves. Empson, soon to be joined by I. A. Richards, quickly became a favorite with his revelation of the resonant possibilities of the poem itself. As for Hardy, I absorbed everything I could find, poetry and fiction, while Graves' poetry and prose transported me into a mythic wonderland, especially when supplemented by *The Golden Bough* (in college, for six pence I picked up James Frazer's own inscribed copy of Lady Charlotte Guest's *The Mabinogion*, and still treasure it). Even today I can remember the excitement I felt reading my extra-curricular discoveries. People have described this sensation in different ways. Matthew Arnold, for example, described it as a "vibration," a shiver up the spine. I don't claim to feel quite the same youthful sensation today, no matter how much enjoyment I experience. However, thinking about this essay and searching about for ways to describe that early excitement, I recalled an incident from some years ago when I was staying on Ossabaw Island off the coast of Georgia. A friend had trained his high-powered binoculars on a large Spanish moss-bedizened live oak and waved me over. Pointing, he handed me his glasses. "There!" he whispered, and, after some excited searching—there indeed! I had never seen anything like it. My sight was flooded and filled with colors there's no point in trying to portray. The richness, the vision took me over. A well-named nonpareil or painted bunting!

A tiny bird that now seemed as big as my brain. I did not want to hand the glasses back. The bird solved my dilemma by flying off. If I didn't want to sound overly dramatic, even clichéd, I'd say that for an instant it took my breath with it. I was transported.

**

True poetry exists in the engendering dark, giving and receiving light. The language of poetry resonates like whale-song. The words shimmer with their long journeys, their history. They echo their past at their core and around the edges where they flicker with suggestiveness, elusive linkages, which is why translation is only successful when equivalent echoes are created. Words live from their roots. Cut off, they are just implements. It is good for poets to know some etymology, some linguistics, the history of the language, and of the words they work with whose roots are deep in our ancient being, perhaps pre-alphabetical and even pre-linguistic, from a time using "a mode of thought based on diffuse multidimensional configurations," (André Leroi-Gourhan), a way of consciousness using "things to think with" (Claude Lévi-Strauss). Words in poetry are living tissue. A word is, radically, breath, something spoken. It is muscular.

**

If true poetry lives in the dark, it also lives in space, in reverberative vacancy, so visual and auditory intelligence is called for. The page's wholeness is air, its life emptiness. Here words can rise from the linear plane and inhabit whiteness, floating but not free, for there is no such thing as free verse any more than there is free movement; movement is constrained and shaped by structure. A poem's "plot" is its inevitable trajectory. The precise knit, the coruscation of imagery, the flow and break of rhythm, the expectation and frustration, the music, the pulse and breath, these make up the poem's connective tissue, its body, what it looks, feels and sounds like, its "meaning," its "idea", for "meaning" (from OE *maenan*, to tell, recite, speak) is simply the relating, the breathing-speaking, and "idea" is the same root as Latin *video/videre*, the look of a thing. There is nothing to "prove". An idea in a poem is something "thoroughly incarnate," in George Eliot's phrase, its wisdom to be known and understood by looking deeply, the way of the "seer." "I see" and "I understand" are synonymous, but "understand" is a mysterious word, (contrast another synonym, "comprehend.") This deceptively simple word evokes almost a mythic memory, something like the central sacrificial Mithraic rite where an initiate *stood under* the grille and was drenched, bathed in the blood of the bull, transformed. The best way to understand the "meaning" of a poem is to stand under it, soak it in, be trans- and re-formed. Perhaps with this word we can see an example of what Ernst Cassirer in *Language and Myth* termed "the bond between linguistic and mytho-religious experience," expressed in the fact that verbal structures appear as "mythical entities" where the word becomes "a sort of primary force."

**

A word in a poem is an event (compare Hebrew *dabar*, which means both "word" and "event"). The "life-world" of a poem is never remote, felt "reflexively". The expression of a truth is sensed as itself always as event. The poem enacts its own being. It dances its own attitudes. There is no paraphrasable prose content. The language of poetry is not transparent. You can't see through it to a prose "meaning", though prose is a keen tracker, albeit with a limp. There is just more body, more poem, (we talk of "the body" of a poem); there is more "spirit," to use Kant's word, more beauty "born of the spirit and born again," where *spirit* is the invisible vitalizing force of breath, *spiritus*, mind-breath, continuous, animating and re-animated by another's sensibility. In a sense, following Beloit Mandelbrot and his fractals, one might even talk of the "self-similarity" of poems. Or one might say that "meaning" in poetry occurs when ambiguities focus and balance dynamically so they strain their bonds and almost seem to be about to break free, like Michelangelo's prisoners. Or one could also note the importance of the lyric's musical component which, as Eugenio Montale said, can make a poem's "meaning" slippery, hard earned, as one tries to reconcile the "literal meaning" and "the musical sense," since the two can present different degrees of incompatibility (or compatibility), between "rational import," which may be "evident," and the verbal music which can be "secret, concealed, almost beyond our grasp" (afterword to Lucio Piccolo's 1956 volume *Canti barocchi*). Poets have often stressed the importance of music and voice, the sound of a poem, and C. K. Williams even said that "meaning" arrives after the music has been established and, mysteriously, is contained in it ("On Whitman: The Music"). For me, it all has to do with *texture*, the weaving of the *text*, the integrated inter-tissue, something sensuous, a fabric you can hold and wear, taste, smell, and see (remember Denise Levertov's *O Taste and See*, 1964), a tangible intangibility that *is*, a kind of being that expresses itself in harmony.

**

It could be that the search for "meaning" is the reason so many intelligent people find poetry "difficult". Today, poetry may not be just the skillful re-expression of familiar or general truths or sentiments, "what oft was thought, but ne'er so well expressed." But it is still available to anyone ready to engage it on its own terms, prepared to be prodded and enticed out of familiarity with self and world, even with poetry itself. All that is required is a sense of and taste for emotional and intellectual adventure, an openness to risk, even in those scary cases where "the reader is placed in an unprecedented condition of estrangement from his reading habits" (Pasolini on Zanzotto). An ability to tolerate or even enjoy uncertainty and ambiguity is helpful, perhaps essential, since a poem is almost always about something else, as befits its close relationship with riddle, one of the roots of lyric, a connection which Susan Brind Morrow claims goes back at least four thousand years to the poetic riddles of the Egyptian "Pyramid Texts." Though Jan Huizinga in *Homo Ludens* doubts that contemporary civilization is capable of appreciating and nurturing poetry's "special language," he notes that this relationship with riddle "is never entirely lost," tracing it back to the Greeks who "required a poet's word to be dark," to the Icelandic *skalds* who considered "too much clarity" to be "a technical fault," and to the troubadours for whom "special merit was attributed to the *trobarclus*—the making of recondite poetry." Riddle, after all, as Aristotle pointed out, is metaphor, which means we can never really know what something is because we are defining it by what it isn't, knowing it by its connections, changing it, carrying it across, trans-lating, trans-porting it (Greek *metafora* signifies "carrying across"). So "meaning" is "process." Perhaps Emily Dickinson's riddling lines say it best: "And through a Riddle, at the last—/ Sagacity must go."

**

Poetry is much older than prose. Poetry does not create "isolated mental entities or abstractions" (Eric Havelock, *Preface to Plato*) to describe the world objectively and impersonally. It generates a physiology, a tangible thick world of imagistic continuity via sensual pleasure, making it difficult for us to separate ourselves from it, which was the reason Plato rejected it, insisting on abstract language to describe and explain experience, thus bringing us closer to pure "forms," invisible ideals which artists degrade and distort. In addition, following Havelock, Walter J. Ong has pointed out how in oral-aural cultures words are more "celebration," "events," "happenings" and less "tools," or "work." This is still true of that poetry today which keeps close contact with the core. And this core seems to exist in a deep part of the brain where "thinking" works apart from logic, not divorced but in a different register, where connections are made quickly, as perhaps they were at a time when quick and decisive action was a matter of life and death. It should not be forgotten, however, that "rational import" is an integral part of poetry's texture. It would be a mistake to say that there is no logic in poetry, no structure of reason, that it is all "emotion". For not only is there an intense logic of image, there is the particularization in the way components interact, projecting an "argument" that "adds up," that "makes sense." This includes the sorting and discriminating of hints and echoes, the evaluation of leads, calling for something like detective skills, the way of "riddle."

**

In oral cultures words are alive, part of a sentient world with human and other-than-human beings. They are "interactive," "participatory," as Dennis Tedlock and others have noted. Moreover, Native American oral narratives which used to be translated into prose as "stories" are now, following the lead of Tedlock and, in particular Dell Hymes, translated and presented as "poetry," into formats showing their complex rhythmic, dramatic and patterned structures. In this vein, it is interesting to note that narratives in oral cultures are often thought of as living entities. Among certain Algonquian-speaking people, for instance, the story is a person accustomed to walking all over the world whose story cannot be told until it stops and makes camp. It does what you do. It is what you are. There is no separation between what is told, who tells it, and you the listener. Curiously, this is something like the way I feel when I read a good poem: non-separation. I am drawn into it as into myself, as if it were part of me. I have the sensation that the poem is flesh, something palpable I can touch, grasp, and as I do so I become different (I experience a similar reaction in front of a beautiful painting, when I am somehow the movements, the shapes; they are inside me, a reciprocal physical fit).

**

Plato somewhere describes the mysterious way in which, during the course of an ordinary day, we are attracted and moved by something we cannot explain or understand. The kind of poetry that means a great deal to me begins in and is rooted in such an experience, the wonder of what Paul Falkowski calls our improbable, "almost magical" existence (*Life's Engines*), when, for example, something we might have seen a thousand times catches the attention and this time holds it. A tree, horses in a field, a sparrow on the sidewalk, or something we didn't know we had remembered bubbles up, or what the photographer Robert Frank characterized as "some moment I couldn't explain." Then the poem spins out reverberating images with the appearance and feel of permanence; it embodies a sensation, making a moment mysterious and valuable in our throw-away culture. Even when a poem is complete, however, it can never tell us everything it knows. It is always holding something back, the way of the dream. Poetry re-enchants the world, mixes "as if" and "it is", *as if* becoming *it is* and vice versa. It rephrases boundaries. It is "oceanic thinking" (Jean Gebser's phrase). It is "also" and "not only" whereas in "mental thinking" only "either-or" is valid. It is "as if" the world's vibratory field calls at unpredictable moments and in unexpected places. I remember Magritte who, after a visit to a working-class Brussels beer-hall, wrote that he found the door-moldings "endowed with a mysterious life," and he remained "a long time in contact with their reality." And when William Carlos Williams saw a red wheelbarrow "outside the window of an old negro's house on a backstreet" in Rutherford he wrote that the sight impressed him somehow "as about the most important and most integral that it had ever been my pleasure to gaze upon." (Recently, I was glad to read that awe, wonder and beauty promote lower, healthier levels of cytokines, whose elevated levels are tied to depression). A poem lives in the numinous and, as Paul Ricoeur noted, becomes "the representation of a presence." The ancient world, like some traditional tribal cultures still today, was filled with presence, continually remaking itself. Poetry tries to call things back from the positivistic brink, away from what Rilke termed "America," where "empty, indifferent things pour over us." The history of the west is the removal of mind or spirit from phenomena. A poem calls us back to the world's beautiful strangeness, the uniqueness of everything and the way things are related, linked in a place at once us and not us.

**

Philip Larkin once famously said, "Oh, for Christ's sake, one doesn't *study* poets! You read them, and think: 'That's marvelous, how is it done, could I do it?' And that's how you learn." Of course, that's true. But my experience of the marvelous in the form of a small bird led me to learn as much as I could about it, and that led me to an interest in ornithology. You can never know or learn too much, despite William Stafford's remark that you can be "too well prepared for poetry." I know what he means, but when you feel clogged up you can always go for a walk and keep an eye out for birds.

**

II) Prose poem:
**

Which brings me to prose poems, devious things. They want you to think they are four-sided, square, stable, when in fact they roll around picking up whatever sticks. Prose poems are poetry packed into a box in order to trick you into thinking they are prose. That way they can get away with all sorts of things, "all sorts of fantastic details," as Robert Bly noted. They are particularly adept at camouflage. They can be whatever they want, something like the quantum world that eludes scientists trying to agree on a single picture of what's really going on. They are shape-shifters, they are the Trickster of literature, encompassing opposites. The form is inherently ironic. As you walk on it, it pulls away from under your feet. As you look, it slowly disappears before your eyes. But does not vanish. Far from it. It has a lot of fun playing with ideas and concepts such as "poetry," "fiction," "nonfiction," and so on. It is not afraid to mix styles and genres, be excessive and way-out. For instance, what goes for normal in a prose poem might be called bravura in a novel. The prose poem can pretend to be linear but it has no need for what Nicholson Baker termed "the clanking boxcars of plot." However, something that looks like prose but has no plot might be a bit scary. Something that has no pegs for readers to hang their progress from so they won't get lost could be rather frightening. Which makes the prose-poem chuckle and smile, and toss out a few pieces of string for you to mark your passage. (When I write about the prose poem I feel that I am writing one, that I have been hoodwinked by the prose poem into writing a prose poem). The prose poem can seem continuous middle, whatever parts it may have interchangeable, simultaneous. It does not rely on a schema of beginning, middle, end. You can almost dive in anywhere. In a society devoted to winning and losing, the kind of prose-poem I love escapes the curse of success and failure by virtue of its insistent presence, its vital insouciance. Prose poems are both warm companions and a lovely shape for alienation: alienation as companion, (I think of prose poems as a kind of person). They are always turning corners, often on a whim, seldom arriving anywhere in ways to which we are accustomed, calling us over and keeping us off, a rich tease, witty, cheeky, unpredictable, crystalline but not transparent, a shimmering cabinet of wonders (the wonderful, "*le merveilleux*," is a core concept of surrealism), and the objects on view are words, each a cabinet in itself, reflecting off each other, slipping on, over, into each other with what Michael Benedikt calls "visionary thrusts."

**

I think that poetry retains an ancient way of "thinking" and "being", and that prose poetry is one of the few remaining wild places at a time when the world is being covered with people and concrete; where wilderness, which generates mythological thinking, has been cordoned off into national parks or made into playgrounds for ATVs, skiis, skidoos, recreational hunters and Bigfoot enthusiasts. I might think of poetry as a garden, dug, planted, tilled and tended yet full of out of the way places, surprising, coigns of vantage, kind of neolithic. I tend to think of the prose-poem as a place and time in which to live by one's wits, relaxed but on the qui vive, gathering good stuff, tracking quarry, aurochs or angels, unafraid of failure, a bit rough and ready perhaps, sometimes irresponsible even, but rangy, relaxed, full of all sorts of things, kind of paleolithic.

**

The prose poem is an ecumenical entity *in se*. It is not, as Donald Hall once wrote, "a fashion," a station on the journey to a "more varied and useful free verse." Verse is welcome to take what it wants, but that won't affect the prose poem. The prose poem may still not yet be fully appreciated, but it doesn't care—Oh, it's off again! It just thought of something else, something just struck it, something's caught its attention. "Perhaps I am a post-modern ethnologist," it thinks. "Mmm. 'Beyond truth and immune to the judgment of performance.' I may even be Anishinabe, it could happen," he mutters, quoting Judy Tenuta. "Yes, 'I could curse the monologue and praise the comic holotrope'. And what is my name? Nanabozho is it, Ma'ii or Iktomi or Laks? How about Pihneefich, Sinawavi, Wehixamukes or Kwakwadek? Who knows, and what's in a name anyway? Who the hell cares?" It laughs a huge laugh and takes off anonymously for the horizon at a fair clip.

"I Think I Would Rather Be/A Painter"

Over the years, I've published drawings in journals such as *Exquisite Corpse, Caliban, City Lights Review, Kayak, Boulevard,* and *Parnassus,* and have painted on and off for as long as I can remember, mostly in blue because I never knew how to handle color, and blue is my favorite. Then, some twenty years ago, my wife and I purchased a house on the side of a mountain in the western Catskills. Here, with more space than in a Manhattan apartment, I began to play around with all sorts of materials: colored inks and paper, acrylics and oils, chalks, pastels, pens and pencils, brushes, knives, various kitchen utensils, glue, sprays and lotions, bottles and bottles of Wite-out, "multi-media" with a vengeance, even though I'd read that much modern and contemporary art was in danger of disintegration because of the materials used in the making. Each morning when I went to my desk I half expected to find my paintings had fallen apart or crumbled to dust (I still half expect it). But on I went, covering sheets of paper seldom bigger than foolscap (aptly named, since, as Arthur C. Danto has wryly remarked, using paper undermines art's seriousness). In the process, I discovered that my technique only worked on this scale, though when a slide of the painting was projected onto screen or wall the parts, magnified, still held together, kept their relative proportions, and there was more to look at, like a stained-glass window. Briefly, they became louder and attained the importance of size (Danto also noted that making a painting large is "a condition for making it big," so for an evanescent moment I made it big).

While I worked, time collapsed and paintings emerged, materializing before me. In a converted bedroom, on my writing desk among scraps of paper, drafts, notes, poems, books and the above mentioned means of production, sometimes I could complete more than one painting a day, and they piled up. Today, now that I can look back at them in sequence, I see how they have changed. I wonder how I learned to handle color, and think of the paintings in almost musical terms: rhythms, phrases, tones, modulation, "color."

When a painting decided it was done, I found myself looking at something someone else had made, or as if I was a victim of trompe l'oeil, hoaxed. I'm not one for mysticism,* but it was as if the shapes, scenes, sounds and sensations that populated my slow wanderings in field and forest had sunk in, modulated into some sort of emotional equivalent; not so much a case of "the influence of natural objects" as a sort of metaphoric metabolic infusion, a kind of participation, perhaps what Mallarmé would have called "the effect the thing produced." It was the opposite of those dreams

---

* I am not knocking the mystical, though I have only had two or three experiences of what I imagine might be called a mystical experience. One was whole rowing in CUBC trial eights, which used to be held on the raised Bedford Level. Both boats raced in a straight line for about four miles above the Cambridgeshire fens, mist all around dissolving space, time melting into rhythmic repetition, creating the sensation of flying. The second experience occurred in the fragrant dark under the fan vaulting of King's College Chapel, when, taking a break from crew ("I suppose someone has to pole a bit of wood up and down the river," sneered my un-athletic tutor, Dr. John Holloway) as a member of the Cambridge University Musical Society (CUMS), I sang in one of the eight five-part choirs that made up the full choir for Thomas Tallis' ineffably gorgeous motet "*Spem in alium*." In the echoic polyphony, I felt transported. The only other "mystical" occasion I can recall was when I smoked marijuana for the first and last time, though time didn't exist. Inhaling, I understood the meaning of life, and wrote it down, until my painting of blue fig leaves began to come off the wall at me, and when the wall itself started to buckle I panicked but could not escape. When I was finally in a condition to read what I had written it turned out to be gibberish.

in which you find yourself flying or playing the piano, but when you wake up you can neither fly nor play. But I flew, I played. I was even reminded, immodestly, of Caedmon, the illiterate farm laborer from Whitby in ancient Northumbria, who woke from dreams to sing of first things, *frumsceaft*, creation. Then I became blasé, assuming the process would go on forever. But it didn't. It stopped about the time we decided to sell the house and move back to the city full-time. The paintings and slides were packed up and placed at the back of filing cabinets along with old tax records, journals and letter files.

I have shown my little paintings to just a few friends. One, a well-known art historian, found them "surprising." I was unwilling to ask what she meant, or what she had expected, and she didn't elaborate. Another found them "dark," but I think she had her sunglasses on. When I was younger, I knew quite a few artists, but now, despite teaching at an art school, I no longer know any. In the '70s, however, I was friends with the wonderful painter John Wesley and his equally wonderful novelist wife, Hannah Green. One summer we shared a cottage in Vence where, in addition to supplying me with paper and acrylics with which to immortalize the leaves of the fig tree that grew outside my door, Jack allowed me to hang out in his studio while he painted. Watching him work on *The Very Last Fish* from preliminary gridded cartoon to exciting completion, I thought how great it was to be an artist. When done, Jack signed the cartoon, dedicated and gave it to me. It hung in my city study until taken upstate to hang near my desk. It is now back in the city. I know what Frank O'Hara meant when he wrote: "I think I would rather be/a painter."

Brian Swann

The following poem is from my 2013 collection *In Late Light*.

THE WAVES

> *Where's the past? It's here or nowhere ...*
> —Italo Calvino, *Invisible Cities*
>
> *Awake I dream ...*
> —Hannah Green, *The Dead of the House*

We level out and all's well. I reach for the *Times* stuffed into
the seat pocket and flip through, stopping at an article on his
"blockbuster" retrospective at the Venice Biennale, with a photo
and him remarking of the huge sign "emblazoned" with JACK

WESLEY, "That is really something, isn't it?" Where has he been?
Where have I been? I sleep, and then we are over the water at La Guardia.
I fold the paper to take with me, remembering where I put Jack's cartoon
he gave me for *The Very Last Fish*, and am about to stand up when

I realize I've taken off my pants. Is this really happening? Waves
are lapping at my ankles and I'm with him and Hannah after our drive
south to visit one of her Columbia students near Livorno, arriving late,
and the four of us dashing to the empty beach, shedding our clothes

and heading into the dark sea and Hannah, bountiful Hannah,
laughing over the surge, is letting go of Jack's hand, then turning
to beckon me further in, but I'm holding back, afraid of what
    I cannot see,
what might be hidden under the waves that do not frighten her.

—*In memoriam*, Hannah Green (1927–1996)

Work Riff

Work as unpleasant necessity, work as punishment, working by the sweat of one's brow—this is the legacy of Adam and Eve. It reflects mythically that moment when the more easygoing Paleo- and Mesolithic gave way to the hard-working, town-building Neolithic.

*

I am lucky in that I have never had to think of work as an unpleasant necessity, perhaps because I consider my profession, teaching, a kind of privilege (most of the time). For me, real work is physical and doesn't take place in an office. Work means sweat (the fact that I emerge sweaty from teaching complicates the issue). I come from a long line of hard workers, paid-up members of the English working class: coal miners, ship-builders, plumbers, blacksmiths, housewives, truck, bus and train drivers, all of whom left school at 15 or younger. My father ran away from home at 14 and spent thirty years in the engine rooms of Royal Navy ships, five of those years in the North Atlantic during WWII.

*

I do not want to romanticize work, because while it can dignify it can also be boring and dangerous. In fact, men I worked with spent a good deal of time and ingenuity trying to avoid it. If I do romanticize work from time to time, it may be because "'tis distance lends enchantment to the view," and because my time as a worker was always temporary, no matter for how long. I knew I could get out. But those memories left strong impressions which I've drawn on all my life.

*

If ever I praised my fellow-workers to my father he was not impressed. From time to time he predicted a career for me as a "dustman" (garbage collector), but in more optimistic moments thought the civil service, where he had ended up, would be a good fit, if only for the pension. And on the surface, this wasn't a bad solution for someone whose high school career was not that distinguished at the Cambridgeshire High School for Boys (the "County"). This was the school, if I may digress, that produced most of Pink Floyd, from Roger Waters, whose mother was my primary school teacher at the Morley Memorial, to Storm Thorgerson and Roger Barrett, who became "Syd" by adopting the first name of my uncle and godfather Sid Barrett, whose jazz band Syd followed. (David Gilmour didn't go to my high school, but he was the grandson of Uncle Ted Swann the butcher). Toward the end of his life, Syd went to live with his mother in a semi-detached house on St. Margaret's Square, next door to my sister's family who were regularly startled by Syd burning his paintings in the backyard or by firemen responding to clogged, backed-up drains, thanks to Syd stuffing sanitary napkins down his toilet. In line with this musical digression, I might note that my headmaster was a fine Welsh baritone named Brin Newton-John, who was father of Olivia, the songbird, as well as my primary school friend Rhoda, who was involved with the Profumo scandal. When the judge at the Old Bailey asked her occupation, "Whore, m' lud," she replied. Finally, the County was the school that gave rise in 1979 to "Brick 2" of *The Wall*, and its rousing lines "We don't need no education,/ We don't need no thought control." Waters, the author, recently wrote that "some of the teachers locked into the idea that young boys needed to be controlled with sarcasm and the exercise of brute force to subjugate us to their will. That was their idea of education." Extreme, but containing enough truth. I remember those teachers, and bear scars, not just from sarcasm but from canings, or being held up by your sideburns until your toes scarcely touched the floor, or from chalk and board erasers hurled at you, or from being beaten on your backside with your own gym shoe in front of the class, or from head-slappings. I even recall a violent mugging by a German teacher of a mild-mannered young man who survived to become a bishop in the Church of England. "Such, such were the joys." Martin Amis also went to this school, and he too hated it, but I also remember teachers who made all the difference in my life, who stirred the desire to be a teacher—and who helped me to avoid having to join the civil service. I name them here to thank and honor them: the late George Barlow who taught me history, and Derek Pearsall, my English teacher, who retired not long ago as Gurney Professor of English Literature at Harvard.

*

My first job (though to me it was just fun) was working on the farm across our street, driving the cows, all ten of whom had names and were of different breeds, to and from pasture, milking them, delivering the milk in a horse-drawn cart, cleaning out barn and shippen. I did this up to the age of ten, when my family left Wallsend, my mother's home town, for Cambridge, my father's. I loved being among animals and having the men who took care of them treat me as an adult, especially when it was time for the cows to be served by our old, reluctant, bored bull, Bill, who always needed a hand, literally. Then in high-school holidays there was getting up before dawn to ride my big red GPO bike across town to sort and deliver the mail, or on my own treasured Raleigh, again before dawn, riding off to Histon to pick fruit for Chivers, who sent it on to the specialized luxury Covent Garden Market in London, though many a luscious purple Victoria plum ended in my stomach. I still recall sitting up a tree with a plum, the cool morning dew still on it, delaying the pleasure of biting into it. In one of the gardens I found a tree of magical apples, some of which I brought home. My father surprised me by eating one and getting hooked. I kept him supplied as long as I could and he talked about those apples until he died, which was puzzling since he hated apples, saying them smelled of fish. Strangely, he loved fish.

*

My fruit-picking skills were put to the test when, a year or so later, as a member of the university's Travelers' Club, though I had never traveled anywhere, I signed up for a charter flight to the US. When this was canceled, I was given the choice of a refund or a charter to Israel. I chose the latter, though I had barely heard of the country. The only Israel I knew was in the Bible. I spent the summer of 1962 working at Kibbutz Yad Mordechai, not far from Ashkelon and the Gaza Strip, laboring and picking fruit with a rifle strapped across my back.

*

In school and college vacations there were many non-manual, non sweat-inducing jobs. My favorite was working at Heffers bookstore in Cambridge where once I sold a collection of Wordsworth's poems to Benjamin Britten. To cover my shyness,

I pretended I didn't know who he was, so I never asked him, or Peter Pears, for their autographs. I spent my lunch breaks up in the gallery that ran around the store reading all eleven volumes of *The Golden Bough*. When I wasn't selling books, I was driving in a small van all over Norfolk buying up libraries from the wives of deceased clergymen and schoolmasters.

*

After graduating from college, I taught for a year at Manchester Grammar School, the experience of which caused me to leave the UK forever. Subsequently, there were other jobs, including a well-paying position with Esso Standard Italiana in Rome, a comic interlude at the Magistero in Cassino, and the teaching of English to various Italian actresses. But I move ahead of myself. Let us go back a bit.

*

In other college vacations I stacked planks and boards in a woodyard or worked as a "porter" (orderly) in Addenbrook's Hospital. My specialty was wheeling patients about and helping in the morgue with its ghoulish attendant who, after hosing down the post-autopsy floor, would sit down on his stool for a sandwich lunch with bits of flesh sticking to his high yellow boots. And then there was working for the city at a new housing estate, digging drains in heavy, stinking, blue fen clay. Shay and Shaun were twin Irish navvies whose shoulders were too wide to fit into the trench so one or the other would start the dig and I would finish it. They entertained themselves, and the housewives peeking out from behind curtains, by fashioning giant gray phalloi, balls to match, and being inventive with them. It was amazing to me how the work actually got done, because, when not entertaining the housewives and hurling clay lumps at each other we spent most of time inside the construction tent. Our foreman, a fellow Geordie, kept an eye on the sky for any signs of a cloud. When one appeared, no matter how flimsy or far off, "Howay, lads," he'd say. "Rain," and in we'd go where much tea was brewed and consumed, along with something stronger. Since this was England, there was a lot of rain.

*

I've always had a thing for digging. At the age of 15 I dug up an overgrown half-acre allotment for my father to grow potatoes in. Then, decades later, when my wife and I bought our house and ten acres upstate, I surprised and alarmed her because even before we'd moved the furniture in I'd grabbed a spade and rushed out back to dig a hole for no reason save the sheer joy of digging in the earth after years in the concrete city. She called the hole "Swann Lake," though it seldom retained any water. During years that followed I dug a three-foot-deep ditch in hardpan, filling it with buckets of cow and horse manure from a neighbor's field as well as buckets and buckets of duff from old and rotten trees. The trench became a long-maintained, ever-growing garden stretching in a half-moon around the house.

*

After a year as a Proctor Fellow at Princeton, I spent the summer of 1965 working for Weyerhaeuser in Longview, WA. I'd gone west with the romantic notion of being a lumberjack, toting my ax among giant redwoods but, since I was deemed too tall and not nimble enough to get out of the way of falling trees, I ended up in a foul-smelling factory making plywood at a lathe and trying to avoid the fate of my predecessor who somehow managed to fall among the machete-sized knives used to strip bark off trees and turn them to chips. All they found, some time later, was part of a silver watchband embedded in a roll of paper. I boarded at a Finnish guesthouse where I became friendly with one of the brothers-in-law of a local jeweler who ran a wife-swapping group. Since I had no wife, the jeweler kindly offered to lend me one. He had two, he said, both named Judy.

*

Nowadays, the only physical work I do is at the gym, two or three times a week. On the rowing machine I sweat and relive my glory days. Ah, rowing, "a strenuous yet sedentary occupation," as Max Beerbaum called it. I never lost a race, then or now, so far.

Also by Brian Swann:

POETRY

The Whale's Scars (New Rivers Press, 1975).

Roots (New Rivers Press, 1976).

Living Time (*Quarterly Review of Literature* Contemporary Poetry Series, 1978).

Paradigms of Fire (Corycian Press, 1981).

The Middle of the Journey (University of Alabama Press, 1982).

Song of the Sky: Versions of Native American Songs (University of Massachusetts Press, 1993).

Wearing the Morning Star: Versions of Native American Song-poems (Random House, 1996).

Autumn Road (Ohio State University Press, 2005).

Snow House (Pleiades Press/LSU Press, 2006).

In Late Light (Johns Hopkins University Press, 2013).

St. Francis and the Flies (Autumn House Press, 2016).

Companions, Analogies (Sheep Meadow Press, Fall, 2016).

FICTION

The Runner (Carpenter Press, 1979).

Unreal Estate (Toothpaste Press / Coffee House Press, 1981).

Elizabeth (Penmaen Press, 1981).

Another Story (Adler Publishing Co., 1984).

The Plot of the Mice (Capra Press, 1986).

Dogs on the Roof (MadHat Press, 2016).

TRANSLATION

The Collected Poems of Lucio Piccolo, with Ruth Feldman (Princeton University Press, 1972).

Selected Poetry of Andrea Zanzotto, with Feldman (Princeton University Press, 1976).

Shema: Collected Poems of Primo Levi, with Feldman (Menard, 1975).

Collected Poems of Primo Levi, with Feldman (Faber and Faber, 1988).

The Dawn Is Always New: Selected Poems Of Rocco Scotellaro, with Feldman (Princeton University Press, 1979).

The Dry Air of the Fire: Selected Poems of Bartolo Cattafi, with Feldman (Ardis/ Translation Press, 1981).

Primele Poeme / First Poems of Tristan Tzara, with Michael Impey (New Rivers Press, 1976).

Selected Poems of Tudor Arghezi, with Impey (Princeton University Press, 1976).

Currents and Trends: Italian Poetry Today, edited, with many translations, with Feldman (New Rivers Press, 1979).

Euripides' The Phoenician Women, translated with Peter Burian (Oxford University Press, 1981).

The Hands of the South: Selected Poems of Vittorio Bodini, with Feldman (Charioteer Press, 1981).

Rain One Step Away: Selected Poems of Milih Cevdat Anday, with Talat Halman (Charioteer Press, 1981).

Rome, Danger to Pedestrians, by Rafael Alberti (*Quarterly Review of Literature* Contemporary Poetry Series, 1984).

Garden of the Poor: Selected Poems of Rocco Scotellaro, with Feldman (Cross Cultural Communications, 1992).

CHILDREN

The Tongue Dancing (Rowan Tree Press/ Simon and Schuster, 1984).
The Fox and the Buffalo (Green Tiger Press, 1985).
A Basket Full of White Eggs (Orchard Books / Franklin Watts, 1988).
Turtle and the Race Around the Lake (Sierra Oaks Publishing, 1996).

The House With No Door: African Riddle-poems (Browndeer Press/ Harcourt Brace, 1998).

Touching the Distance: Native American Riddle-poems (Browndeer Press/ Harcourt Brace, 1998.)

EDITING

Smoothing the Ground: Essays on Native American Oral Literature (University of California Press, 1982).

Recovering the Word: Essays on Native American Literature, with Arnold Krupat (University of California Press, 1987).

I Tell You Now: Autobiographical Essays by Native American Writers, with Krupat (University of Nebraska Press, 1987).

Poetry From The Amicus Journal (Tioga Press, 1990).

On the Translation of Native American Literatures (Smithsonian Institution Press, 1992).

Coming to Light: Contemporary Translations of the Native Literatures of North America (Random House, 1995).

Native American Songs and Poems, An Anthology (Dover Publications, 1996).

Here First: Autobiographical Essays by Native American Writers, with Krupat (Modern Library, 2000).

Poetry Comes Up Where It Can: Poems from the Amicus Journal, 1990–2000 (University of Utah Press, 2000).

Voices From Four Directions: Contemporary Translations of the Native Literatures of North America (University of Nebraska Press, 2004).

Algonquian Spirit: Contemporary Translations of the Algonquian Literatures of North America (University of Nebraska Press, 2005).

Born in the Blood: On Translating Native American Literature (University of Nebraska Press, 2011).

Sky Loom: Native American Myth, Story, and Song (University of Nebraska Press, 2014).

Bio Note:

BRIAN SWANN was born in Wallsend, England, in 1940, graduated as Foundation Scholar in 1963 from Queens' College, Cambridge, with a Double First in English and came to Princeton in 1964 as a Proctor Fellow. After two years, he left for Europe, before returning in 1968 as a Princeton National Fellow, earning a PhD in 1970, and becoming a U.S. citizen in 1980.

He has published many books in a number of genres, from poetry and fiction to children's books, poetry in translation and Native American literature, the most recent of which is *Sky Loom: Native American Myth, Story, and Song* (University of Nebraska Press, 2014). He was founder and series editor of the Smithsonian Series of Studies in Native American Literatures and is founder and series editor of "Literatures of the Americas" for the University of Nebraska Press.

He has won a number of awards and prizes, including a National Endowment for the Arts fellowship in fiction, the John Florio Prize for the best Italian translation published in the UK, and the Italo Calvino Award from Columbia University's Translation Center. In addition he won the University of Alabama Press open poetry prize for *The Middle of the Journey*, the Ohio State University Press/*The Journal* prize for *Autumn Road*, the Lena-Miles Wever Todd Poetry Prize for *Snow House*, and the Autumn House Poetry Prize for *St. Francis and the Flies*. In the fall of 2016, Sheep Meadow will publish his twelfth poetry collection, *Companions, Analogies*.

His work has appeared in many scholarly journals, such as *English Literary History, Novel,* and *Nineteenth Century Fiction*, as well as anthologies and literary magazines, including *The New Republic, The New Yorker, Paris Review, Hudson Review, American Scholar, Poetry, Yale Review, Harvard Review, Partisan Review, Raritan, American Poetry Review,* and *Southern Review*. His art work is represented by Pierogi Gallery in NYC. He has taught at Princeton and Rutgers

Brian Swann

and was director of the Bennington Writing Workshops for five years. He is Professor of Humanities at the Cooper Union for the Advancement of Science and Art in New York City.

www.ingramcontent.com/pod-product-compliance
Lightning Source LLC
Chambersburg PA
CBHW020349170426
43200CB00005B/100